ADVANCED IMAGE ACQUISITION, PROCESSING TECHNIQUES AND APPLICATIONS

Edited by **Dimitrios Ventzas**

Advanced Image Acquisition, Processing Techniques and Applications
Edited by Dimitrios Ventzas

Published by InTech

Janeza Trdine 9, 51000 Rijeka, Croatia

Publishing Process Manager Vana Persen

Technical Editor Teodora Smiljanic

Cover Designer InTech Design Team

Additional hard copies can be obtained from orders@intechopen.com

Advanced Image Acquisition, Processing Techniques and Applications,
Edited by Dimitrios Ventzas
p. cm.
ISBN 978-953-51-0342-4

For EU product safety concerns:
IN TECH d.o.o., Prolaz Marije Krucifikse Kozulić 3, 51000 Rijeka, Croatia,
info@intechopen.com or visit our website at intechopen.com.

Meet the editor

Dr Dimitrios E. Ventzas received the B.Sc. degree from the University of Thessaloniki, Greece, Electrical Eng Dpt in 1979 and the M.Sc. and Ph.D. degrees in Control and Instrumentation Engineering from the University of Bradford, UK, in 1980 and 1983, respectively, where he worked as a Research Assistant in multiphase flow. He served as a full-time Network, System, Control and Instrument Engineer of DPCS at HARSA, Athens. He joined the Biomedical Engineering Department at TEI of Athens, in 1987, as Biomedical Eng Professor and served as Chairman of the department from 1990 through 1992. He has been Control and Instrumentation Professor at TEI of Lamia, Electronics Dpt from 1993 through 2001 and he is currently Professor of Control and Digital Signal and Image Processing in Computer and Telecommunications Engineering Dpt at TEI of Larissa. He taught at postgraduate courses of Mechanical Eng, Agricultural Control Eng and Computer Science. He is the author of over 100 technical articles in international Journals, Conferences with over 50 citations. He has been member of professional societies including IEE, IEEE, InstMC and ISA. He is involved in the development of image processing in 2D software tools in Sensors Design, computer and robotics vision, Traffic Control and old images restoration.

Contents

Preface

This book presents a wide range of applications on image processing that fits areas of engineers such as acquisition, sensing, optimization, medicine, biomedicine, materials, agriculture and text image processing. It is suggested to students, scientists and researchers in the field. Its most important feature is the way the authors allow newcomers with a little background in mathematics to go through all the topics presented without getting lost or discouraged to actually understand image acquisition, enhancement, restoration, preparation, and compression. The mathematical principles are clearly explained by the authors. Another nice distinctive characteristic of the book is the detailed explanation on practical issues and fully developed applications that allow the reader to thoroughly understand how to solve problems professionally and how to implement standard and advanced image processing algorithms.

The book covers many topics that one expects to find in a modern image application book such as a coded structured light projection method for high-frame-rate 3D image acquisition, high density devices applied to a gamma-camera implementation, adipose measurement using micro MRI, image processing quality analysis for particle based peptide array production on a micro chip, digital restoration by denoising and binarization of historical manuscripts images, applications of image processing technique in porous material characterization, accurate spectral measurements and color infrared imagery of excised leaves exhibiting Gaussian curvature from healthy and stressed plants and a comparative study of some Markov random fields and different criteria optimization in image restoration.

The various algorithms suggested in the book, are a valuable tool for experimenting and helping the reader to grasp the secrets associated with the advanced image processing techniques and algorithms. This book fits the needs of image acquisition and applications engineers to many application fields.

Professor Dr. D.E. Ventzas
Department of Computer Science and Telecommunications,
Technological Educational Institute of Larissa,
Greece

1

A Coded Structured Light Projection Method for High-Frame-Rate 3D Image Acquisition

Idaku Ishii
Hiroshima University
Japan

1. Introduction

Three-dimensional measurement technology has recently been used for various applications such as human modeling, cultural properties recording, machine inspection of industrial parts, and robot vision. The light-section method and coded structured light projection method are well-known active measurement methods that can accurately obtain three-dimensional shapes by projecting light patterns on the measurement space. These active measurement methods have been applied to practical systems in real scenes because they are robust regarding texture patterns on the surfaces of the objects to be observed, and have advantages in calculation time and accuracy. Following recent improvements in integration technology, three-dimensional image measurement systems that can operate at a rate of 30 fps or more have already been developed [1, 2]. In many application fields, dynamic analysis tools to observe dynamic changes in high-speed phenomena in three-dimensional shapes at high frame rates are required. Off-line high-speed cameras that can capture images at 1000 fps or more have already been put into practical use for analyzing high-speed phenomena; however, many of them can only record high-speed phenomena as two-dimensional image sequences.

In this chapter, we propose a spatio-temporal selection type coded structured light projection method for three-dimensional shape acquisition at a high frame rate. Section 2 describes the basic principle and related work on coded structured light projection methods. Section 3 describes our proposed coded structured light projection method that can alternate a temporal encoding and a spatial encoding adaptively according to the temporal changes of image intensities so as to accurately obtain a three-dimensional shape of a moving object. In section 4, several experiments were performed for several moving objects, and our proposed algorithm was evaluated by capturing their three-dimensional shapes at 1000 fps on a verification system comprising an off-line high-speed camera and a high-speed DLP projector.

2. Coded structured light projection method

Our proposed three-dimensional measurement method can be described in terms of the coded structured light projection method proposed by Posdamer et al. [3]. In this section, we describe its basic principles and the related previous coded structured light projection methods.

2.1 Basic principle

In the coded structured light projection method, a projector projects multiple black and white 'zebra' light patterns whose widths are different onto the objects to be observed, as shown in

Figure 1. A three-dimensional image is measured by capturing the projection images on the objects using a camera whose angle of view is different from that of the projector. When n patterns are projected on the objects, the measurement space is divided into 2^n vertical pieces, corresponding to the black and white areas of the zebra light patterns. Thereafter, we can obtain the n-bit data at each pixel in the projection image, corresponding to the presence of the light patterns. The n bit data is called a space code, and it indicates the projection direction. Based on the relationship between such a space code and the measurement directions that are determined by pixel positions, we can calculate depth information at all pixels of an image using triangulation.

2.2 Related work

Posdamer et al. [3] have used multiple black and white light patterns with a pure binary code as shown in Figure 1. In this case, serious encoding errors may occur, even when there is a small amount of noise, because the brightness boundaries of the multiple projection patterns with a pure binary code exist at the same positions. To solve this problem, Inokuchi et al. [4] proposed a technique for minimizing encoding errors using boundaries introduced in the form of multiple light patterns with a gray code. Bergmann [5] proposed an improved three-dimensional measurement method that combines the gray code pattern projection method and a phase shift method; in this method, the number of projection patterns increases. Caspi et al. [6] proposed an improved gray code pattern projection method that can reduce the number of projection patterns using color patterns. In these methods, three-dimensional shapes can be measured as high-resolution three-dimensional images because depth information is calculated at every pixel; however, it is difficult to accurately measure the three-dimensional shapes of moving objects because multiple light patterns are projected at different timings.

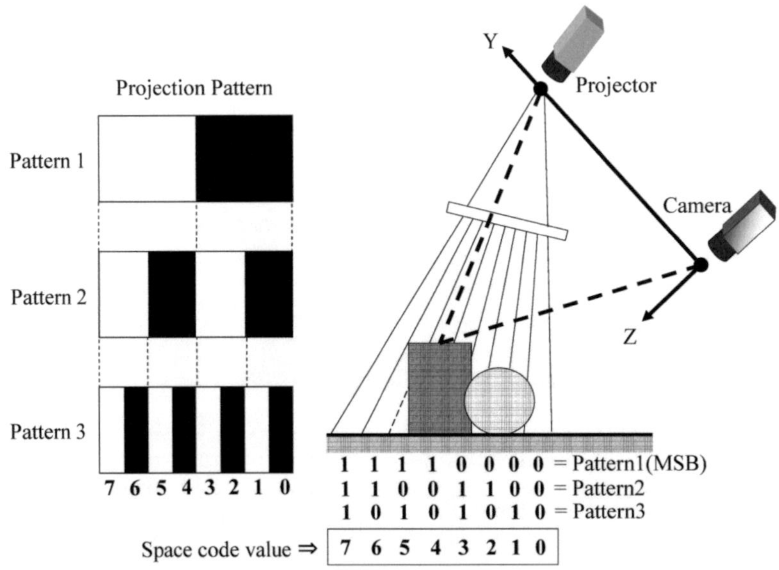

Fig. 1. Coded structured light projection method.

On the other hand, several three-dimensional measurement methods that use only a single projection pattern for spatial encoding have also been proposed. Maruyama et al. [7] proposed a method that can measure three-dimensional shapes by encoding the spatial codes on the basis of slits when a light pattern with multiple slits of different lengths is projected on the object to be observed. Durdle [8] proposed a measurement method based on a single light pattern that periodically arranges multiple slits with three grayscale levels. These methods have a disadvantage that some ambiguity exists in spatial encoding when there are pixels whose brightness are the same as that of its spatial neighborhood. To improve this ambiguity in spatial encoding, several methods introduced color slit pattern projections based on de Bruijin sequences as a robust coded pattern projection [9, 10]; this spatial encoding depends on the color surface reflectance properties of the object to be observed. These spatial encoding methods can measure the three-dimensional shapes of moving objects by projecting only a single light pattern; however, their spatial resolution is not as accurate as those obtained with the methods that use multiple light patterns because most of them assume local surface smoothness of objects in spatial encoding with a single light pattern projection.

3. Spatio-temporal selection type coded structured light projection method

3.1 Concept

As described in the previous section, the coded structured light projection method using multiple light patterns enables highly accurate three-dimensional measurement of static objects. The projection method using a single light pattern is robust when the object to be observed is moving rapidly. In this chapter, we propose a spatio-temporal selection type coded structured light projection method that attempts to combine the advantages of both temporal encoding methods and spatial encoding methods, that is, high accuracy in the case of a static object and robustness in the case of a moving object. The main features of our proposed method are in the following:

- Projection of multiple coded structured light patterns that enable both temporal encoding along the time axis and spatial encoding in the spatial domain.
- Adaptive selection of encoding types in every local image region by calculating the image features that are dependent on the measured object's motion.

Consequently, temporal encoding using multiple light patterns is selected so as to allow accurate three-dimensional measurement in the case in which there is no motion, while spatial encoding using a single light pattern is selected for robust three-dimensional measurement in the case in which the brightness changes dynamically. The concept of our proposed coded structured light projection method is shown in Figure 2.

3.2 Proposed coded structured light pattern

In the spatio-temporal selection type coded structured light projection method, when the size of a projected binary image $I(x,y,t)$ is given by $I_x \times I_y$ pixels and the space code is n bits, $I(x,y,t)$ can be expressed by the following equation:

$$I(x,y,t) = G\left(\left\lfloor \frac{x}{m} + t \right\rfloor \bmod n, y\right), \tag{1}$$

where $\lfloor x \rfloor$ is the greatest integer less than or equal to x, and m is the unit width of a light pattern in the x direction. $G(k,y)$ represents n types of one-dimensional gray code patterns

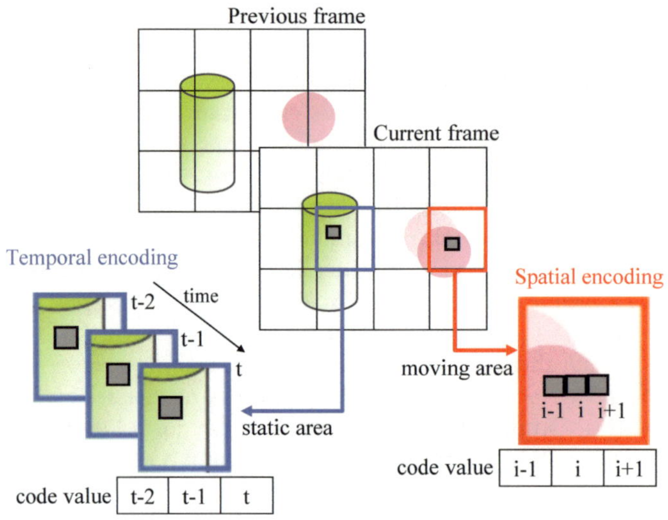

Fig. 2. Concept of our proposed algorithm.

in the y direction ($0 \leq k \leq n-1$), which can minimize encoding errors on code boundaries. $G(k,y)$ is given by:

$$G(k,y) = \left\lfloor \frac{y \times 2^k}{I_y} + \frac{1}{2} \right\rfloor \bmod 2. \tag{2}$$

The coded pattern defined by Eq.(1) has the following properties:

- The coded pattern has a periodic branched pattern based on the gray code.
- The coded pattern shifts in the x direction over time.

These features of the coded pattern enable spatio-temporal selection type encoding that can select not only encoding along the time axis, but also encoding in the spatial domain.

As an example of the coded patterns, the coded patterns at time $t = 0, 1, 2,$ and 3 are shown in Figure 3 when the number of bits of the space codes is set at $n = 8$. The numbers $k(= 0, \ldots, 7)$ at the bottom of each image indicate that the one-dimensional pattern in the y direction is set to $G(k,y)$. In Figure 3, the space code can be generated only using spatial neighborhood information because eight gray code patterns from $G(0,y)$ to $G(7,y)$ are periodically arranged in a single image. From Eq.(1), the projection pattern also shifts to the left after a certain period of time; the gray code pattern on the same pixel changes $G(0,y), G(1,y), G(2,y), \ldots$, every unit time. Similarly, a space code can be obtained at each pixel along the time axis.

3.3 Spatio-temporal selection type encoding algorithm

3.3.1 Calibration between a projection pattern and a captured image

When the shifting light pattern is projected using a projector to measure the three-dimensional shape of objects; the projection results are captured as an image by a camera whose angle of view is different from that of the projector. To calculate space codes using this captured image,

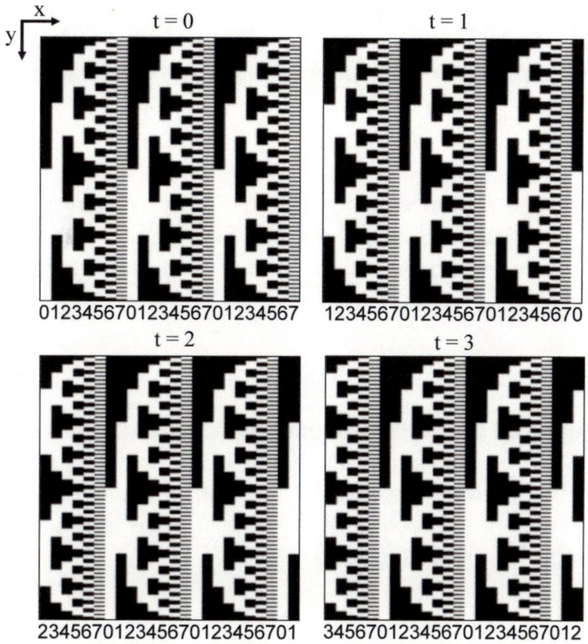

Fig. 3. Coded structured light patterns for spatio-temporal selection.

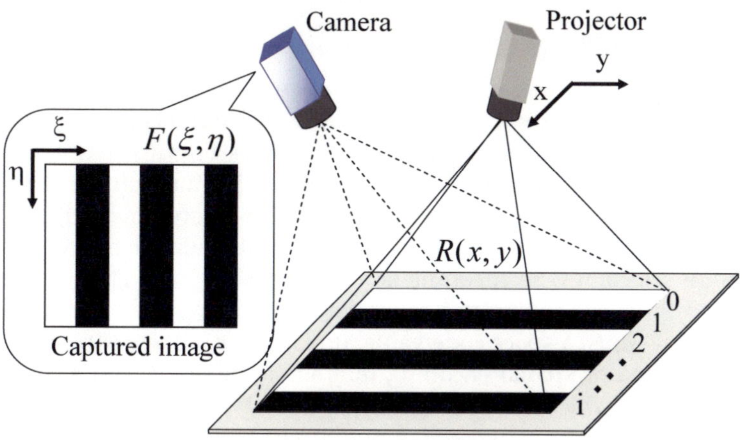

Fig. 4. Spatial relationship between a projector and a camera.

the type of gray code patterns expressed in Eq. (1), $G(0, y), \ldots, G(7, y)$, that is projected at each pixel on the captured image must be identified after the captured image has been binarized.

Figure 4 shows the spatial relationship between the xy-coordinate system of a projector and the $\xi\eta$-coordinate system of a camera. It is assumed that the x-axis and ξ-axis are parallel for light patterns projected from the projector and images captured by the camera.

Here, a region corresponding to a gray code pattern $G(k, y)$ is assumed to be a rectangular area in the captured image. When the number of rectangular areas is assumed to be i, the i-th rectangular area r_i on the projector coordinate system can be defined as follows:

$$r_i = \left\{ (x, y) \mid \left\lfloor \frac{x}{m} \right\rfloor = i \right\}. \tag{3}$$

Here, a rectangular area r_i is assumed to be projected onto a rectangular area r'_i in the camera coordinate system. To make a correspondence between r_i and r'_i, the following light pattern $R(x, y)$ is projected as a reference pattern that divides the measurement space on the captured image into multiple rectangular areas:

$$R(x, y) = \left\lfloor \frac{x}{m} + 1 \right\rfloor \bmod 2. \tag{4}$$

$F(\xi, \eta)$ is the image captured when the reference light pattern $R(x, y)$ is projected; the region number at pixel (ξ, η) can be matched with that at $h(\xi, \eta)$. $h(\xi, \eta)$ is defined as the number of switching obtained by counting the changes in brightness until reaching pixel (ξ, η) when scanning $F(\xi, \eta)$ in the positive direction of the ξ-axis. A rectangular area r'_i on the camera coordinate system can be assigned as follows:

$$r'_i = \{ (\xi, \eta) \mid h(\xi, \eta) = i \}. \tag{5}$$

In the space encoding discussed below, the initially given map $h(\xi, \eta)$ can uniquely specify the number of a rectangular area i at a pixel (ξ, η) in the captured image via Eq. (5). Thus, we can judge which gray code pattern of $G(0, y), \ldots, G(7, y)$ is projected on pixel (ξ, η) at time t.

3.3.2 Space encoding types

Next, we put forward a method of space code calculation that can select coded patterns temporally and spatially according to brightness changes in the captured images, which are strongly dependent upon an object's motion in the images. Figure 5 shows the types of gray code patterns that are projected onto a part of the given line for eight frames when the light patterns defined by Eqs. (1) and (2) are projected. In the figure, the vertical axis represents time, and the horizontal axis represents the number of rectangular areas. We show an example of spatio-temporal selection type encoding at a given pixel (ξ, η). There are four bits in the time direction and three bits in the space direction; they are referred to to obtain space code values at pixel (ξ, η). Thus, a space code value at pixel (ξ, η) in a rectangular area i uses not only temporal encoding or spatial encoding in a single direction, but also spatio-temporal selection type encoding (which refers image information both temporally and spatially).

In this study, we introduce n selectable space code values ${}^pX(\xi, \eta, t)$ at pixel (ξ, η) at time t, whose number of referred bits in time and space (excluding the specified pixel) are $(n - 1, 0), (n - 2, 1), \ldots, (0, n - 1)$, respectively. Here, n is the number of bits of space code, and $p (= 1, \ldots, n)$ is an alternative parameter for space coding; the space encoding is close to the space pattern selection when p is small, whereas it is close to the temporal one when p is large.

Here, $g(\xi, \eta, t)$ is a binarized image obtained from a camera at time t; it corresponds to coded structured light patterns. The binarized image $g(\xi, \eta, t)$ belonging to a rectangular area i

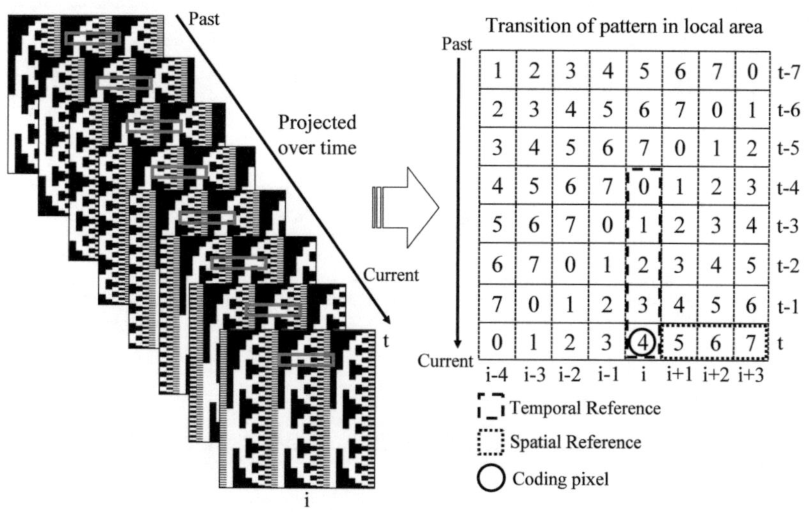

Fig. 5. Spatio-temporal selection type encoding ($p = 4$).

is abbreviated as ${}^i g_t$. The space code ${}^p X(\xi, \eta, t)$ is abbreviated as ${}^p X_t$. Eqs. (6)–(13) are enumerated as examples of selectable space code values when $n = 8$.

$$
\begin{aligned}
{}^1X_t &= {}^i g_{t-4}\,{}^i g_{t-3}\,{}^i g_{t-2}\,{}^i g_{t-1}\,{}^i g_t\,{}^i g_{t-7}\,{}^i g_{t-6}\,{}^i g_{t-5}\,, && (6)\\
{}^2X_t &= {}^i g_{t-4}\,{}^i g_{t-3}\,{}^i g_{t-2}\,{}^i g_{t-1}\,{}^i g_t\,{}^{i+1} g'_t\,{}^i g_{t-6}\,{}^i g_{t-5}\,, && (7)\\
{}^3X_t &= {}^i g_{t-4}\,{}^i g_{t-3}\,{}^i g_{t-2}\,{}^i g_{t-1}\,{}^i g_t\,{}^{i+1} g'_t\,{}^{i+2} g'_t\,{}^i g_{t-5}\,, && (8)\\
{}^4X_t &= {}^i g_{t-4}\,{}^i g_{t-3}\,{}^i g_{t-2}\,{}^i g_{t-1}\,{}^i g_t\,{}^{i+1} g'_t\,{}^{i+2} g'_t\,{}^{i+3} g'_t\,, && (9)\\
{}^5X_t &= {}^{i-4} g'_t\,{}^i g_{t-3}\,{}^i g_{t-2}\,{}^i g_{t-1}\,{}^i g_t\,{}^{i+1} g'_t\,{}^{i+2} g'_t\,{}^{i+3} g'_t\,, && (10)\\
{}^6X_t &= {}^{i-4} g'_t\,{}^{i-3} g'_t\,{}^i g_{t-2}\,{}^i g_{t-1}\,{}^i g_t\,{}^{i+1} g'_t\,{}^{i+2} g'_t\,{}^{i+3} g'_t\,, && (11)\\
{}^7X_t &= {}^{i-4} g'_t\,{}^{i-3} g'_t\,{}^{i-2} g'_t\,{}^i g_{t-1}\,{}^i g_t\,{}^{i+1} g'_t\,{}^{i+2} g'_t\,{}^{i+3} g'_t\,, && (12)\\
{}^8X_t &= {}^{i-4} g'_t\,{}^{i-3} g'_t\,{}^{i-2} g'_t\,{}^{i-1} g'_t\,{}^i g_t\,{}^{i+1} g'_t\,{}^{i+2} g'_t\,{}^{i+3} g'_t\,, && (13)
\end{aligned}
$$

where ${}^i g'_t = {}^i g'_t(\xi, \eta, t)$ is a value obtained via spatial neighborhood processing, and which is set to 0 or 1. The value 1 is taken when the numbers of 0, 1 of the binarized image $g(\xi, \eta, t)$ are counted in the ξ direction for the nearest i-th rectangular area to pixel (ξ, η).

Figure 6 shows eight space encoding types as defined by Eqs. (6)–(13). The example in Figure 5 is a case of $p = 4$: four bits are referred to in the time direction and four bits are referred to in the spatial neighborhood. When the objects to be observed are not in motion, space encoding that refers only to information along the time axis ($p = 1$) is effective, that is, it is equivalent to the conventional gray code pattern projection method [4]. In the case of $p = 8$, the space encoding type, it refers only to information in a single projected image; this encoding type is effective in measuring the three-dimensional shapes of moving objects because its accuracy is completely independent of the motion of objects. However, there is a disadvantage in that measurement errors increase when undulated shapes are measured because the space encoding measurement when $p = 8$ assumes spatial smoothness for the shape.

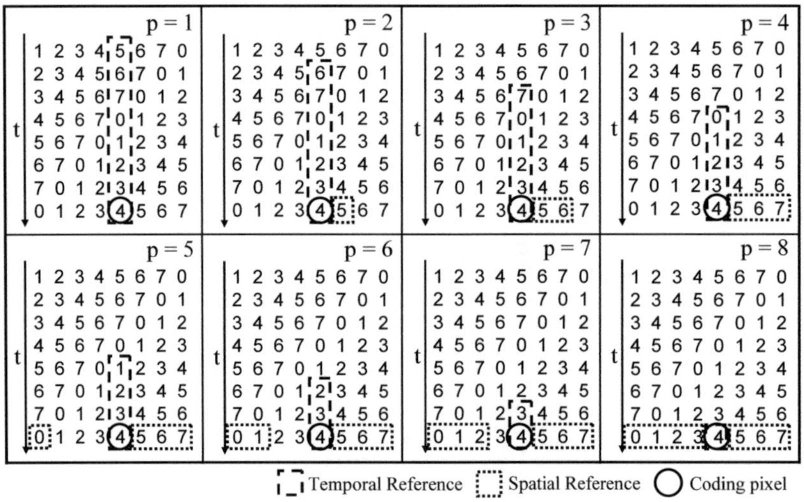

Fig. 6. Types of encoding.

3.3.3 Adaptive selection of encoding types

Considering the brightness changes in space code images, we introduce a criterion for the adaptive selection of encoding types defined by Eqs. (6)–(13). In the introduced criterion, we use the frame differencing feature obtained by differentiating a space code image $T(\xi, \eta, t)$ at time t from a space code image $S(\xi, \eta, t-1)$ at time $t-1$. $T(\xi, \eta, t)$ is the space code image that refers only to information along the time axis, and $S(\xi, \eta, t-1)$ is the space code image in a previous frame selected using the following equation:

$$D(\xi', \eta', t) = \sum_{(\xi,\eta) \in q(\xi',\eta')} T(\xi, \eta, t) \oplus S(\xi, \eta, t-1), \tag{14}$$

where $\oplus$ refers to the logical exclusive OR operation, and $q(\xi', \eta')$ refers to the ξ'-th and η'-th $s \times s$-pixel block area in the ξ and η directions, respectively. $T(\xi, \eta, t_0)$ is initially set to $S(\xi, \eta, t_0 - 1)$ at the start time t_0 to generate the space codes. After differentiation, the criterion $D(\xi', \eta', t)$ is provided for every divided square image region (each unit of which is $s \times s$ pixels), by calculating the summation of the differentiation result in Eq. (14). $D(\xi', \eta', t)$ corresponds to the number of pixels where the values of $T(\xi, \eta, t)$ are different from those of $S(\xi, \eta, t-1)$ in the block area $q(\xi', \eta')$.

When moving objects are measured, the space code image $T(\xi, \eta, t)$ is not always encoded correctly because it refers only to the information along the time axis, which requires multiple images at different frames. However, the space code image $S(\xi, \eta, t)$ generated by the spatio-temporal selection type encoding defined by Eq. (15) is robust to errors caused by moving objects. Thus, the criterion $D(\xi', \eta', t)$ can be defined with a frame differencing calculation for every block area to detect the coding errors caused by motion.

Based on the criterion $D(\xi', \eta', t)$, the spatio-temporal encoding type $p = p(\xi', \eta', t)$ is selected from the encoding types ${}^pX_t$, which are defined by Eqs. (6)–(13) for every block area $q(\xi', \eta')$ at time t. In this study, a spatio-temporal selection type space code image $S(\xi, \eta, t)$ at various times t is determined using the calculated encoding types for all the block areas as follows:

$$p(\xi', \eta', t) = \begin{cases} n & (D(\xi', \eta', t) = s^2) \\ \left\lfloor \dfrac{nD(\xi', \eta', t)}{s^2} \right\rfloor + 1 & (\text{otherwise}) \end{cases} . \tag{15}$$

Figure 7 shows an example of our newly introduced criterion for spatio-temporal encoding

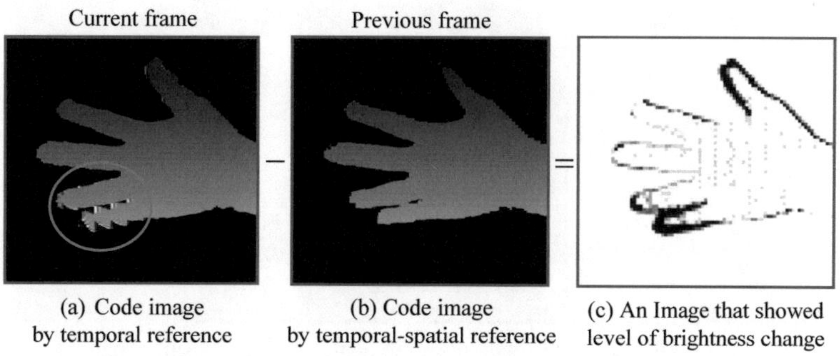

Fig. 7. Criterion for spatial-temporal encoding.

when a human extends and contracts his fingers. In the figure, (a) a space code image $T(\xi, \eta, t)$ coded using temporal reference, (b) a space code image $S(\xi, \eta, t-1)$ coded using temporal-spatial reference in a previous frame, and (c) selected spatial encoding types $p(\xi', \eta', t)$, are shown. In (c), the value of p increases when the gray-level tone becomes darker. It can be observed that the number of the spatio-encoding type, p, increases if code errors are caused by the motion of fingers, whereas p decreases in the area in which motion is slight. This fact indicates that space codes that are robust to motion are selected for the dynamically changing scenes, and space codes that enable accurate shape measurement are selected for the static scenes. Thus, the spatio-temporal encoding type can be selected both adaptively and according to the defined criterion based on frame differencing features for space code images.

3.4 Correction of misalignment in the projected image

Next, we consider a misalignment problem in the projected image, and introduce a correction method to reduce misalignment errors in space code images. Figure 8 shows a framework for our method of correcting the misalignment of the projected image. When ideally projecting, as shown in (a), the projected black and white zebra patterns are accurately matched with the initially assigned rectangular areas r'_i, and we can always observe the same value of 0 or 1 at all the pixels on a certain line segment in the ξ direction in the same rectangular area when the projected zebra pattern has a width of several pixels. However, when there is a certain displacement between the projected zebra patterns and the initially assigned rectangular areas, as shown in (b), there are cases in which there are both black and white pixels on a certain line segment, even in the same rectangular area. This ambiguity may generate errors, especially around the edge boundaries of the black and white zebra patterns, when computing space code images in the coded structure light projection method.

To avoid this ambiguity (caused by the displacement between the projected zebra patterns and the initially assigned rectangular areas), the pixel values of 0 or 1 in the same rectangular

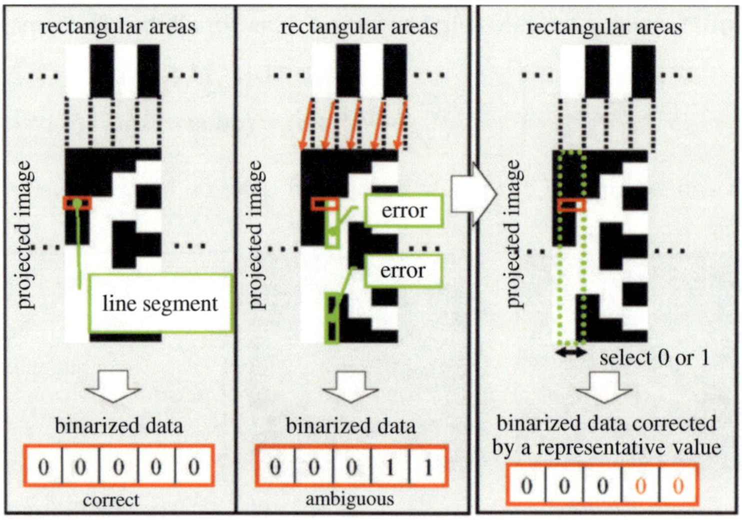

(a) no misalignment (b) with misalignment (c) correction method

Fig. 8. Correction of misalignment in the projected image.

area are calibrated by replacing with a representative value on a certain line segment in the ξ direction; the representative value on a certain line segment in the ξ direction is determined to have the pixel value of 0 or 1 when its number surpasses that of its opposite value on the given line segment in the same rectangular area, as shown in (c). Thus, we can reduce the influence of the misalignment of the projected image and correct the correspondence between the projected zebra patterns and the initially assigned rectangular areas.

As an example, Figure 9 shows the corrected space code images when a human hand is observed using our structured light projection method. Before correction, many slit-like noises can be observed around the edge boundaries of the black and white stripe patterns. By introducing the correction process, we can reduce this slit-like noise and obtain the correct space code images, which correspond to the fact that the hand shape smoothly varies in space.

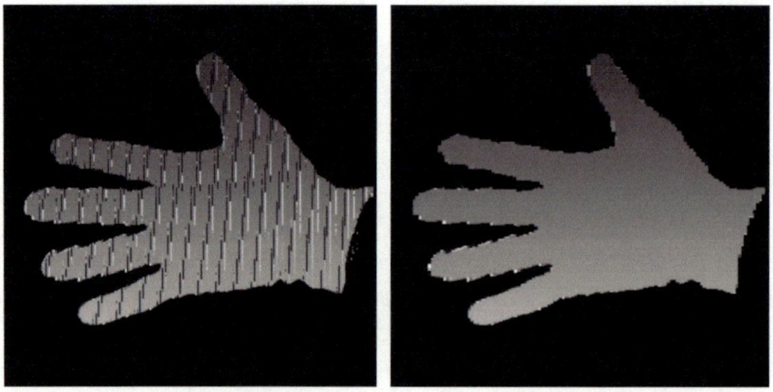
(a) before correction (b) after correction

Fig. 9. Corrected space code images for a human hand.

3.5 Calculation of three-dimensional information

To obtain three-dimensional information from the space code image $S(\xi,\eta,t)$, it is necessary to transform $S(\xi,\eta,t)$ using the relationship between the location of the camera and the projection; this requirement was common in the previously-reported structured light pattern projection methods. In this chapter, the space code image is transformed into three-dimensional information at each pixel using the method described in [4].

The three-dimensional coordinate $\boldsymbol{X}(t)$ is obtained from the pixel position (ξ,η) on the camera. Its corresponding space code value $S(\xi,\eta,t)$ is obtained by solving the following simultaneous equation with a 3×4 camera transform matrix $\boldsymbol{C}$ and a 2×4 projector matrix $\boldsymbol{P}$,

$$H_c \begin{pmatrix} \xi \\ \eta \\ 1 \end{pmatrix} = \boldsymbol{C} \begin{pmatrix} \boldsymbol{X}(t) \\ 1 \end{pmatrix}, \tag{16}$$

$$H_p \begin{pmatrix} S(\xi,\eta,t) \\ 1 \end{pmatrix} = \boldsymbol{P} \begin{pmatrix} \boldsymbol{X}(t) \\ 1 \end{pmatrix}, \tag{17}$$

where H_c and H_p are parameters, and the camera transform matrix $\boldsymbol{C}$ and the projector matrix $\boldsymbol{P}$ must be obtained by prior calibration. All of the pixels in the image are transformed using Eqs. (16) and (17). We can obtain a three-dimensional image as the result of our proposed coded structured pattern light projection method.

4. Experiments

4.1 Experimental system

To verify the three-dimensional measurement method proposed in the previous section, off-line experiments for three-dimensional shape measurement are performed using an off-line high-speed camera and a high-speed DLP projector. Figures 10 and 11 show its location configuration and an overview, respectively. We used an off-line high-speed video camera, FASTCAM-1024PCI (Photron Ltd., Tokyo, Japan), that can capture a 1024×1024-pixel 10-bit gray-level image at 1000 fps. The high-speed DLP projector comprises a DMD (Direct Micro-mirror Device) Discovery 1100 controller board (Texas Instruments Inc., Dallas, USA), an ALP controller module (ViALUX GmbH, Chemnitz, Germany), and an LED

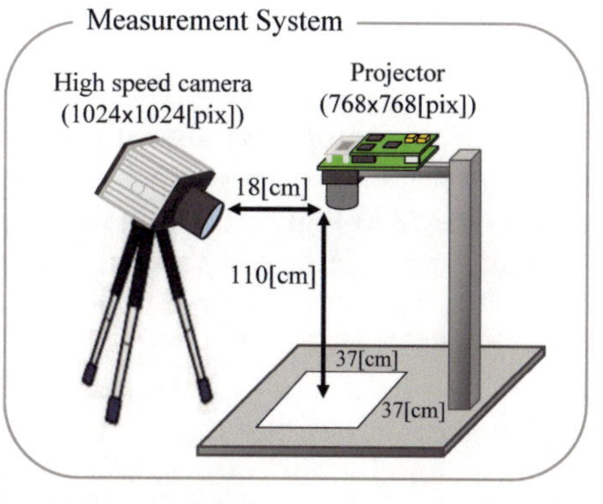

Fig. 10. Configuration of experimental system.

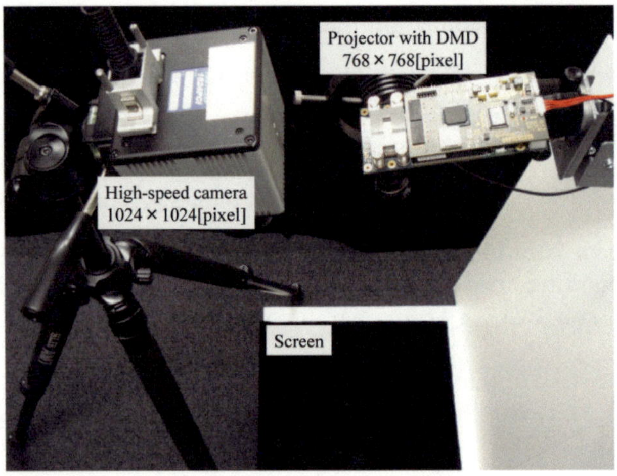

Fig. 11. Overview of experimental system.

Integrated Optical Module (ViALUX GmbH, Chemnitz, Germany). The projector can project 1024×768-pixel binary images at a frame rate of 1000 fps or more.

In the experimental setup, the camera is located at a distance of approximately 18 cm from the projector; and a background screen is placed at a distance of approximately 110 cm from the camera and projector. Light patterns from the projector are projected over an area of 37 cm × 37 cm on the screen. Here, the camera is positioned such that the rectangular areas in the x direction are not distorted, even if the heights of the measured objects vary. In the experiments, a 768×768-pixel light pattern defined by Eq. (1) is projected at 1000 fps. The number of bits of space codes and the width of rectangular areas are set to $n = 8$ and $m = 4$, respectively. The high-speed camera is synchronized with the projector electrically, a 1024×1024-pixel image is captured at 1000 fps so that the projected light patterns are settled in the captured image. To reduce errors caused by illumination or surface properties, the image for space encoding is binarized by differentiating a pair of positive and negative projection images that are generated by projecting a consecutive pair of light patterns whose values of black and white are reversed. The size of the block area is set to 8 × 8 pixels ($s = 8$) to calculate the criterion $D(\xi', \eta', t)$ for the selection of encoding types.

4.2 Experimental results

To demonstrate the effectiveness of our proposed algorithm using the off-line high-speed camera and the high-speed DLP projector, we show three-dimensional shape measurement results for three types of moving objects in Figure 12; (a) a rotating plane, (b) a waving piece of paper, and (c) a moving human hand. First, we show the measured result for a rotating plane object; the measure object is a 8.5 cm × 10.0 cm plate. It is rotated at approximately 5.5 revolutions per second (rps) by a DC motor. Figure 13 shows the images captured by a video camera at a frame rate of 30 fps on the left; the three-dimensional color-mapped images calculated using our proposed method are on the right. The image interval is set to 0.03 s. It can be observed that three-dimensional shape information can be obtained at a high frame rate even when the measured object moves too quickly for the human eye to see it.

Next, we show the measured result for a waving piece of paper; the measure object is an A4 paper of 297 mm $\times$ 210 mm size. The piece of paper is waved in the vertical direction. Figure 14 shows the images captured by a video camera at a frame rate of 30 fps on the left;

(a) rotating plane (b) waving paper (c) moving human hand

Fig. 12. Measurement objects.

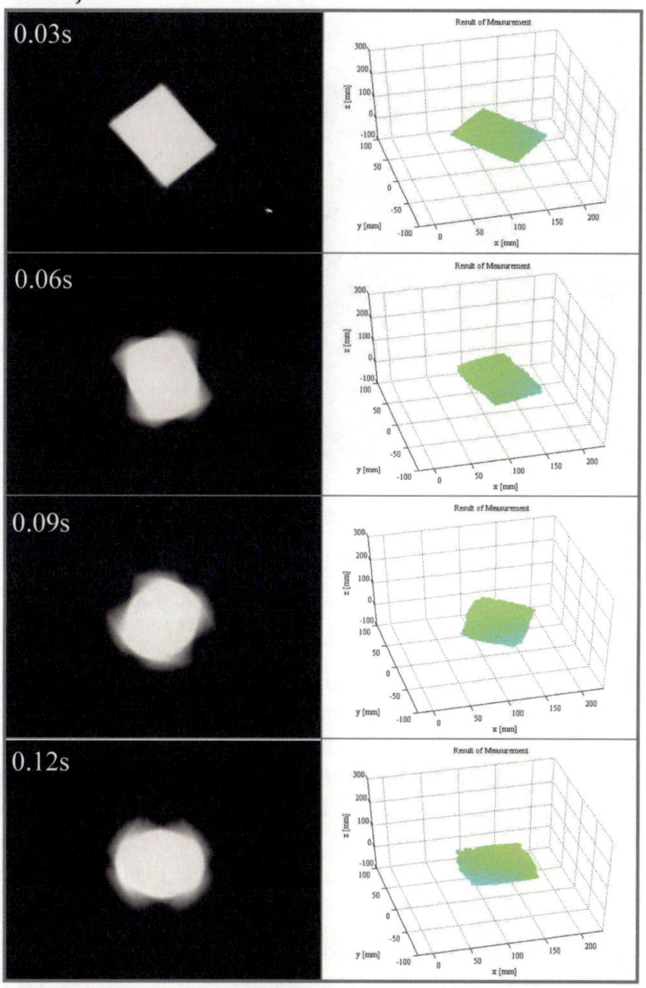

Fig. 13. Experimental result for a rotating plane.

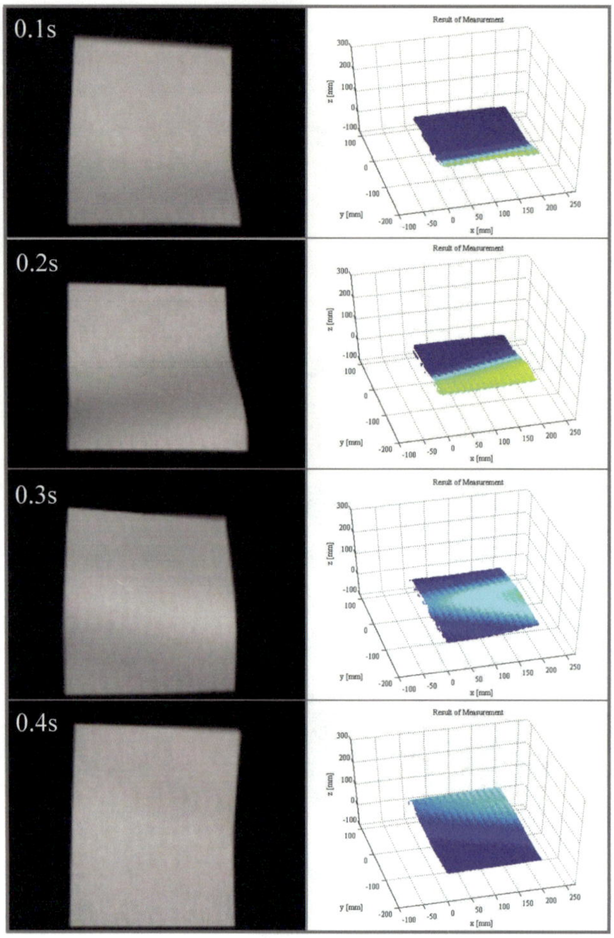

Fig. 14. Experimental result for a waving piece of paper.

the three-dimensional color-mapped images calculated using our proposed method are on the right. The image interval is set to 0.1 s. It can be observed that the temporal changes in the three-dimensional shape, which are generated by wave propagation, become visible in detail.

Finally, we show the measured result for a human hand whose fingers move quickly. Here, a human changes his fingers' shape from "paper" to "scissors" in rock-scissor-paper game with a duration of approximately 0.1 s. Figure 15 shows the images captured by a video camera at a frame rate of 30 fps on the left; the three-dimensional color-mapped images calculated using our proposed method are on the right. Their interval is set to 0.03 s. It can be observed that the three-dimensional shape of a human hand, a complicated shape, can be acquired, and that quick movements of the fingers or changes in the height of the back of the hand can also be accurately detected in the form of a three dimensional shape.

Figure 16 shows the examples of the selected spatial encoding types in these experiments. When the gray-level tone becomes darker, p increases, that is, the spatial encoding becomes more dominant. When the tone becomes brighter, p decreases, that is, the temporal encoding

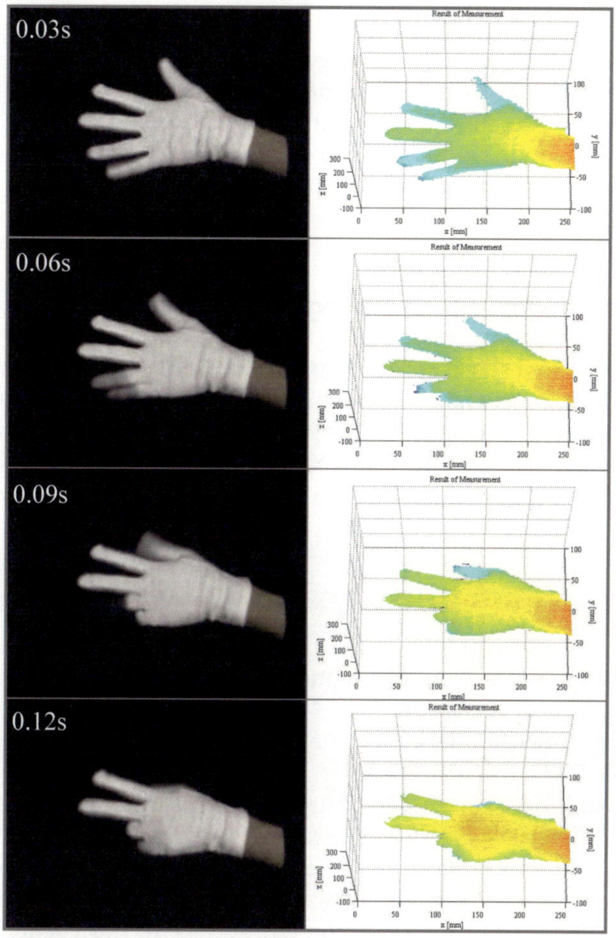

Fig. 15. Experimental result for a moving human hand

(a) rotating plane (b) waving paper (c) moving human hand

Fig. 16. Selected spatial encoding types spatio-temporal encoding types.

becomes more dominant. In all the snapshots, the dark pixels exist around the edges of the moving objects, because the depth changed primarily at the pixels around these spatial discontinuities (between the object and its background); temporal selection type encoding was mainly performed on the inner side of the object, where the depth largely did not change. In the snapshots for the waving piece of paper, it can be observed that the selected spatial encoding types varied spatio-temporally with the waving movement.

5. Conclusion

In this chapter, a spatio-temporal selection type coded structured light projection method is proposed for the acquisition of three-dimensional images at a high frame rate. The proposed method can select adaptive space encoding types according to the temporal changes in the code images. Our proposed method was verified off-line using a testbed that was composed of a high-speed camera and a high-speed projector. We evaluated its effectiveness by producing experimental results for various three-dimensional objects moving quickly, at a high frame rate such as 1000 fps, which is too fast for the human eye to observe their three-dimensional motion in detail.

6. References

[1] S. Yoshimura, T. Sugiyama, K. Yonemoto, and K. Ueda. "A 48kframes/s CMOS image sensor for real-time 3-D sensing and motion detection," in *ISSCC Tech. Dig.* , 94–95, 2001.

[2] Y. Oike, M. Ikeda, and K. Asada. "A CMOS image sensor for high-speed active range finding using column-parallel time domain ADC and position encoder," *IEEE Trans. Electron Devices*, 50(1), 152–158, 2003.

[3] J.L. Posdamer and M.D. Altschuler. "Surface measurement by space-encoded projected beam systems," *Computer Graphics and Image Processing*, 18(1), 1–17, 1982.

[4] S. Inokuchi, K. Sato, and F. Matsuda. "Range imaging system for 3-D object recognition," in *Proc. Int. Conf. Pattern Recog.*, 806–808, 1984.

[5] D. Bergmann. "New approach for automatic surface reconstruction with coded light," in *Proc. Remote Sensing and Reconstruction for Three-Dimensional Objects and Scenes*, SPIE 2572, 2–9, 1995

[6] D. Caspi, N. Kiryati, and J. Shamir. "Range imaging with adaptive color structured light," *IEEE Trans. Pattern Anal. Mach. Intelli.*, 20 (5), 470–480, 1998.

[7] M. Maruyama and S. Abe. "Range sensing by projecting multiple slits with random cuts," *IEEE Trans. Pattern Anal. Mach. Intelli.*, 15 (6), 647–651, 1993

[8] N.G. Durdle, J. Thayyoor, and V.J. Raso. "An improved structured light technique for surface reconstruction of the human trunk," in *Proc. IEEE Can. Conf. Elect. Comput. Eng.*, 874–877, 1998.

[9] L. Zhang, B. Curless, and S.M. Seitz. "Rapid shape acquisition using color structured light and multi-pass dynamic programming," in *Proc. Int. Symp. 3D Data Processing Visualization and Transmission*, 24–36, 2002.

[10] J. Salvi, J. Batlle, and E. Mouaddib. "A robust-coded pattern projection for dynamic 3d scene measurement," *Int. J. Patt. Recog. Lett.*, 19, 1055–1065, 1998.

2

High Density Devices Applied to a Gamma-Camera Implementation

Griselda Saldana-Gonzalez[1], Uvaldo Reyes[2], Humberto Salazar[2], Oscar Martínez[2], Eduardo Moreno[2] and Ruben Conde[2]
[1]*Electric and Electronics Department, Universidad Tecnologica de Puebla*
[2]*Physics and Mathematics Faculty, Benemerita Universidad Autonoma de Puebla*
Mexico

1. Introduction

Image processing is considered to be one of the most rapidly evolving areas of information technology, with growing applications in all fields of knowledge. It constitutes a core area of research within the computer science and engineering disciplines given the interest of potential applications ranging from image enhancing, to automatic image understanding, robotics and computer vision. The performance requirements of image processing applications have continuously increased the demands on computing power, especially when there are real time constraints. Image processing applications may consist of several low level algorithms applied in a processing chain to a stream of input images. In order to accelerate image processing, there are different alternatives ranging from parallel computers to specialized ASIC architectures. The computing paradigm using reconfigurable architectures based on Field Programmable Gate Arrays (FPGAs) promises an intermediate trade-off between flexibility and performance.

In the present work a prototype for reconstruction of two-dimensional images based in FPGAs is presented. The front-end includes two main modules, the data acquisition electronics and a hardware architecture for data processing. The read out electronics consists mainly of a Discretized Positioning Circuit (DPC), analog-to-digital converters and a FPGA Virtex IV of the Xilinx's family. This module reads the electrical signals produced by a Position-Sensitive Photomultiplier Tube (PS-PMT) coupled to a Cerium-doped Lutetium Yttrium Orthosilicate (LYSO) crystal. The hardware architecture takes the digitized signals produced by the acquisition module and processes them to determine the positions of the interactions based on the logic of Anger to form a planar image. The architecture performs arithmetic operations, formats the data and stores them in memory blocks to be sent to the displaying stage. The final image obtained represents a 2D histogram for the intensity distribution of the radioactivity. Both systems interact to operate at a clock frequency of 322 MHz reducing the processing time to reach real time performance. Using parallelism techniques and an appropriate management of memory, the necessary logic to implement the system has been developed improving flexibility for adjustment to new requirements or new algorithms. The main contribution of this work consists on validating the use of FPGAs in the image processing stage in a nuclear medicine application, such as gamma camera.

This chapter shows a brief introduction to the physics involved in the operation of a gamma camera. Some details regarding the characteristics of the sensors used to obtain signals and the mechanism to interpret them and to relate them with the formation of a gammagram are presented. Details of the acquisition systems and image formation architecture proposed are explained. The obtained results are shown highlighting the benefits that can be provided by a system implemented with FPGA technology and reconfigurable computing. Finally some conclusions are presented.

2. Physics of the gamma camera

The discovery of radioactivity and the natural radioactive elements at the end of the last century marked the beginning of a series of important discoveries that completely changed the idea of the matter structure. This allowed the use of radiation for medical applications and in other areas.

Nuclear Medicine is based on the detection of nuclear radiation emitted by a human body after inserting a radiopharmaceutical. Although its birth has not an exact date, it begins with the discovery of polonium by Pierre Curie and Marja Sklodowska-Curie in 1898, however, the concept of producing images for diagnosis using radioactive materials is more recent. The first medical report on the use of a radioactive substance was made by Eugene Bloch and the French physicist Henri Danlos when they placed radio in contact with a skin lesion caused by tuberculosis.

One of the most significant developments in image instrumentation was the scintillation camera developed by Anger in 1952 (Anger, 1958). This camera is also known as gamma camera or Anger camera, it is of great use in nuclear medicine due to it allows to obtain useful medical images called gammagram (see Fig. 1).

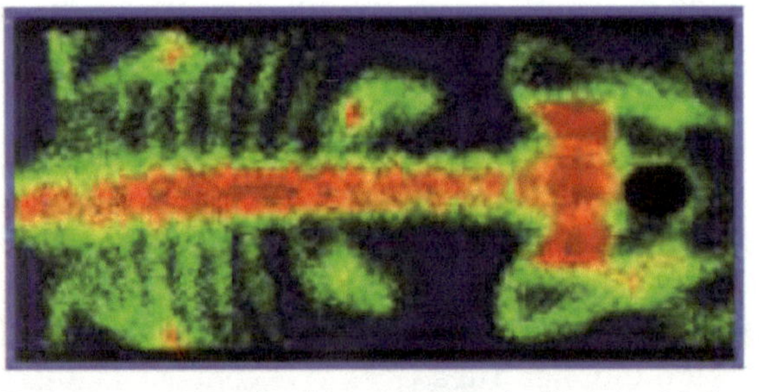

Fig. 1. Gammagram. Hot areas are marked in red; they indicate a higher radiopharmaceutical concentration. Cold areas have a less concentration

Nuclear medicine, as diagnostic method, highlights biochemical and functional processes for a particular organ or tissue; radioactive elements emitting photons or positrons joined to drugs are used. The amount of radiation emitted from the host tissue describes its metabolism.

Unlike x-ray diagnosis, which uses an x-ray emitting source, from where a percentage interacts with the patient and the resulting beam is analyzed on a detector film, in the gamma camera diagnosis, the patient is the radioactive emitter source of gamma photon and using the appropriate detector certain information from the target tissue is obtained.

2.1 The energy of radiation

In general, radioactive elements are those which have an excess of protons or neutrons. When the number of neutrons equals the number of protons is more difficult that the strong nuclear force hold them together. Eventually, the imbalance is corrected by release of excess neutrons or protons in the form of α particles (*He* nucleus) and particles that can be electrons or positrons.

These emissions lead to two types of radiation:

- α radiation, which lightens the atomic nucleus by four mass units and changes the atomic number two units.
- β radiation, which does not change the mass of the nucleus as it involves the conversion of a proton into a neutron or vice versa and change the atomic number in a single unit (positive or negative, depending on the emitted particle, either an electron or a positron).

There is also a third type of radiation in which high-frequency photons called γ radiation are emitted. This type of radiation is due to the nucleus passes from an excited state of higher energy to a lower energy state. γ radiation is a very penetrating electromagnetic radiation because the photons have no electrical charge.

In the case of protons, electrons, neutrons, α particles, heavy ions, etc., the E energy is the kinetic energy given by the classical equation:

$$E = \frac{1}{2} m v^2 \tag{1}$$

Where m is the mass and v the particle speed. The Joule, J, is the energy unit in the international system.

On the other hand, radiations provide a vehicle for transporting energy from one place (the source) to another (the absorber). The electron volt [eV] is the unit used in radiation physics and it is defined as the energy acquired by a particle with electric charge e (electron electric charge of 1.6×10^{-19} C) in a potential difference of 1 Volt. The equivalence with the Joule is $1\text{eV}=1.60\times10^{-19}$ J.

Since light has wave-particle duality, at times it behaves as particle and some other shows wave characteristics. Thus, a photon has an energy given by:

$$E = h v \tag{2}$$

Where h is the Planck constant (equal to 6.626×10^{-34} Js) and υ is the wave frequency.

Photons travel at the speed of light in vacuum c, as:

$$v = \frac{c}{\lambda} \tag{3}$$

Where λ is the wavelength.

One result of the relativity theory is the possibility of converting mass into energy and vice versa obeying the formula:

$$E = m c^2 \tag{4}$$

2.2 Radiation sources

In this work the referred radiation is the one caused by jumps of electrons around the nucleus, which is called X-rays, but mainly to the radiation originated from transitions within the nucleus, gamma rays.

Most sources used for radiation measuring are radioisotopes that decay by emission of a beta-less. This process can be described as follows:

$$ {}_{Z}^{A}X \rightarrow {}_{Z+1}^{A}Y + \beta^- + \bar{\nu} \quad (5)$$

Where X and Y are the nucleus of the initial and final elements, and $\bar{\nu}$ is an antineutrino. The nucleus of the initial element is called the father nucleus and the nucleus of the final element is called a son nucleus. Due to neutrinos and antineutrinos have a low probability of interaction with matter, they are virtually undetectable, and thus ionizing radiation produced by beta decay is the fast electron or beta particle.

After a beta less decay the nucleus is in a metastable state and to reach its base state it emits a gamma photon. As the nuclear states have well defined energies, the gamma ray energy emitted in the transition from state to state is also well defined.

All the above processes can be displayed in a decay scheme as shown in Fig. 2, where a horizontal line represents the father nucleus, and the final horizontal line represents the son nucleus. The horizontal lines between these two lines represent intermediate excited states. A diagonal line to the left shows an electron capture decay, a small vertical line followed by a diagonal line to the left indicates a β^+ or alfa decay, and a right diagonal line indicates a β^- decay. Vertical lines indicate the emission of gamma rays.

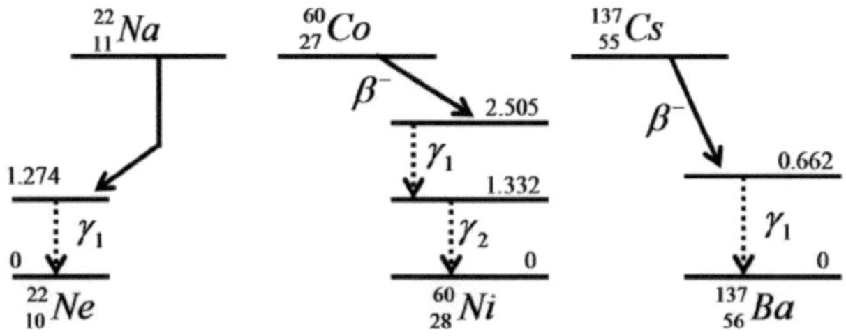

Fig. 2. To the left is the decay scheme of ^{22}Na. At the center is the decay scheme of ^{60}Co. To the right is the decay scheme of ^{137}Cs

In order to calibrate the systems, four sources of radiation: ^{22}Na, ^{57}Co, ^{60}Co and ^{137}Cs are commonly used. Their decay schemes are shown in Fig. 2. The ^{22}Na decays by the process of β^+ emitting a gamma photon of 1.274 MeV when the nucleus is stable, but also emits two gamma photons of 511 keV product of the annihilation of positron. The ^{60}Co decays to ^{60}Ni via a β^-, it emits two photons of 1.173 and 1.332 MeV. ^{137}Cs decays to ^{137}Ba also by a β^- process, 6.5% of the time decays directly to ^{137}Ba and 93.5% decays to ^{137}mBa emitting a gamma photon of 662 keV, 85% of the times.

Reference sources are an essential accessory to measure radiation in a laboratory. Usually, they are samples of radioisotopes of few microcuries encapsulated in plastic disc. The thickness of the package is enough to stop the radiation from the father nucleus decay allowing the passage only to the gamma radiation produced by the decay of the son nucleus.

2.3 Photon-matter interaction

When X-rays or gamma rays pass through a medium, the interaction between photons and matter can be noticed by the result of energy transferred to the medium. Due to the abundance of electrons in any substance, the most common interaction process of different radiations is with the electrons in the material, giving rise to the ionization and excitation phenomena. Through these processes, radiations usually deposit almost all their energy on the substances with which they collide. A high percentage of this energy ends up as heat, raising the temperature of the material, but part of the energy deposited can also cause chemical reactions and changes in the material structure.

The attenuation of a photons beam by an absorber material is mainly caused by four types of interactions: coherent scattering, photoelectric effect, Compton effect and pair production. Each of these processes can be represented by its own coefficient of attenuation, which varies according to the incident photon energy and atomic number of absorber material.

2.3.1 Coherent scattering

Coherent scattering is also known as classic scattering or Rayleigh scattering. This interaction consists of an electromagnetic wave that passes near an electron and makes it oscillate. The oscillating electron re-radiates energy at the same frequency as the incident electromagnetic wave. In this way, there is no change in energy and there is not absorbed energy by the medium, there is only a photon scattering effect for small angles. The coherent scattering is probable for materials with high atomic numbers and low energy photons.

2.3.2 Photoelectric effect

The photoelectric effect is a phenomenon in which a photon interacts with an atom and ejects an orbiting electron as shown in Fig. 3. In this process the photon's energy $h\upsilon$ is absorbed by the atom and then it is transferred to the electron. The kinetic energy of the ejected electron (called a *photoelectron*) is equal to $h\upsilon - E_B$, where E_B is the binding energy of the electron. Interactions of this kind can take place with electrons in layers *K, L, M* or *N*.

After that the electron has been ejected from the atom, a hole is created in this orbital; with this the atom is in an excited state. The hole can be filled by another electron from the external orbital, emitting radiation known as X-ray.

2.3.3 Compton effect

The Compton effect is a logical extension of the photoelectric effect. The difference is that in this case the photons are generally more energetic than when the photoelectric effect occurs (X-rays or gamma rays) and as a result, all its energy is not used to remove and accelerate an electron. In this case, there is excess energy and the photon does not disappear completely.

In this interaction the incident photon with energy E_0 and an associated wavelength, λ_0, from Equation (2), interacts with an electron that is free in the material, Fig. 3. The result is a low energy photon E_λ and an electron that goes back with a kinetic energy T depending on the angle of the leaving new photon.

It is common that the Compton effect occurs when the incident photons falls within a range from 0.05 MeV to several MeV. The energy range overlaps with the photoelectric energy range. With very low photon energies, the photoelectric effect is dominant, but becomes less common with increasing photon energy. The Compton effect begins slowly at low levels of energy and becomes dominant from 0.1 to 0.15 MeV and onwards, see Fig. 4.

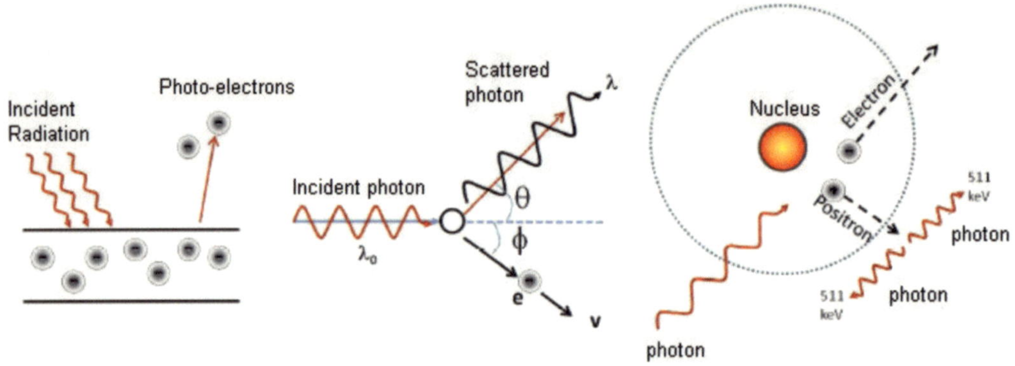

(a) Photoelectric effect (b) Compton effect (c) Pairs production

Fig. 3. In photoelectric effect, a material emits electrons when electromagnetic radiation incides on it. In Compton effect, the electromagnetic radiation striking out a surfaces goes out with a wavelength greater than the input. In pair production a photon interacts with a nucleus, completely disappears and results in the creation of a particle-antiparticle pair, electron-positron

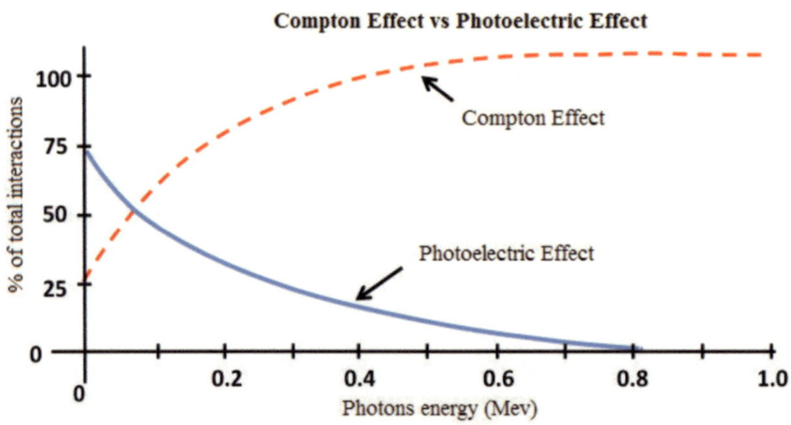

Fig. 4. With very low photon energies, the photoelectric effect is dominant. The Compton effect becomes dominant from 0.1 to 0.15 MeV and onwards

2.3.4 Pairs production

In this process the photon full energy is converted within an atom in a positron-electron pair, Fig. 3. As in the photoelectric effect, pairs production requires the presence of a body with large Z. Furthermore, in this process the photon must have energy greater than or equal to 1.022 MeV.

2.4 Ionizing radiation detection

Since the ionizing radiation is generally not perceptible by the senses, it is necessary to use appropriate tools to detect its presence. Many types of radiation detectors have been developed and each one is sensitive to certain types of radiation and energy range, therefore it is essential to select the appropriate detector for the radiation to be measured.

Radiation detectors have been developed based on the interactions of ionizing radiation with matter described above. The idea is to measure the lost energy or deposited by radiation when passing through the detector. Radiation detectors convert the energy deposited in a measurable electrical signal of few volts, which is achieved by constructing a diagram called characteristic energy spectrum (see Fig. 5). If there is mono-energetic radiation incident, variations in the measurements of that energy would appear due to an incomplete deposit of the incident radiation. For example, in a gamma camera some of the incident photons of 82 keV can have one or more Compton scatterings depositing part of their energy and then leave the detector.

The continuous proportion in the energy spectrum shown in Fig. 5 is due to partial energy deposits. The peak position marks the average energy of the incident radiation (after a full deposit in the detector).

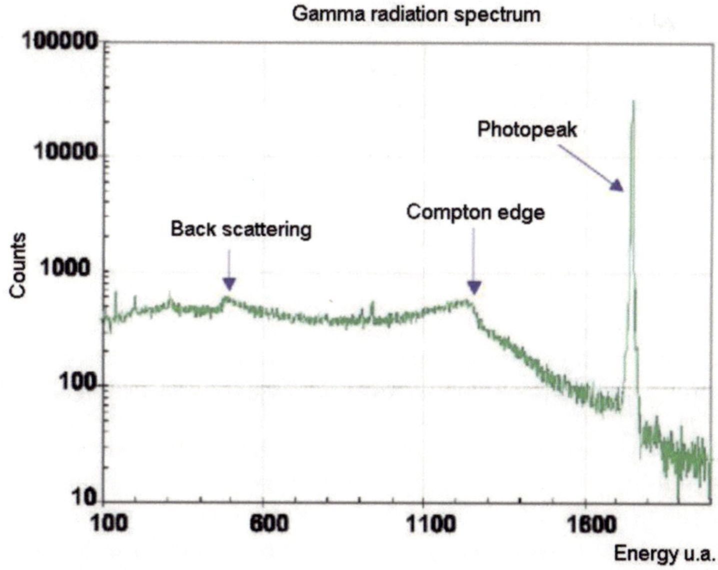

Fig. 5. Typical spectrum of gamma radiation, where the photopeak, the Compton edge and the backscattering peak are shown

The width of this peak (called photopeak) shows the effect of fluctuations for energy deposits for a mono-energetic photon. The detector's ability to accurately measure the energy deposited is an important parameter and is characterized by the width of the photopeak in the energy spectrum, referred to as the energy resolution of the system.

Radiation detectors generally used in the mini gamma cameras are called scintillation detectors. They are composed of an inorganic crystal (scintillator) and a photodetector. The scintillator crystal emits photons with wavelengths in the visible after radiation-matter interaction occurs inside the crystal. The photodetector is used to detect and measure the number of photons emitted by an interaction in the scintillator crystal. The number of photons due to scintillation (or intensity) is generally proportional to the energy deposited within the crystal. Due to the high atomic number, and therefore high density, scintillator detectors give high braking efficiency for photons of about 500 keV.

3. The mini gamma camera

The mini gamma camera is an imaging device commonly used in nuclear medicine as a diagnostic tool. The radiation comes from the patient who is previously injected, usually intravenously, with a radioactive tracer. The mode of conducting the clinical diagnosis is called scintigraphy.

The radioisotope tracer can be monitored inside the patient's body by the mini gamma camera and making easier to establish a medical diagnosis. The analysis offered by the gammagrams is especially functional rather than anatomical such as x-rays. They serve to assess whether a patient's metabolism is working properly adhering tracers, for example in platelets, red blood cells or other cells where a correct operation is checked. It is possible to mark the glucose molecules to assess which areas of the brain are activated (consume more glucose) at certain times.

Without loss of generality it can be say that a gamma camera consists of three components: a head or radiation detector, a data acquisition system and image reconstruction algorithms, as shown in Fig. 6.

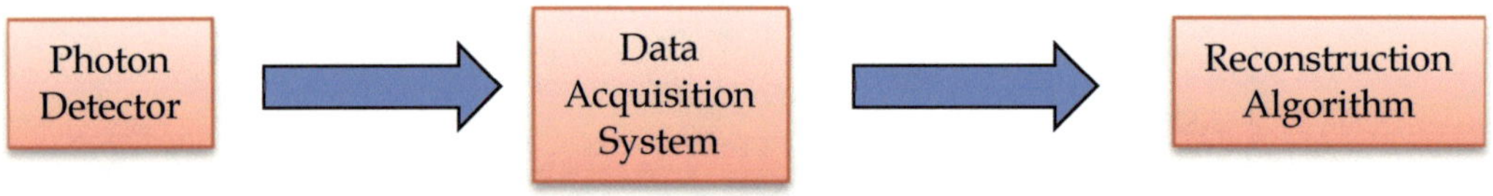

Fig. 6. Schematic of the gamma camera parts. The three components are: a head or radiation detector, an electronic data acquisition system and image reconstruction algorithms

The photon detector is responsible for converting the radiation-matter interaction into analog electrical pulses; it is usually composed of a collimator, a scintillator crystal and a photomultiplier tube (PMT). The collimator allows the passage only of radiation emitted perpendicular to the head and is usually constructed of lead or tungsten. In the scintillator crystal take place radiation-matter interaction processes between photons and the material that constitute the scintillator crystal, usually sodium iodide, $NaI(Tl)$ or Cesium Iodide, $CsI(Tl)$, both activated with thallium, to deliver lower energy photons (ultraviolet radiation).

The PMT is able to detect ultraviolet photons and turn them into a measurable electrical pulse in order to be processed by the appropriate electronics.

3.1 Photon detector

A radiation detector is a device used to track and identify high-energy particles, such as those produced by radioactive decay, cosmic radiation or reactions in a particle accelerator. In nuclear physics, radiation detectors capable of identifying energies in the order of keV are used.

The photon detector for the mini gamma camera consists of a collimator, a scintillator crystal, an array of photomultiplier tubes and positioning electronics.

3.2 Collimator

Leaning on the detector is the collimator; it is an element that is chosen according to the needs of study (Simon et al., 2003). It is made of lead or tungsten and is crossed by a distributed set of holes with different geometric patterns. The lead bricks between the holes are called *septas*. The collimator improves the system detection.

3.3 Scintillator crystal

In high-resolution mini gamma camera or micro PET equipment, the scintillator crystals can be cut into small blocks that are grouped into a matrix, separated by a reflective material. This configuration of segmented crystals (also known as pixilated crystals) is the dominant commercial high-resolution equipment and it is intended that each crystal behaves as a small waveguide for optical photons, in order to avoid that the light produced in the interaction of gamma rays is spread.

The materials most commonly used in the mini gamma cameras have been the sodium iodide activated with thallium (*NaI:Tl*) (Sánchez et al., 2004), bigermanate of bismuth (*BGO*) (Zhang et al., 2002), the oxi-ortosilicato of gadolinium (*GSO*), oxi-ortosilicato of lutetium (*LSO*) (Demetri & Jonathon, 2005) and its variants, the last two, doped with cerium. The most interesting features of these crystals and other novel materials are shown in Table 1.

3.4 Photomultiplier tube

The photomultiplier tubes used in mini gamma cameras are sensitive to the position (PSPMT). The first requirement in this design is the use of an electron multiplier structure which maintains a spatial separation between the electrons clouds multiplied (from the photoelectrons generated in different positions on the photocathode). One of the electron multiplier structures is the metal channel dynodes.

In the structure of metal channel dynodes gives a crosstalk effect during the multiplication of secondary electrons. This is due to the emitted electrons from the photocathode go to the first dynode by the focus grille, then they flow toward the second dynode, the third, until the last dynode and finally to the anode. Fig. 7 shows this type of structure. The common method of reading the outputs of the PS-PMT is a resistive arrangement; see Fig. 8, which allows calculating the position of interaction of radiation in the scintillator crystal.

	Maximum wavelength (nm)	Refractive index	Decay Time (μs)
Alkaline			
NaI(Tl)	415	1.85	0.23
CsI(Tl)	540	1.80	0.68, 3.34
CsI(Na)	420	1.84	0.46, 4.18
slow inorganic			
BGO	480	2.15	0.30
$CdWO_4$	470	2.13	1.1, 1.45
ZnS(Ag)	450	2.36	0.2
Fast inorganic without activator			
BaF_2	220		0.0006
CsI	305		0.002, 0.02
CeF_3	310	1.68	0.005, 0.027
Cerium activated fast inorganic			
GSO	440	1.85	0.056, 0.4
YAP	370	1.95	0.027
YAG	550	1.82	0.088, 0.302
LSO	420	1.82	0.047

Table 1. Properties of some inorganic crystals

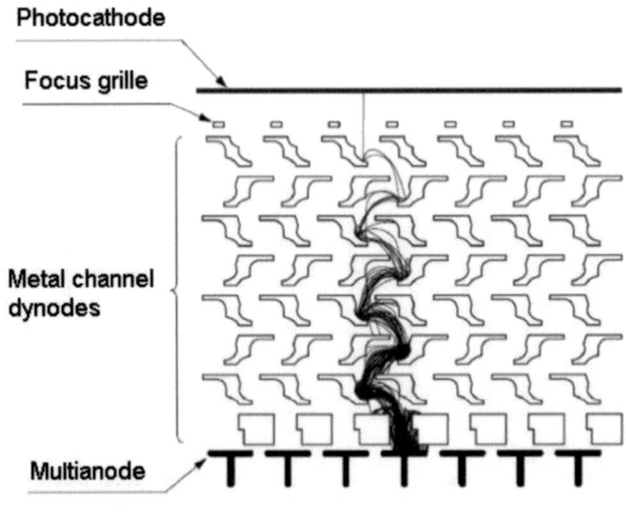

Fig. 7. Dynode structure and electrons trajectory

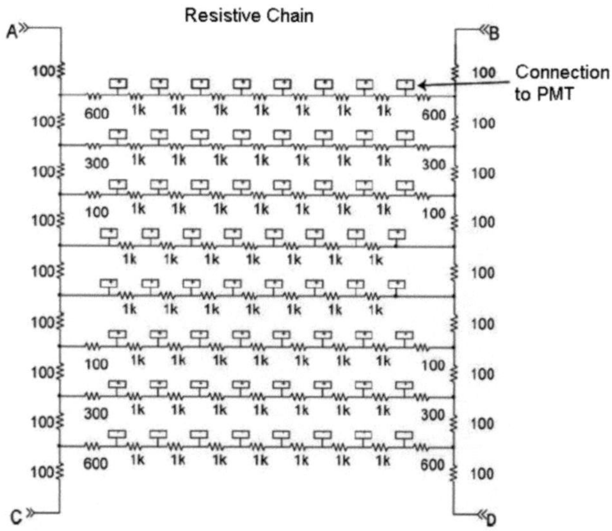

Fig. 8. Positioning circuit consisting of an array of resistors, commonly known as resistive chain

3.5 X, y positions calculation

In general to calculate an average position, the best estimate of the true value of $\vec{x}$ is given by the weighted average given by the following expression:

$$\vec{x} = \frac{\sum_i P_i \vec{x}_i}{P_i} \tag{6}$$

$\vec{x}$ indicates the position (x, y) of the event, P_i are the weights and x_i are the positions of the elements in question.

If the amount of light detected by a PMT is inversely proportional to the lateral distance between the place of interaction and the center of the PMT (Simon et al., 2003), as illustrated in Fig. 9. Ideally, the ratio between the signal amplitude in relation to the center of a PMT should be linear. In addition, the maximum measurable voltage at points A and B of the resistive chain, are also linear in relation to the center of signals delivered by the PMT. This allows calculating an event position by taking a weighted average or centroid of the PMT signals.

In this case the problem lies in knowing the position of a gamma photon interaction on the surface of the scintillator crystal. Assuming that the position of interaction is given by the values (x, y), as shown in Fig. 10, the known values are the maximum voltages (V_A, V_B, V_C and V_D) and the positions where these voltages are measured (x_1, y_2), (x_2, y_2), (x_1, y_1) and (x_2, y_1). Using equation (6) the position (x, y) is:

$$x = \frac{(V_A + V_C)x_1 + (V_B + V_D)x_2}{V_A + V_B + V_C + V_D} \tag{7}$$

$$y = \frac{(V_C + V_D)y_1 + (V_A + V_B)y_2}{V_A + V_B + V_C + V_D} \tag{8}$$

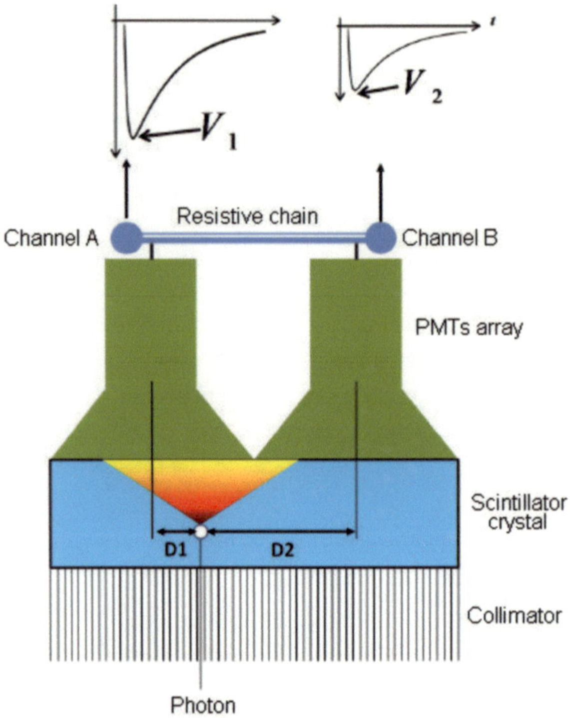

Fig. 9. Illustration of gamma radiation interacting with the photomultiplier tube

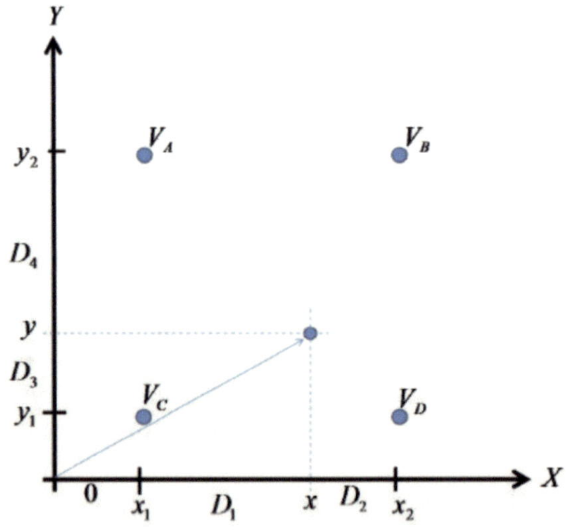

Fig. 10. Scheme to describe the process of event detection. In the Cartesian system position identifies the four voltage signals, V_A, V_B, V_C and V_D, and the position (x, y) of gamma photon interaction on the crystal

Equations (7) and (8), indicate that the sought position is a function of the maximum values, which change over time, and the known positions x_1, x_2, y_1 and y_2.

In order to remove the dependence on the known positions the following variables are defined: $D_1 = x - x_1$, $D_2 = x^2 - x$, $D_3 = y - y_1$, $D_4 = y_2 - y$, $D = D_1 + D_2$ y $D' = D_3 + D_4$, see Fig. 10. In this way, $D = x_2 - x_1$ y $D' = y_2 - y_1$, and doing simple calculations leads to the following equations:

$$x' = \frac{D_1}{D} = \frac{V_B + V_D}{V_A + V_B + V_C +} \tag{9}$$

$$y' = \frac{D_3}{D'} = \frac{V_A + V_B}{V_A + V_B + V_C + V_D} \tag{10}$$

The photon energy that interacted with the scintillator crystal is proportional to the sum of the maximum voltages:

$$E \propto V_A + V_B + V_C + V_D \tag{11}$$

As can be seen, the resistive chain helps to reduce the number of signals from the photomultiplier tubes to only four. This is not the only system to reduce the number of signals, but it is the simplest to build (Demetri, 2005).

The most important thing from equations (9), (10) and the proportionality given by (11) is that only the maximum voltage values of the four signals from the resistive chain V_A, V_B, V_C and V_D are involved. That is, it is not important to know the exact information from the whole pulse, it is enough to find its maximum value in voltage, in order to know the relative position (x, y) of the interaction on the scintillator crystal and an approximation of the energy deposited.

3.6 Data acquisition system

A data acquisition system takes analog electronic signals to generate data that can be manipulated by a computer or other electronic system (digital system). This procedure takes a set of physical signals; it turns them in current signals and digitized them in order to be processed on a computer. It is required a conditioning stage, which adapts the signal to levels compatible with the element that makes the conversion to digital. The element that makes this transformation is the digitalization module or data acquisition board. A data acquisition system is basically composed of:

- The signal sources, which are of two kinds:
  1. Direct measurement elements. They produce a signal as a result of electrical measurements, such as voltage, current, resistance, frequency, etc.
  2. Transducers. They are devices that sense physical phenomena and convert non-electrical parameters into electrical signals; examples are resistance temperature detectors, pressure transducers, among others.
- Elements of signal conditioning. These elements amplify, isolate and filter signals to make more accurate measurements.
- Data processing and display. Allows the signals visualization. Data can be displayed in analog or digital way, numerically or graphically.

3.7 Image reconstruction algorithms

The principle of image reconstruction in all forms of tomography is that an object can be reproduced exactly from a set of its projections taken from different angles. In the last two decades, several algorithms have been developed, they can be considered as methods to approximate the inverse Radon transform. They can be implemented for different tomography reconstruction modalities. It is noteworthy that these methods are not all equivalent.

3.8 Energy resolution

The energy resolution is a measure of the system's ability to distinguish between particles or photons of different energies. That can be determined by irradiating the detector with monoenergetic particles or photons and measuring the width of the Gaussian peak in the resulting heights spectrum of the acquired signals. A wider Gaussian peak implies a poorer energy resolution. The width of the Gaussian peak is usually measured at half its maximum height, as illustrated in Fig. 11, which is called *the full width at half-maximum* (FWHM). In this way the energy resolution is expressed as:

$$R = \frac{FWHM}{M} \times 100\% \qquad (12)$$

R is the energy resolution and M is the energy value correspondent to the maxim Gaussian peak.

For example, the energy resolution of a crystal of 5 cm in diameter and 5 cm thick, coupled to a PMT and exposed to gamma rays of 662 keV of ^{137}Cs, is typically about 7% to 8%.

4. Materials and methods

The camera presented in this work is composed of a Hamamatsu H8500 Flat Panel PS-PMT (Hamamatsu Photonics, 2007), a LYSO scintillator (Chen, 2007), a resistive chain, a data acquisition system and a hardware architecture for image reconstruction. Fig. 12 shows a block diagram of the implemented system.

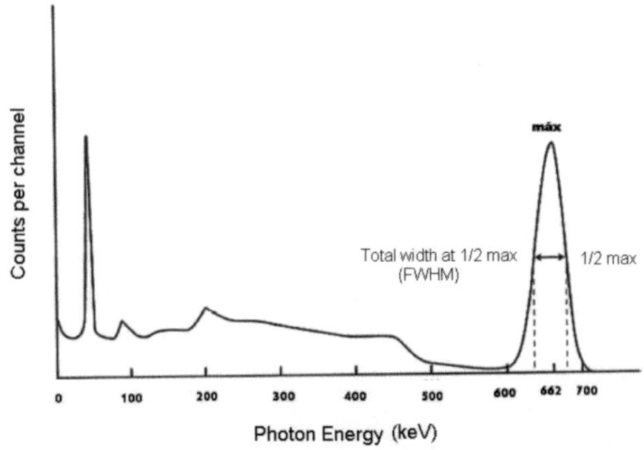

Fig. 11. Energy resolution of a height pulse spectrometer. The spectrum shown corresponds to ^{137}Cs, obtained by a scintillator *NaI* (*Tl*) coupled to a photomultiplier tube.

The scintillation structure is composed of 20×20 LYSO crystal. The H8500 Flat Panel PS-PMT has an external size of 52.0×52.0×27.4 mm^3 with an active area of 49×49 mm^2; the gain of the H8500 is about 10^6 for -1000V.

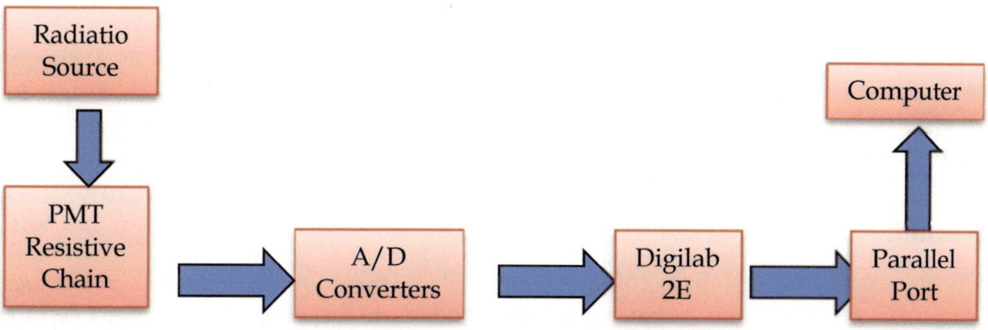

Fig. 12. Main camera connected to the data acquisition hardware

The multiplied charge is collected by an array of 8×8 anodes and the size of each anode is 5.8×5.8 mm^2. The resistive chain is composed of one board (60×60×3 mm^3) mounted orthogonally with respect to the PS-PMT according to Fig. 13 (Olcott, 2006), combined with two dedicated compact 2-channel ADC board developed in the faculty laboratory. The ADC board contains two 10 bits analogue-to-digital converters with 100 MSPS, an on-chip voltage reference of 1V to 2V p-p single-ended. The ADC boards are connected to a 2E board which allows to pick up the maximum values of the signals and stores them in a FIFO memory (data transmission is 100 MHz). The 2E board is connected to a Virtex IV based board, which allows calculating x, y position values for each event based on the Anger's logic (Equations 9, 10 and 11).

Fig. 13. Scintillator structure coupled with the resistive chain

The system allows to display planar histogram in real time mode (1s refresh time). To build a 2D image, the x and y values are used to determine a location on the image and the brightness of the pixel at that position corresponds with the histogram value calculated (Equation 11). This process is performed until a desired number of counts on total acquisition time are reached. In order to display the results, the data are sent to a VGA monitor. The test was carried out using a ^{137}Cs point source (1microCi activity) emitting 662 keV (99%) gamma-ray lines. The architecture has been implemented using VHDL and synthesized to a XC4VFX20-FF672 Virtex IV FPGA with the Xilinx Synthesis Technology (XST) tool and placed and route with Foundation ISE 10. Inside the Virtex IV the Anger logic (Wong, 2006) is implemented profiting parallelism inherent to operation in order to achieve real time performance.

5. Results

When the acquisition system is complete, the energy spectrum of the crystal and its decay constant are obtained, the pulses shape obtained with the acquisition system for these values are presented. Finally the ^{137}Cs source is placed in a corner on the scintillator crystal and the energy resolution of the system and the first scintigraphies are obtained.

The voltage pulses registered caused by radiation from the scintillator crystal are in the range of 40 to 400 mVolts, as shown in Fig. 14. By comparing the emission spectrum of LYSO crystal is identified that he voltage range (50 to 250 mV) should match to the range of the emitted energy in the crystal, which corresponds to wavelengths from 380 to 460 nm therefore the system must be calibrated.

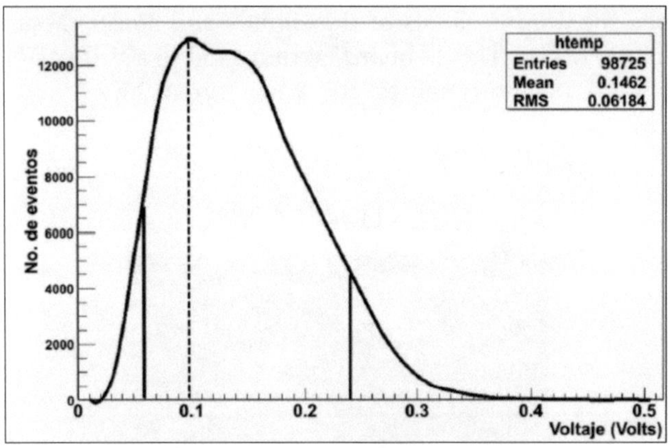

Fig. 14. Emission spectrum for the scintillator crystal

In data acquisition, 15 traces are obtained for each pulse, from these the one appearing in the fourteenth position is taken, see Fig. 14. The time in which occurs (140 ns) is known, the maximum and the trace value at 140 ns is also known. Using the following equation for different voltage pulses the histogram shown in Figure 8 is obtained.

$$\lambda = \frac{1}{t} ln \left[\frac{v(t)}{V_{max}}\right] \tag{13}$$

V_{max} is the maximum voltage, v(t) is the voltage measured at t time. The decay constant for the crystal is 41,03 ± 9,6 ns.

In order to calculate the energy resolution, first a histogram of the emission spectrum of ^{137}Cs was obtained as can be seen in Fig. 15. It is possible to identify the photopeak and using equation (12) the energy resolution is calculated.

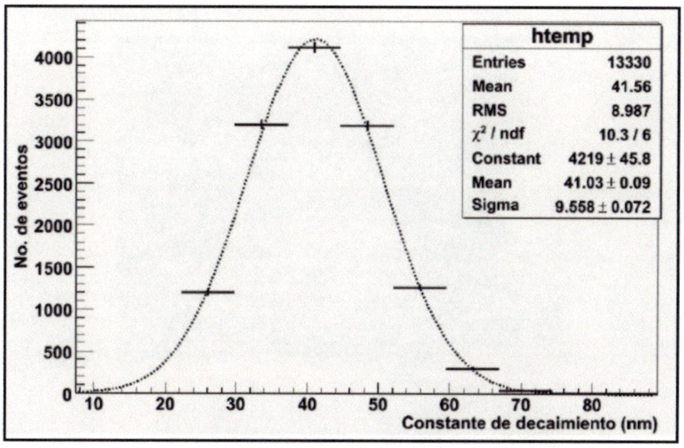

Fig. 15. Histogram to determine the decay constant of the scintillator crystal, which resulted in 41ns

The H8500 has PSPMT non-uniformity. It is known that the photomultiplier is pixilated into an array of 8×8 pixels. It is expected that each pixel has a different answer to the same power source. That is why the different responses of each pixel must be quantified and standardized with respect to the greatest response.

When the resolution of the system for all pixels is calculated, a resolution of 34% is obtained. This value is mainly affected by the PSPMT non-uniformity. For this reason the energy resolution for a single pixel was obtained, which is 19%. This result is promising because it is within the values reported in the literature (Knoll, 2000).

The image obtained with the LYSO crystal, the source of ^{137}Cs the adquisition block and the Virtex IV board can be seen in Fig. 16. The system is operating at a frequency of 322 MHz, which will give the system the capability of real time operation. The amount of area used by

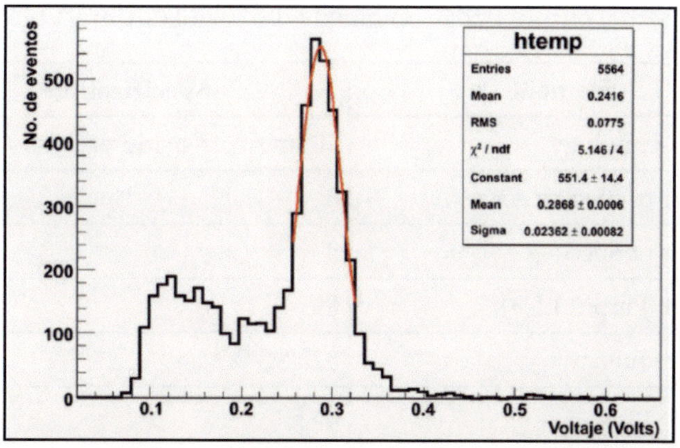

Fig. 16. Energy spectrum for the ^{137}Cs source. The value obtained was 19%

the implementation is considerably reduced, around 25% of total available in the FPGA; this is due to the implemented operations are really simple and performed in parallel. Furthermore each processing block is re-used by the data incoming to the architecture. Technical data for the FPGA architecture are resumed in Table 2.

Fig. 17. Two dimensional output image obtained with the FPGA in a VGA monitor

Element	Specification
FPGA technology	90nm triple-oxide process
Number of Block RAMs	3
Number of Slices	53
Number 4 input LUTs	89
Clock frequency	322 MHz
Area Occupancy	25%

Table 2. Technical data for the FPGA architecture

6. Conclusions and future work

In this paper the implementation of a read out electronics prototype for a gamma camera has been presented. The system has successfully included reprogrammable devices in order to accelerate a two-dimensional image construction. A board containing a Virtex IV FPGA was used for implementation where parallel techniques and an efficient management of data and a reduced access to memory were used. The obtained system provides enough flexibility for adjustment to new requirements or new algorithms. The main contribution of this work consists on validating the use of a FPGA in the image processing stage for a nuclear medicine application.

Nowadays this application is being developed looking for the reconstruction to be performed in real time. Based on results obtained for planar images; as future work it is proposed the implementation of the filtered back projection algorithm for image reconstruction inside the FPGA in order to accelerate it.

Even though ^{137}Cs is not the most commonly source used in a gamma camera, in the present work it was employed due to as future work it is planned to extend the prototype to the implementation of a PET system.

7. References

Anger, Hal O. (1958). Scintillation Camera, *Review of scientific instruments*, Vol.29, No.1, (January 1958), pp. 27-33, ISSN 0034-6748.

Simon R., et al. (2003). *Physics in Nuclear Medicine*, Elsevier, ISBN 9780721683416, Philadelphia, USA.

Sánchez, F., Et al. (2004). Design and tests of a portable mini gamma camera, *Medical Physics*, Vol.31, No.6, (May 2004), pp. 1384-1396, ISSN 0094-2405.

Zhang, N., et al. (2002). Anode Position and Last Dynode Timing Circuits for Dual-Layer BGO Scintillator With PS-PMT Based Modular PET Detectors, *IEEE Transactions on Nuclear Science*, Vol.49, No.5, (October 2002), pp. 2203-2207, DOI: 10.1109/TNS.2002.803815

Demetri, P. & Jonathon A. (2005). Compact Readout Electronics for Position Sensitive Photomultiplier Tubes, *IEEE Transactions on Nuclear Science*, Vol.52, No.1, (February 2005), pp. 21-27, DOI: 10.1109/TNS.2004.843134

Hamamatsu Photonics, Electron Tube Center, H8500 Data Sheet (2007).

Chen, J., et al. (2007). Gamma-Ray Induced Radiation Damage in Large Size LSO and LYSO Crystal Samples, *IEEE Transactions in Nuclear Science*, Vol.54, No.4, (August 2007), pp. 1319-1326, ISSN 9781-4244-3962-1.

Olcott, P. D., et al. (2006). Compact Readout Electronics for Position Sensitive Photomultiplier Tubes, *IEEE Transactions in Nuclear Science*, Vol.53, No.5, (October 2006), pp. 2698-2703, ISSN .

Wong, W. (2006). A High Count Rate Position Decoding and Energy Measuring Method for Nuclear Cameras Using Anger Logic Detectors, *IEEE Transactions in Nuclear Science*, Vol.45, No.3, (June 2006), pp. 1122-1127, ISSN.

Knoll, G. F. (2000). *Radiation detection and measurement*, John Wiley, ISBN 978-0-471-07338-3,Michigan, USA.

3

Adipose Measurement Using Micro MRI

Yang Tang and Rex A. Moats
University of Southern California, Children's Hospital Los Angeles
USA

1. Introduction

The increased incidence of obesity and well-documented co-morbidities, have lead to the recognition that obesity is a public health epidemic (Mann, 1974; Larsson et al., 1984). Excess adipose tissue is a high risk factor for cardiovascular and metabolic syndrome (Manson et al, 1990). These two diseases both rank high on the list of leading causes of morbidity and mortality not only in the developed world but now also in the developing world..

The now well established relationship between excess adiposity and disease, has spurred obesity research which has been supported both by public institutions and private companies. In most of adiposity research, the experiment designs require the assessment of the adipose load and the development of the associated biological or medical issues. The measurement of fat tissue is a fundamental task. Studies covering both the nature history of obesity and the development of obesity associated diseases often require repeated longitude measurements during the course of the experiments. This is especially true of protocols assessing interventions through outcome analysis. This chapter focuses on the measurement of adipose tissue in animal models by micro MRI in combination with an automated method for adipose measurement. The emphasis is on the logic, development and application of the computational methodology for virtual fat extraction.

1.1 Adipose imaging technique

Classic adipose measurements have been based on weight or Body Mass Index (BMI). Recently imaging technologies have emerged as powerful tools for refined adipose assessment (Zhao et al., 2006; Luu et al., 2009). Imaging can provide not only the size of an adipose depot, but also its location. Often this more accurate information is of critical importance to the adipose researches.

For adipose measurement, a variety of imaging techniques have been adopted in both human beings and small animals. Computed tomography (CT) is a widely used technique. It has the merits of high resolution and low cost. It has been developed in both humans (Zhao et al., 2006; Ohshima et al., 2008) and animals (Luu et al., 2009; Lublinsky et al., 2009). Compared to CT, Magnetic Resonance Imaging (MRI) (Gray, 1991; Gronemeyer, 2000) has advantageous in adipose research. Because MRI is radiation free, it is good for radiation sensitive research and desirable for longitudinal studies where the effects of radiation would be additive. This is especially true at the high resolution covered here.

1.2 Animal model and micro MRI

Experiments on Human subjects have obvious appropriate limitations. The mouse has emerged as the human surrogate in a large body of obesity research. In drug development and translational medicine research, preclinical research of animal models plays a significant role. Thus, researchers studying adipose tissue and the associated disease processes are actively pursuing preclinical studies using mouse models (Bechah et al., 2010; Church et al., 2009).

Micro MRI (small animal MRI) is a powerful tool for in vivo fat measurement using small animal models. As described before, micro MRI can provide quantitative information about fat volume as well as depot locations (Ranefall et al., 2009). In adipose research it is often important to obtain spatial information related to the mechanism of pathogenesis and disease onset.

1.3 Post processing

1.3.1 Manual measurement

Although micro MRI provides a powerful imaging tool, the post processing of the image dataset is intense time consuming work for both technicans and experts. Especially, for accurate abodomial adipose measurement, 3D volume instead of 2D slices are obtained for each animal. Therefore, a typical experiment on a group of mice will generate thousands of images requiring adipose measurements. This is an obstacle for high throughput and efficient discovery. In order to get the exact adipose region, manual drawing Region of Interests (ROI) is usually carried out. In such procedures, the errors and variations are inevitable.

In the case of manual measurements, intra- and inter-operators' variations result in repeated measurements and statistical complexity. Furthermore adipose tissue has irreguar shapes and located in various depots throughout the body. Thus expertise are required to detect the adipose from the organs in the MRI images. All these factors decrease the accuracy for fat measurement.

1.3.2 Automatic measurement

Considering the above limitation and complexity added by manual analysis, automated or semi-automated techniques are urgently demanded for adipose measurements which can relieve the researcher from the tedious operational burdens as well as reduce the operator-dependent errors.

In order to accomplish automatic measurement, many tasks have to be considered.

For fat measurement, the total size and locations of the fat tissues is basic information needed. From the imaging and image-processing viewpoint, how to extracting the fat pixels from the MR image is the first task.

This task require matched and optimized imaging protocols and customized algorithms. Based on the observation that fat is relative bright in T1 weighted images, the adipose tissues are often extracted from the images by applying a threshold to the intensities (Ranefall et al., 2009; Sijbers et al.,1998; Chae et al., 2007). To deal with the inhomogenity of the MR images due to the inhomogeneitis in the magnatic field, local and adaptive threshold methods have been adapted (Sijbers et al.,1998; Chae et al., 2007). Beyond threshold based methods; fuzzy logic methods have been applied. In fuzzy logic, each pixel is assigned a fuzzy membership to indicate the probability that the pixel is fat. Then the fat is extracted by minimizing the membership function instead of being based solely on a threshold (Positano et al., 2004; Positano et al., 2009). More mathematically complex models have been created to compensate for the inhomogeneities in the intensity images (Hou, 2006; Vovk et al., 2007). But methods based only on intensity are in general limited because other tissues or objects in the background exhibit similar intensities and complicate the separation. An exmaple can be seen in Figure.1, where the fat and non-fat region are close in intensity. (Tang et al., 2011)

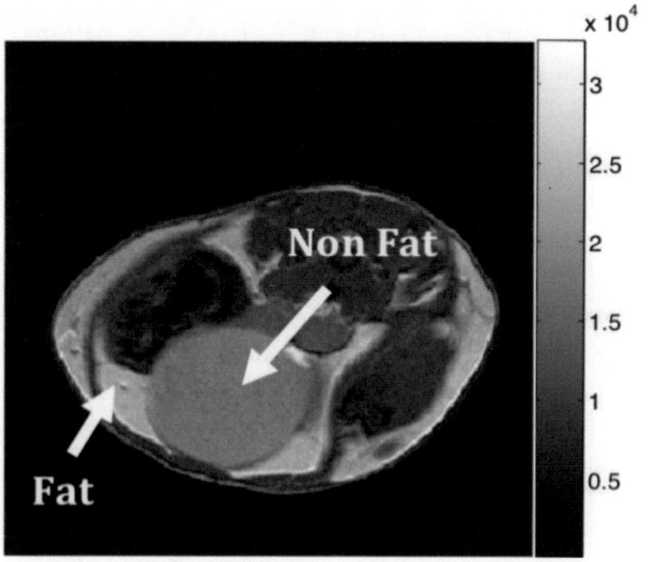

Fig. 1. The similar intensity of fat and non fat pixels in this case in the bladder. (Tang et al., 2011)

As a result, image acquisition techniques have been proposed to provide better discrimination. For example, the water-saturation technique (Dixon et al., 1984; Reeder et al., 2005; Peng et al., 2005). However, analogous techniques have not been implemented for small animals at micro MRI due to magnetic field inhomogeneities at high field that can lead to artifacts and due to the increased difficultly of implementing strictly analogous pulse programs.

For fat measurement, the location of fat depots has been shown to provide important information relevant to disease states. For example, the amount of abdominal visceral fat has been shown to be related to hypertension and cardiovascular disease, cerebrovascular disease, insulin resistance and type 2 diabetes (Ross et al., 2002; Snijder et al., 2006). Thus, an important issue in fat analysis is to assign the fat depot type to associated anatomical location, which usually includes the subcutaneous fat and visceral fat. To identify different fat depots, one common methods is based on region growing algorithms (Siegel et al., 2007; Ranefall et al., 2009), which start from the seed points planted in the different fat depots and grow to include nearby pixels with similar intensity into the same group and therefore depot. But the region growing method is difficult to apply in thin mouse with scattered fat tissues. Automated placement of the seed is still an unmet challenge in most cases.

In order to separate the visceral and subcutaneous fat, curve deformation methods (Positano et al., 2004; Positano et al., 2009; Zhao et al., 2006) have also been reported. These methods deform a curve inwards from skin contour to locate a muscle layer. Because the muscle layer lies between the subcutaneous and visceral fat, the different fat depots are separated by default.

1.4 Automatic fat measurement on micro MRI

Fat measurements using imaging technique have been established in humans (Siegel et al., 2007; Ohshima et al., 2008) at lower field strengths, fat measurement in mice models using micro MRI has not been adequately addressed.

Here we summarize our fat measurement system using micro MRI. As the schematic representation illustrated in Figure 2, the system includes an imaging and post processing module. In the imaging module, the mice are subject to a MRI scanning on the abdominal region with multiple echo sequence. In the post processing module, fat is first extracted from the multiple echo images with a multi-part algorithm based both on intensities and each pixels T2 translation relaxation time. In our system, the fat extraction is accomplished by adopting a fuzzy c mean clustering algorithm in the T1 weighted image and then selecting clusters into fat regions aided by the additional T2 information.

For fat depot recognition, we developed a method which utilizes a knowledge-based framework for image post acquisition image processing, which takes advantages of the a priori anatomical knowledge and automatically segments each depot into visceral fat or subcutaneous fat using fuzzy logic techniques.

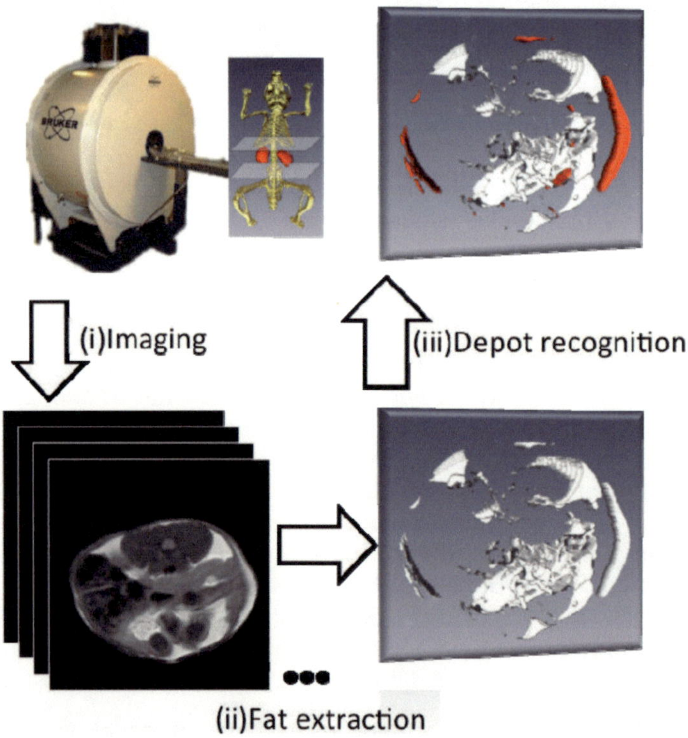

Fig. 2. The schematic representation of adipose measurement system using micro MRI

In this chapter, we will describe how we perform the fat measruement in typical mouse model of obseity, detailing how to perform the imaging, fat extraction and depot separation. Most of the content of this chapter comes from our groups previous and ongoing research work (Tang et al., 2010; Tang et al., 2011). For each section, section 2 presents the imaging protocol and animal groups for image acquisition; section 3 introduces the fat extraction method; section 4 describes the depot separation algorithm. In section 5, the automatic results is compared to manual reference for validataion. After that, the conclusion and acknowledgement is given in section 6 and section 7 respectively.

2. Image acquisition

2.1 Imaging sequence on micro MRI

The experiments were performed on micro MRI scanner (70/16 Bruker PharmaScan, Germany). The field strength of the instrument is 7.05 Tesla and the maximal gradient strength is 400mTesla/m.

To provide adequate signal to noise and coverage, slices were collected with 1mm thickness. An optimized Bruker multiple-slice-multiple-echo (MSME) sequence (TR=5300ms, TE=12~120ms, 10 echoes) was adopted to get the high signal to noise ratio. The field of view was 3*3cm and matrix size was 256*256, in-plane resolution was 117um.

In the imaging, we focus on the abdominal fat. For this purpose, mice were placed prone in a semi cylindrical holder. In previous research (Luu et al., 2009), the abdominal region has been defined from L1 to L5 of the spine in the CT images. Because in the MRI, bone hypointense is not as easily differentiated as it is in the CT, we define the abdominal region in micro MRI using the kidneys as a reference. Data starts at the slice at the top of the left kidney and ends at the end of right kidney.

2.2 Animal population

In order to validate the measurement system, the experiments were tested on an animal population with 26 wild type C57BL/6 mice.

There are 4 groups in the mice population with different adipose ratio, which is differentiated by feeding strategies. Mice received regular chow or a high fat diet respectively. In the regular chow group, mice were placed into 3 litters with different sibling numbers that provided different nutritional conditions due to competition or lack of competition. The details of animal experiments are listed in Tab.1 including large litter (LL), normal litter (NL), small litters (SL) and high fat (HF) groups. (Tang et al., 2011)

Group	Mouse num (Male, Female)	Feed	Little	Sibling num
LL	M=6 F=1	Chow	LL	12
NL	M=4 F=1	Chow	NL	7
SL	M=7 F=2	Chow	SL	3
HF	M=2 F=3	High Fat	LL,NL,SL	5

Table 1. Animal population for the experiments (Tang et al., 2011)

3. Adipose extraction

3.1 Principle

In the MR image, due to the high proton density, fat tissues usually has relative high intensity values. But only intensity information is not sufficient to allow segmentation due to complicated mechanisms resulting in high intensities in other organism as well. Therefore in the multi-component method, we combine pixel intensity information with transverse relaxation time to aid in the automated extraction of the fat tissues.

The basic idea is illustrated in Figure 3 (Tang et al., 2011). Here the first echo image is selected because of its high signal to noise ratio(SNR) compare to other echo images. In the first echo image, instead of the explicit threshold, the fuzzy c means (FCM) clustering approach (Dunn, 1973) is adopted to classify all pixels into groups. With the cluster image, we can first exclude the mouse body from the background by sorting the average intensity in each cluster. The cluster with their average intensity less than minimium threshold is considered to be background.

To deal with problem of the non fat tissue with high intensity in the T1 weighted image, the T2 parametric image based primarily on relaxation is explicitedly calculated from the multiple echo images. Because the T2 value reflects the transverse relaxation time of tissues, the T2 parametric image can help to separate the fat and non-fat tissues. An example is displayed in Figure 4, where the T2 parametric image exhibits a larger range of statitstially distinguishable values and thus aids us in seperating the fat from the non-fat tissues.

Prior to the fat extraction, an image filter is applied to the image data to reduce the noise level. All the technical details are summarized as following.

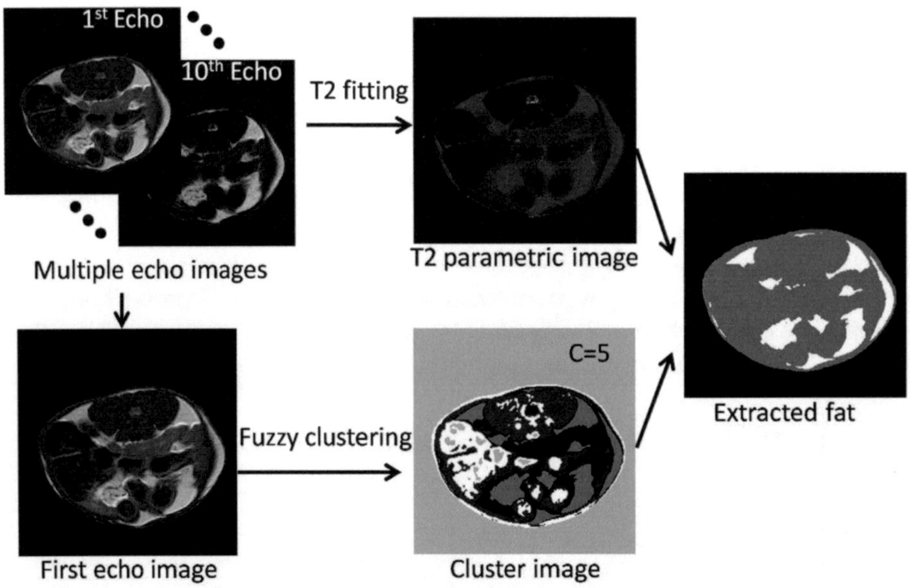

Fig. 3. The schematic representation of adipose measurement system using micro MRI.(Tang et al., 2011)

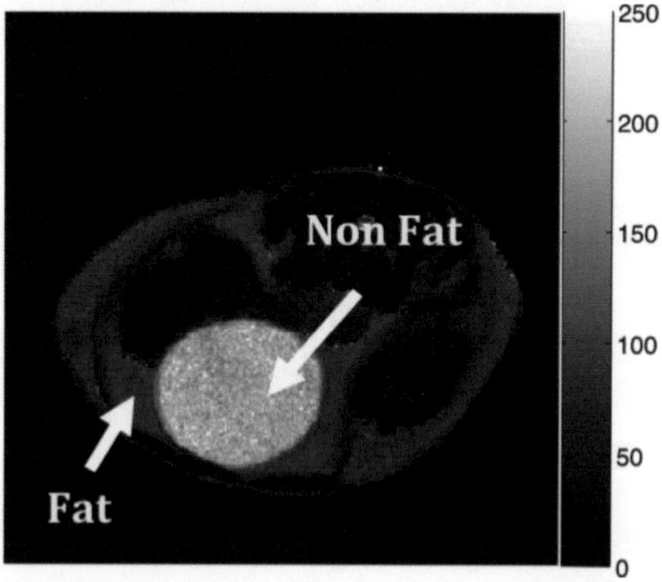

Fig. 4. The fat and non fat tissues in T2 parameter image.(Tang et al., 2011)

3.2 Image filter

The pre-processing step is necessary for reducing noise and thus enhance the image in specific ways. Filtering technique are often used for this purpose. Most image filters replaces the signal of a pixel according to the neighbouring pixels. Filtered image can be regarded as a convolution between original image and the kernel. The filter kernel, typically a matrix, represents the number of pixels nearby taken into account.

There are two typical filters including the linear and nonlinear filters used in image processing. The linear filter only takes into consideration the relative position in kernel, and remains constant throughout the whole image filtering. Nonlinear filters are relative to the target pixel and the coefficients are calculated as a function of local variations of the signal (Bonnya et al., 2003). For example, in the linear filter class, average and Gaussian filers are often used. Among the nonlinear filters, the median filter is popular. A selective blurring filter (Wang et al., 1981) is often used, which emphases the pixels with similar intensity to the target pixel. A bilateral filter (Tomasi&Manduchi, 1998) is an edge preserving technique proposed recently and has been widely used in image processing. In comparison to the selective blurring filter, not only the intensity similarity but also the spatial similarity is taken into account.

In this section, we try to give some examples of common filters for the adipose image and finally choose the bilateral filter for our system. Figure 5. shows the different results from both linear and nonlinear filters. For better insight, an amplified region of the whole image was displayed.

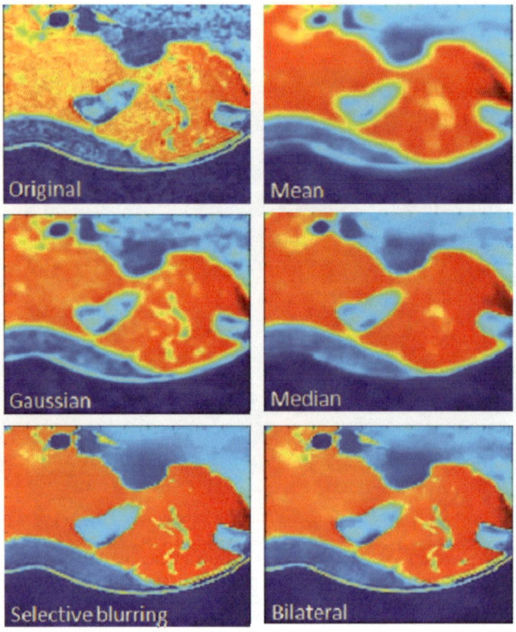

Fig. 5. The image of adipose tissue after the application of common image filters. (Tang et al., 2010)

3.3 Cluster image

Clustering is an important technique for image analysis, which can sort all the pixels in the image into different clusters according to their similarities. In our measurement system, the fuzzy c means (FCM) clustering approach (Dunn et al., 1973) was adopted to classify all pixels into groups and produce the cluster images. In this clustering, as shown in Figure 3 , the first echo image was chosen because of its relatively high SNR compared to later echo images.

In clustering, the cluster number is an important parameter. In the previous research (Positano et al., 2004; Positano et al., 2009; Ranefall et al., 2009), the cluster number was usually defined to be three, corresponding to background, fat and muscles. Nevertheless, in the real anatomy, more organs and tissues are included in the MR image. Three clusters do not well describe the discrepancies between different tissues. We found that increasing the cluster number was necessary to more accurately describe the full data. The fat tissue may display in multiple clusters and it becomes difficult to correctly select the appropriate cluster using intensity-only images. In our method, the clusters are recognized by their T2 values, which allowed us to increase the number of clusters.

3.4 T2 time

Transverse relaxation time (T2) is an important clue for adipose extraction in our system. To accurately measure the T2 time for each pixel of the parametric image, a curve is fitted to the decay of intensity with increasing TE (Vander et al., 2000). For the fitting of fat data, we used the weighted least square method with baseline subtraction and least point requirement. The fitting model and comparison of the fitting methods are described as follow.

3.4.1 Fitting model

The transverse relaxation time measurement of fat appears to satisfy a mono-exponential physical model known as: (Sijbers et al., 1998)

$$Si(S0,T2)=S0*exp(-Tei/T2) \quad (1)$$

with Tei=i*te and S0 is the pseudo-proton density, which is relative to the true proton density, T1 value and receiver coil response.

3.4.2 Fitting methods

T2 value can be calculated by fitting the experimental data to above model in equation (1). To accomplish the fitting, a fitting method should be adopted. Here we have a comparison of the least square and weighted square method.

A least square method (LS) is the common way of fitting the curve, which consists in minimizing the quadratic distance between the fitted curve and the curve represented by the raw data.

$$\phi^2 = \sum_{i=1}^{N} [I_i - S_0 \exp(-Te_i / T_2)]^2 \quad (2)$$

Where I_i is the scanned intensity of intensity images in ith echo.

Weighted least square method (WLS) takes other factors into account using the weight with merit function:

$$\phi^2 = \sum_{i=1}^{N} w_i^2 [I_i - S_0 \exp(-Te_i / T_2)]^2 \quad (3)$$

Where w_i, the weight of ith point, should represent the confidence of the signal. As the low intensity signals are more likely to be noise and according have less certainty, here w_i was simply set as proportion to the intensity.

In figure 6, the calculated T2 and S0 in fitting model are compared using both least square and weighted least square methods. We can see that weighted least square method presents a more consist result compared to least square method. Therefore, we adopted the weighted least square method in our system.

3.5 Adipose separation

With T2 reference, the fat regions are extracted in the cluster image by comparing the clusters' similarities in T2 values. In order to take T2 into account, the average T2 values are calculated for each cluster. A similarity threshold Ts is defined:

$$Ts=|T2cluster-T2fat|/T2fat \quad (4)$$

Here the T2cluster is the average T2 value in each cluster from non-empty pixels and T2fat is the T2 value of fat.

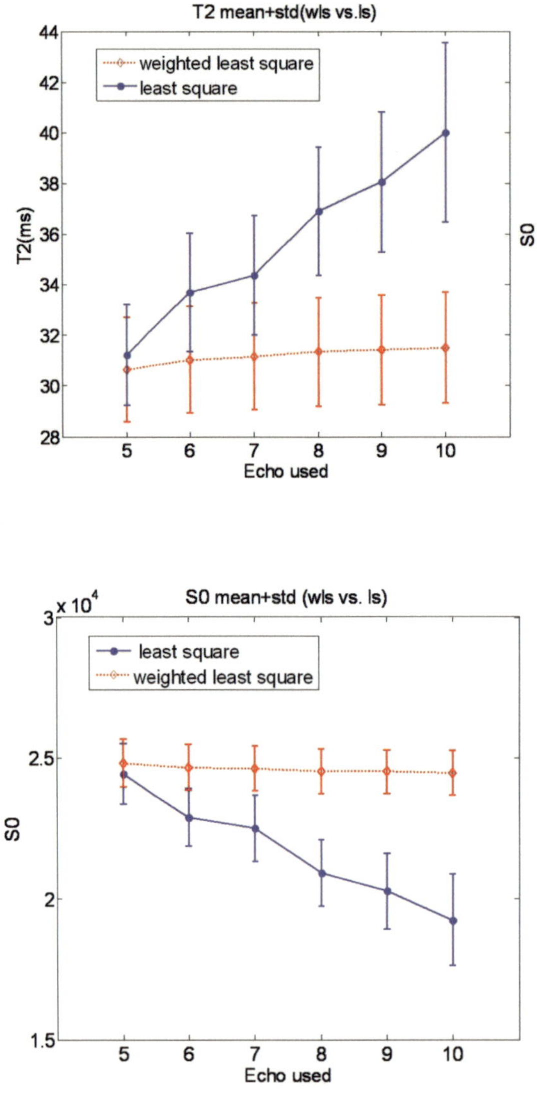

Fig. 6. Comparison of Methods for T2 fitting in the MR images(Tang et al., 2010)

Because the T2 value is related to the magnetic field strength, we suggest that the fat T2 could be defined by drawing a ROI in the known fat region or based on phantoms using the exact same imaging acquisition protocol and instrument.

The similarity threshold in Equation (4) defines a T2 range. The clusters with T2 value in the defined range are considered as fat tissues. Because the T2 values of fat and non-fat tissues are generally distinguishable, a reasonable threshold can be found for each specific application.

Instead of the threshold, a more complicate strategy can also be designed using a confidence image. More details can be found in our previous work (Tang et al., 2010).

4. Depot recognition

The definition of fat depots distribution and volume plays a great role in disease studies. In this study, we present a method to analysis the total adipose tissue (TAT), which employee a knowledge-based framework to separate the subcutaneous adipose tissue (SAT) from the visceral adipose tissue(VAT).

4.1 Principle

The basic procedures of depot separation are illustrated in Figure 7. Before the knowledge is applied, a morphological operation is performed to decompose the fat tissues. Then the unconnected parts are labelled and a knowledge-based method is adopted to recognize each object to be different depots.

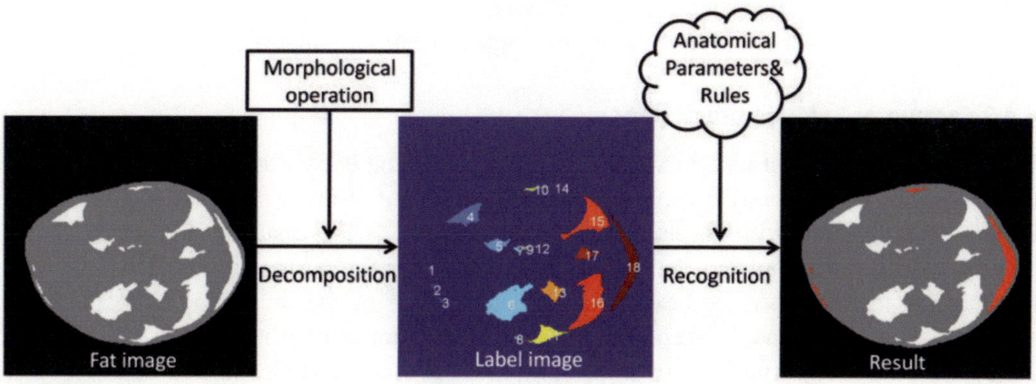

Fig. 7. The procedures of the depot recognition (Tang et al., 2011)

4.2 Decomposition

In the extracted fat image, the subcutaneous adipose tissues and visceral adipose tissues sometimes are accidently connected, which will complicate the depot recognition in further processing. Here a morphological opening operation (Gonzalez & Woods, 1992) is employed to decompose the adjoining parts. The morphological opening is composed by erosion and then dilation operations respectively. In our application, because some slim sections are erased by opening operation as well, the erased sections from pre- and post-morphological operation are saved for later placement into the mostly probable depot.

4.3 Knowledge based recognition

After decomposition, unconnected fat tissues are labelled as individual regions. To sort these individual regions into their likely respective fat depots, we employ a knowledge-based framework. Considering the variance of each feature, the descriptors are expressed by fuzzy logical (Zadeh, 1965). In the fuzzy set, each feature is assigned a grade of membership between 0 and 1. Using the fuzzy set to present the probability of belonging to different depots allows the anatomical variance to be contained in our system.

4.4 Parameters

Four parameters were adopted which contained the a priori knowledge of anatomical features. The parameters are described below and displayed in Figure. 8. (Tang et al., 2011)

4.4.1 Parameter 1: Orientation

Previous research indicates that the abdominal fat in mice tends to accumulate in a bilateral pattern (Calderan et al., 2006). Taking advantage of this a priori information, we implemented an orientation parameter dividing the body into bilateral regions and dorsal/ventral regions (Figure 9). The orientation parameter for each individual region in a polar system with its origin located at the geometrical centroid of the body area is as the mean of the maximum and minimum angles.

$$\text{Orientation}=(\text{maximum angle} + \text{minimum angle})/2$$

4.4.2 Parameter 2: Minimum distance

We define the feature of location, for each pixel inside the body area, which represents its distance to the nearest body contour. As Figure. 9 shows, a distance map is displayed for the inside the body area with the intensity corresponding to the distance. For example, the bright pixel near the centroid denotes a long distance to the body contour. The minimum distance parameter describes how close the outer edge of the fat region is to the body surface and is defined as the minimum value of the distance map in an individual region. This parameter is important for distinguishing the subcutaneous from visceral fat.

4.4.3 Parameter 3: Maximum distance

Similar to minimum distance, maximum distance is used to express the location feature that describes how far the fat tissues are away from the body surface. It is defined as the maximum value of the distance map in an individual region. Both minimum distance and maximum distance have three membership functions defining a confidence score for small, medium and large distance. Taking into consideration the observed regional variances (Calderan et al., 2006), different strategies are used in the bilateral and dorsal/ventral regions.

4.4.4 Parameter 4: Elongatedness

Elongatedness describes the shape of the object. Derived from empirical observations, in the band-like region near the body surface, the subcutaneous fat segments are usually slender along the surface; therefore a priori shape information is exploited in a location feature. An elongatedness parameter is defined to be the ratio of the length to thickness.

$$\text{Elongatedness}=\text{length}/\text{thickness}$$

Where (length=maximum angle-minimum angle) and (thickness=maximum distance-minimum distance).

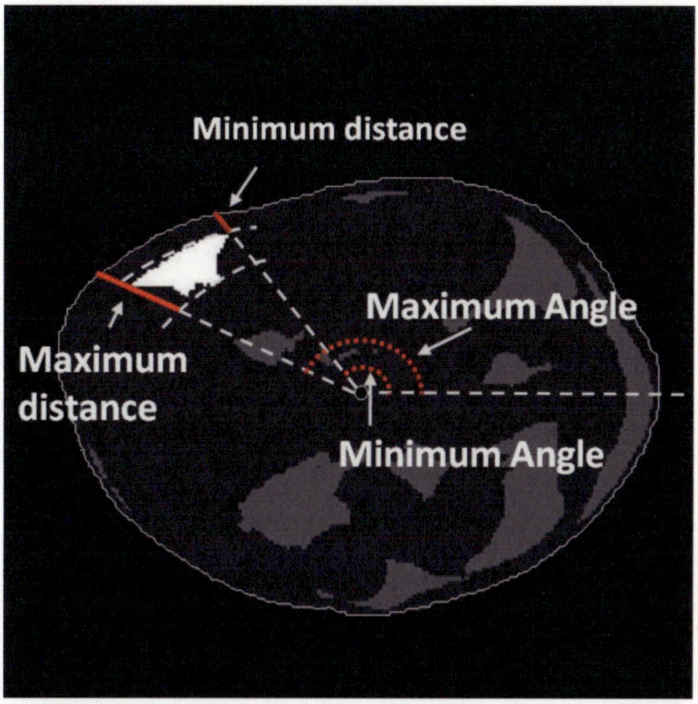

Fig. 8. The description of the parameters. (Tang et al., 2011)

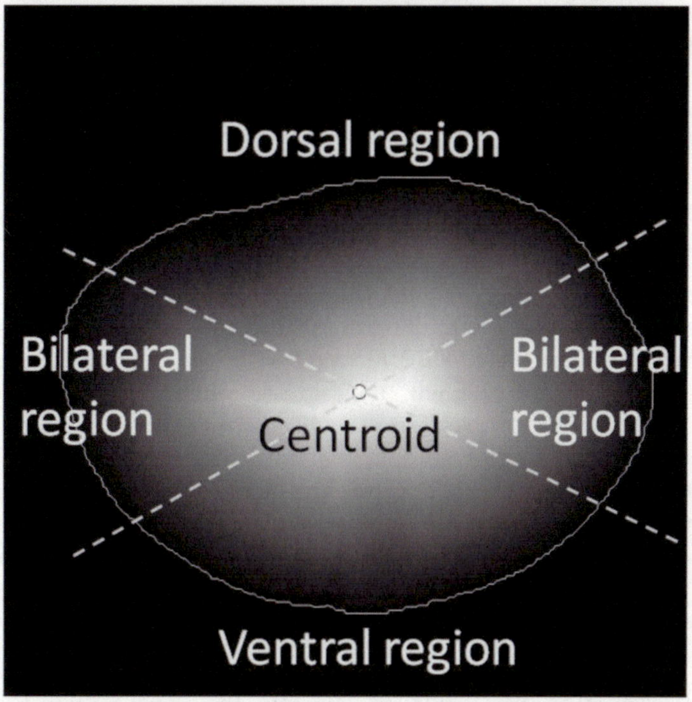

Fig. 9. The bilateral region and dorsal/ventral region. (Tang et al., 2011)

4.5 Inference rules

Utilizing the defined parameters, the depot can be recognized by classical If-Then rules and a min-max fuzzy inference scheme. Tissues are assigned to either the bilateral region or dorsal/ventral region (Fig.9) according to their orientations. Then three rules are employed to distinguish the depots:

Rule1: If maximum distance is small, then it is subcutaneous fat.
Rule2: If minimum distance OR maximum distance is large, then it is visceral fat.
Rule3: If minimum distance is small AND maximum distance is medium AND shape is elongated, then it is subcutaneous fat.

With defined rules, the min-max fuzzy inference scheme will automatically calculate the weights for each rule and assign the depot type in term of the weighted centroid (Zadeh, 1965).

5. Validation

To validate the measurement performed by the automatic process, we compared the automated results to the manual results from multiple observers.

5.1 Manual reference

In order to take inter-operator variations into account, two independent technicians performed the manual segmentations using a customized software tool developed in Matlab. In the software, two basic functions were provided including threshold and ROI analysis. The technicians first select the fat regions by adjusting a threshold. Then multiple manual ROI operations were performed to add or delete the fat regions based on the users experience. The total segmented fat is TAT. To segment the subcutaneous and visceral fat, operators carefully delineated a contour between these two depots. Finally, the fat inside the contour is considered as VAT and the rest of the fat is SAT.

5.2 Quantification results

The first comparison is for the segmented adipose size, which were performed in TAT, VAT and SAT respectively for all mice. A linear regression with 95% confidence ($P<0.001$) was calculated for each comparison. For the first manual result, the R2 for TAT is 0.953 with the regression function $y=1.088x+0.4407$; R2 for VAT is 0.9627 with the regression function $y=1.058x+1.769$; R2 for SAT is 0.8221 with the regression function $y=1.042x+0.8719$. For the second manual result, the R2 for TAT is 0.912 with the regression function $y=1.009x+6.583$; R2 for VAT is 0.9154 with the regression function $y=0.9889x+6.924$; R2 for SAT is 0.8986 with the regression function $y=1.037x+0.3821$. The agreement in the R2 value denotes the linear relationship between the automatic and manual results, and the concordance in the slope of the function provides confidence that the relationship will hold true in a variety of conditions. The agreement between the automatic results and manual results is comparable to the difference between correlation coefficients of the two manual results, which for TAT: R2=0.9514, VAT: R2=0.9195 and SAT: R2=0.8767.

A second comparison was performed to evaluate the voxel-by-voxel overlap of the segmented TAT, SAT and VAT respectively. To qualify these spatial similarities, we adopted the dice coefficient, which is customarily used to compare the segmentation results in medical imaging.

As Equation 5 shows, the Dice Coefficient (DC) describes the average ratio of the intersection between the results (R1) and results (R2). For example, a complete overlap of the segment results will make the DC to be 1.

$$DC = \frac{2|R_1 \cap R_2|}{|R_1| + |R_2|} \tag{5}$$

We calculated the DC in the 26 mice for TAT, VAT and SAT respectively. The average value between automatic result and two manual results are for TAT: DC=0.8839, for VAT:DC= 0.8795 and for SAT:DC=0.873. The detailed statistic DC value (mean value ± standard deviation) for each result is displayed in Table 2. (Tang et al., 2011)

DC	TAT	VAT	SAT
A vs. M1	0.9087±0.0438	0.8999±0.0467	0.8783±0.0546
A vs. M2	0.8591±0.0558	0.840±0.0634	0.8677±0.0435
M1 Vs.M2	0.8846±0.052	0.8717±0.0598	0.8847±0.0491

Table 2. Dice Coefficient (DC) of automatic (A), first manual result (M1) and second manual result (M2). (Tang et al., 2011)

6. Conclusion

In this chapter, we introduce a adipose measurement system for small animal using micro MRI. We have presented the imaging protocol and technical detail of the post-processing methodology. The parameters are well defined yet adjustable and tuneable to new applications. By decreasing the amount of manual operation needed, we hope this technique can reduce the threshold for obesity researchers to use MRI in their research.

7. Acknowledgment

We would like to thank Richard Simerly for the experiments design and adipose research support. We thanks Susan Lee, Priyank Sharma and Marvin Nelson for input in the adipose measurement research. We also would like to thank Seda Mkhitaryan, Anahit Hovsepyan, Kevin Nelson, Harutyunyan Ira, Rozaliya Veytsman-Shpilberg, Vazgen Khankaldyyan and Karapetyan Gevorg for data acquisition/analysis and helpful discussions.

8. References

Bechah, Y.; Paddock,C.D.; Capo,C.; Mege,J.L.; Raoult, D.(2010). Adipose tissue serves as a reservoir for recrudescent Rickettsia prowazekii infection in a mouse model. *PLoS One* , 2010,vol.5,no.1,e.8547.

Bonnya, J.M.; Odile, B.T.; Michel, Z.; Jean-Pierre, R.(2003). Multi-exponential analysis of magnitude MR images using a quantitative multispectral edge preserving filter. *J. Magn. Reson*, 2003, Vol.161, pp.25-34.

Calderan,L.; Marzola, P.; Nicolato, E.; Fabene, P.F.; Milanese, C.; Bernardi, P.; Giordano, A.; Cinti, S.; Sbarbati, A. (2006). In vivo phenotyping of ob/ob mouse by magnetic resonance imaging and H-Magnetic resonance spectroscopy. *Obesity*,2006,Vol.14,pp.405–414.

Chae, Y., Jeong, M.G., Kim, D.(2007). Three dimensional volume measurement of mice abdominal fat in magnetic resonance images. e-Health Networking, *Application and Services*,2007,pp.252–255.

Church, C.; Lee, S.; Bagg, E.A.; McTaggart, J.S.; Deacon, R.; Gerken, T.; Lee, A.; Moir, L.; Mecinović, J.; Quwailid, M.M.; Schofield, C.J.; Ashcroft, F.M.; Cox, R.D.(2009). A mouse model for the metabolic effects of the human fat mass and obesity associated FTO gene. *PLoS Genet* ,2009,vol. 5, no.8, e.1000599.

Dixon, W.T. (1984). Simple proton spectroscopic imaging. *Radiology*,1984,Vol.153,pp.189-194.

Dunn J. C. (1973). A Fuzzy Relative of the ISODATA Process and Its Use in Detecting Compact Well-Separated Clusters, *Journal of Cybernetics*,1973, Vol.3, pp.32-57.

Gonzalez, R.C. & Woods, R.E. (1992). *Digital Image Processing*, 2nd edition, Addison-Wesley Longman Publishing, Boston,MA,1992.

Gray, D.S.; Fujioka, K.; Colletti, P.M.; et al.(1991). Magnetic resonance imaging used for determining fat distribution in obesity and diabetes. *Am J Clin Nutr* 1991, Vol.54, pp.623-627.

Gronemeyer, S.A.; Steen, R.G.; Kauffman, W.M.; Reddick, W.E.; Glass, J.O.(2000). Fast adipose tissue (FAT) assessment by MRI. *Magn Reson Imaging* 2000, Vol.18, pp.815-818.

Hou, Z.(2006). A review on mr image intensity inhomogeneity correction, *Int. J. Biomed. Imag*, 2006, pp.1-11.

Larsson, B.; Svärdsudd, K.; Welin, L.; Wilhelmsen, L.; Björntorp, P.; Tlibblin, G. (1984). Abdominal adipose tissue distribution, obesity and risk of cardiovascular disease and death: 13 y follow up of participants in the study of men born in 1913. *Br Med J Clin Res*, 1984, Vol 288,pp.1401-1404.

Lublinsky, S.; Luu, Y.K.; Rubin, C.T.; Judex, S.(2009). Automated separation of visceral and subcutaneous adiposity in in-vivo microcoputed tomographies of mice. *J Digit Imaging* 2009, Vol.22, pp.222-231.

Luu, YK; Lublinsky, S; Ozcivici E; et al.(2009). In vivo quantification of subcutaneous and visceral adiposity by micro-computed tomography in a small animal model. *Med Eng Phys* 2009, Vol.31, pp.34-41.

Mann, G.V. (1974). The Influence of Obesity in Health. *New England Journal of Medicine*, 1974, Vol. 291, pp.178–185.

Manson, J.E.; Colditz, G.A.; Stampfer, M.J.; et al.(1990). A Prospective Study of Obesity and Risk of Coronary Heart Disease in Women. *New England Journal of Medicine*, 1990, Vol.322, pp.882-889.

Ohshima, S.; Yamamoto, S.; Yamaji, T.; et al. (2008). Development of an Automated 3D Segmentation Program for Volume Quantification of Body Fat Distribution Using CT. *Nippon Hoshasen Gijutsu Gakkai Zasshi* 2008, Vol.64, pp.1177-1181.

Peng, Q.; McColl, R.W.; Wang, J.; Chia, J.M.; Weatherall, P.T.(2005). Water-saturated three-dimensional balanced steady-state free precession for fast abdominal fat quantification. *J Magn Reson Imaging,* 2005,Vol.21,pp. 263–271.

Positano, V.; Christiansen, T.; Santarelli, M.F.; Ringgaard, S.; Landini, L.; Gastaldelli, A. (2009). Accurate segmentation of subcutaneous and intermuscular adipose tissue from MR images of thigh. *J Magn Reson Imaging,*2009,Vol. 29, pp.677-684.

Positano, V.; Gastaldelli, A.; Sironi, A.M.; Santarelli, M.F.; Lombardi, M.; Landini, L.(2004). An accurate and robust method for unsupervised assessment of abdominal fat by MRI. *J Magn Reson Imaging,*2004,Vol. 20,No.4,pp. 684-689.

Ranefall, P.; Bidar, A.W.; Hockings, P.D.(2009) Automatric segmentation of intra-abdominal and subcutaneous adipose tissue in 3D whole Mouse MRI. J *Magn Reson Imaging,* 2009, Vol.30, No.3, pp.554-560.

Reeder,S.B.; Pineda, A. R.; Wen, Z.; Shimakawa, A.; Yu, H.; Brittain, J.H.; Gold, G.E.; Beaulieu, C.H.; Pelc, N.J.(2005). Iterative Decomposition of Water and Fat with Echo Asymmetry and Least-Squares Estimation (IDEAL): Application With Fast Spin-Echo Imaging. *Magnetic Resonance in Medicine,*2005,Vol. 54,pp.636–644.

Ross, R.; Aru, J.; Freeman, J.; Hudson, R.; Janssen, I.(2002). Abdominal adiposity and insulin resistance in obese men. *Am J Physiol Endocrinol Metab,* 2002, Vol.282, pp. 657-663.

Siegel, M.J.; Hildebolt, C.F.; Bae, K.T; et al.(2007). Total and Intra-abdominal Fat Distribution in Preadolescents and Adolescents: Measurement with MR Imaging. *Radiology,* 2007, Vol.242, No. 3, pp.846-856.

Sijbers, J.; Dden Dekker, A.J.; Verhoye, M.; Raman, E.; Van Dyck, D.(1998). Optimal estimation of T2 maps from magnitude MR images, *Proceedings of the SPIE Medical Imaging* 1998,Vol.3338, pp.384-390.

Snijder, M.B.; Van Dam, R.M.; Visser, M.; Seidell, J.C.(2006). What aspects of body fat are particularly hazardous and how do we measure them? *Int J Epidemiol* 2006, Vol. 35, pp.83-92.

Tang, Y.; Lee, S.; Nelson, M.D.; Simerly, R.; Moats,R.A.(2010). Adipose separation of small animal at 7T: a preliminary study. *BMC Genomics,* 2010, 11, S9.

Tang, Y.; Simerly, R.; Moats,R.A.(2011). An Automatic Technique for MRI Based Murine Abdominal Fat Measurement. *Radioengineering.*, vol. 20, no. 4, p. 988-995.

Tomasi, C. & Manduchi, R.(1998). Bilateral Filtering for Gray and Color Images, *Proceedings of the IEEE International Conference on Computer Vision* 1998, pp.839-846.

Vovk, U.; Pernuŝ, F.; Likar, B.(2007). A review of methods for correction of intensity inhomogeneity in MRI. *IEEE Trans Med Imaging.* 2007,Vol.26,pp.405–21.

Wang, D. C.; Vagnucci, A. H.; Li, C.C.(1981). Gradient inverse weighted smoothing scheme and the evaluation of its performance. *Comput Graph Imaging Process,* 1981, Vol.15, pp.167–181.

Zadeh, L.A. (1965). Fuzzy sets. Inform Contr,1965,Vol. 8,pp.338-353.

Zhao, B.; Colville, J.; Kalaigian, J.; et al.(2006). Automated quantification of body fat distribution on volumetric computed tomography. *J Comput Assist Tomogr* 2006, vol.30, pp.777-783.

4

Image Processing Quality Analysis for Particle Based Peptide Array Production on a Microchip

Jenny Wagner[1,2,6] et al*
[1]Kirchhoff Institute for Physics, Heidelberg University
[2]German Cancer Research Centre
[6]Frankfurt Institute for Advanced Studies
Germany

1. Introduction

1.1 Motivation

Highly complex microarray systems based on combinatorial synthesis techniques are in wide-spread use in biological, medical and pharmaceutical research Chee et al. (1996); Cretich et al. (2006); Debouck & Goodfellow (1999). Two prominent examples are micro arrays for the artificial synthesis of arbitrary DNA sequences out of nucleic acids Heller (2002) and peptide synthesis out of amino acids Beyer et al. (2007); Templin et al. (2003). In the case of DNA arrays, these experiments mostly focus on gene identification or gene expression profiling to determine the effects of single genes on cellular evolution. Peptide arrays aim at understanding interactions of peptides with other molecules. As sequences in proteins, peptides are involved in the regularisation of biological activity.

Since a large number of combinations that build a valid molecule chain is possible, both micro array variants require high densities in the range of 10,000 cDNAs or peptides per cm^2. Density and size of the synthesis sites are the critical parameter for such systems, since they limit the number of molecule sorts synthesized per array. Using the micro array in experiments of bio-medical research or in clinical diagnostics means bringing the array in touch with target molecules. Hence, the decreasing size of the synthesis sites, also reduces the amount of target molecules required (i.e. proteins or antibodies), which may be expensive or hard to obtain.

With increasing array complexity, the need for an automated read-out of the results and structuring of the acquired information arises because manual evaluation is tedious and often inconsistent when comparing thousands of synthesis sites with each other. Here, image

---

* Felix Löffler[1,2], Tobias Förtsch[1,2], Christopher Schirwitz[2], Simon Fernandez[2], Heinz Hinkers[3], Heinrich F. Arlinghaus[4], Florian Painke[1], Kai König[1,2,5], Ralf Bischoff[2], Alexander Nesterov-Müller[5], Frank Breitling[5], Michael Hausmann[1] and Volker Lindenstruth[6]
[1]*Kirchhoff Institute for Physics, Heidelberg University, Germany*
[2]*German Cancer Research Centre, Germany*
[3]*Verbundzentrum für Oberflächenanalyse Münster, Germany*
[4]*Institute of Physics, University of Muenster, Germany*
[5]*Karlsruhe Institute for Technology, Germany*
[6]*Frankfurt Institute for Advanced Studies, Germany*

acquisition and image processing based evaluation can be used. While the concept of DNA arrays includes image processing in many ways Angulo & Serra (2003); Bajcsy (2005); Brown et al. (2001), querying the literature yields only a few image processing supported peptide array experiments. In most cases, mass spectrometry data is analysed by means of pattern matching in order to identify peptide sequences for quality analysis Gusev et al. (1993).

Yet, up to now, all image processing tasks have only been used in the *evaluation* step of the array experiment or as a post-processing routine to compensate for irregularities in the quality of the array Wang et al. (2001), but not during array production itself. Contrary to that, we propose a destruction free quality control system based on image acquisition and image processing that is capable of monitoring the peptide array production process to improve the quality of the array with respect to the density of correctly assembled peptides. While post-processing may not always restore the information content of defective synthesis sites, our method detects insufficiencies and errors when they occur, so that subsequent corrections lead to fully functional arrays.

1.2 Outline of the chapter

Section 2 starts with describing the process of peptide synthesis before Section 3 gives an overview of state-of-the-art quality controls that are currently performed in each synthesis step. Section 4 then introduces our new quality control system from the design of the image acquisition setup over full automation to experiments that demonstrate the functionality. Subsequently, Section 5 deals with further applications as well as extensions and modifications of the quality control system that are planned for future research. The conclusion in Section 6 summarises the results gained and discusses the assets and drawbacks of the method.

2. Particle based solid phase peptide synthesis

Since the first peptide synthesis in 1882 by T. Curtius, peptides can be artificially produced by several methods, all basing on the principle of selectively concatenating amino acids of different kinds to create the desired peptides. The most common methods are liquid phase synthesis and solid phase synthesis. The former assumes that peptides are synthesised in solution (i.e. the growing peptides are free to move within the liquid), while the latter requires a solid support with fixed coupling sites to which the first amino acids can couple, so that the growing peptides are bound to their synthesis sites. By design, solid phase peptide synthesis surpasses the method based on liquids in the percentage of correctly assembled peptides as separation and purification of the desired peptide sequences are easier to perform.

Using a solid support, the medium that transports the amino acids to the growing peptides has to be determined. Selecting liquids as transport medium is a commonly used standard Fodor et al. (1991); Volkmer (2009). Nevertheless, it bears some disadvantages: First of all, the form and extension of a liquid drop on a support is hard to control. This means that synthesis spots for different peptides must be positioned on the support in a distance far enough that drops to build different peptides cannot overlap accidentally. Furthermore, there is a minimum size of the drops below which the drop evaporates before it can reach the surface and, at last, there is no control over the amino acids in the drop as they couple to the growing peptide upon contact to the support. This means that incorrectly deposited drops will immediately lead to incorrectly assembled peptides at that spot. In order to overcome these disadvantages, we developed a particle based transport Beyer et al. (2007) that embeds the amino acids in micro particles. Thus, the coupling of the amino acids to the growing peptides is initiated after heating. Along with this new form of transport, the glass slide as solid support was replaced by a CMOS chip König et al. (2010) which facilitates this method of transport as described below.

Hence, our particle based solid phase peptide synthesis consists of the following four processing steps which are also depicted in Figure 1:

1. **Programming of the chip**
   Having equipped the CMOS chip with a chemical surface activation that provides the first coupling sites Stadler et al. (2007), the peptide synthesis can start. On the CMOS chip, each synthesis site is represented by an electrode that can be set up to a positive voltage of 100V. In the first step, all electrodes that are supposed to receive the same sort of amino acids are set to high voltage (usually 100V). All other electrodes are set to 0V, i.e. switched off.
2. **Particle deposition**
   Then, the particles that contain this kind of amino acids are deposited onto the chip: in a special deposition apparatus Wagner et al. (2011), the particles are negatively charged, so that they are guided to their synthesis sites by the electrical field generated by the electrodes, as also described in Löffler et al. (2011).
   After successful deposition of the first kind of amino acids, the chip is reprogrammed for the second kind and particle deposition is repeated using particles containing the second kind of amino acids.
3. **Coupling of amino acids**
   When each electrode is covered with particles, i.e. an entire layer in the peptide synthesis is completed, the chip is heated in an oven until the particles become gel-like. This initiates the coupling of the amino acids contained therein to the coupling sites on the surface activation of the chip.
4. **Chemical washing**
   To prepare the chip for the next layer of amino acids, chemical washing steps provide capping for those coupling sites that did not receive an amino acid, discard the remnants of the particles and activate the freshly deposited amino acids as coupling sites for subsequent depositions.
   Repeating the entire procedure, the amino acids are concatenated layer after layer, until the growing peptides reach their final length.

Fig. 1. Left to right: Solid phase peptide synthesis on CMOS chips: Negatively charged micro particles containing amino acids are guided to their synthesis sites by the selectively programmable electric fields of the CMOS chip, particles containing one specific sort of amino acids are deposited, particles containing all sorts of amino acids for the first layer of the peptide array are deposited, heating initiates the coupling of the first layer of amino acids to the surface, remnants of particles and excess amino acids are discarded in chemical washing, repeating this procedure leads to a complete peptide array (From Beyer et al. (2007). Reprinted with permission from AAAS.)

3. Related work on state-of-the-art quality control for peptide synthesis

Quality checks on each step of the peptide synthesis process are regularly performed. The size of the particles can be measured by means of a Malvern Mastersizer and their form by raster electron microscopy. The percentages of the particle contents are monitored by high-performance liquid chromatorgraphy (HPLC) to ensure that there is an excess of amino acids compared to the coupling sites available on the chip surface.

The deposition quality is checked by experts that investigate the spots on the support under a light microscope to find contaminations and to determine whether enough particles are deposited on each synthesis spot to guarantee a good coupling efficiency. If the spots are homogenously covered with particles, the experts assume that this deposition will result in a good coupling efficiency, having already achieved good synthesis results with such depositions, as demonstrated in Beyer et al. (2007); König et al. (2010).

The coupling efficiency itself can be estimated in the chemical washing step, when the freshly coupled amino acids are prepared to be the coupling sites for the next layer of amino acids. Then, protection groups (Fmoc groups) are removed from the amino acid that has just coupled to the growing peptide. The reaction product of the Fmoc group with the washing solution absorbs UV-light, so that UV spectrometry of the solution yields an estimate of coupled amino acids on the entire support. Yet, this gives no information about the number of coupled amino acids per synthesis spot, only averaged over the entire array. Furthermore, experiments with UV-spectrometry showed high error rates that originated from the fact that the measurements were at the detection limit of the spectrometer. Hence, at this degree of miniaturisation, the amount of reagents already becomes to small to be measured with standard chemical detection reactions.

After termination of the entire process, a selective antibody with a fluorescing molecule on top can be coupled to each peptide to measure the fluorescence signal as evidence for a correct synthesis. Furthermore, there is the possibility to perform a mass spectrometric analysis to investigate the synthesis quality of the assembled peptides. Both reactions are performed routinely Beyer et al. (2007) and are also standard for other types of peptide synthesis Roepstorff (2000). However, as the UV-spectrometry, these measurements are not spatially resolved, i.e. they only provide results for the entire support.

4. Quality control through image acquisition and processing

4.1 Motivation and outline

As discussed in Section 3, the standard quality analysis methods to determine the amount of coupled amino acids or the density of assembled peptides do not yield information about single synthesis spots but only for the entire array. In order to overcome this shortcoming, we developed a quality analysis setup that allows to evaluate single synthesis sites. The method is based on the correlation of two image acquisitions, namely, relating the image of a particle deposition with the respective image of coupled amino acids subsequently acquired by surface analysis, as described further below.

But before the correlation can be established, an image acquisition setup has to be assembled, as described in Section 4.2. Then, we set up a model for particle deposition using the image acquisition setup to compare the theoretical results with experimental tests. As discussed in

Section 4.3, this leads to improvements in the deposition step. Thus, having a tool for particle deposition analysis, Section 4.4 focuses on finding a suitable surface analysis technique that can image the chip surface retrieving signals from coupled amino acids with a resolution below the size of a synthesis spot (i.e. 100μm for the latest chip generation). Since the chosen surface analysis technique, time of flight secondary ion mass spectrometry (TOF-SIMS), destroys the surface during analysis, it cannot be included as quality analysis routine in the peptide array production process. Therefore, the particles deposited on the synthesis spot and the signals from the coupled amino acids in TOF-SIMS imaging have to be correlated to obtain a destruction free quality analysis. In Section 4.5, we define a quality measure based on this correlation that is capable of estimating the quality of single synthesis sites by examining the deposition image. Using this quality measure, we implemented an automated quality control, as described in Section 4.6, that reliably decides whether the density of coupled amino acids is sufficient to yield a predefined density of correctly assembled peptides or not and conveys this message to the peptide array production automaton that can react to the result.

4.2 Image acquisition setup for particle deposition

An image acquisition setup for particle deposition analysis should fulfil the following requirements in order to be suitable for quality analysis:

- The resolution of the entire setup (objective and camera) should be able to resolve the average diameter of the micro particles. Hence, the resolution should be in the range of 1-2μm Wagner et al. (2011).
- The optical imaging should be contactless, without interference of additional material, as for instance, oil immersion.
- If only a chip detail can be photographed, it should contain a satisfactory amount of synthesis sites to obtain a quality analysis evaluation that is representative for the entire chip. Since the experiments in this section are performed without an automated framework, chip details containing 100-160 synthesis sites, i.e. about 1% of the total amount of spots are photographed, as manual control samples showed that this amount already represents the entire chip well.
- The setup should be robust in handling so that all images are taken under comparable conditions, including a uniform illumination of the chip. To monitor the exact deposition for several amino acids, an alignment of the chip is also necessary. Yet, for retrieving a quality evaluation per synthesis site, aligning the images is not required.

Taking into account these requirements, we assembled an image acquisition setup consisting of a conventional inverted light microscope, a Zeiss Axiovert 35, a 10x/0.25 objective, a TV-adaptation of magnification 0.63, and a Progres C5 camera, as shown in Figure 2 on the left. The right hand side of Figure 2 shows a typical image taken from a particle deposition in which particles are depicted in white on the dark grey synthesis sites which are separated by a grid in brown.

4.3 Image processing supported deposition modelling

The image acquisition setup as assembled in Section 4.2 is used to take photos of particle depositions. Thereby, it was noticed that the deposition quality decisively depends on the programmed deposition pattern Löffler et al. (2011). Figure 3 shows some examples: the

Fig. 2. Left: Image acquisition setup to monitor the particle deposition: Zeiss Axiovert 35, 10x/0.25 objective, TV-adaptation with magnification 0.63 and Progres C5 camera Right: Typical particle deposition image: particles (white), synthesis sites (dark grey), grid for separation of synthesis sites (brown)

pincushion effect on the top of the K, the central vertical line-like deposition in the I and the central horizontal line-like deposition in the P.

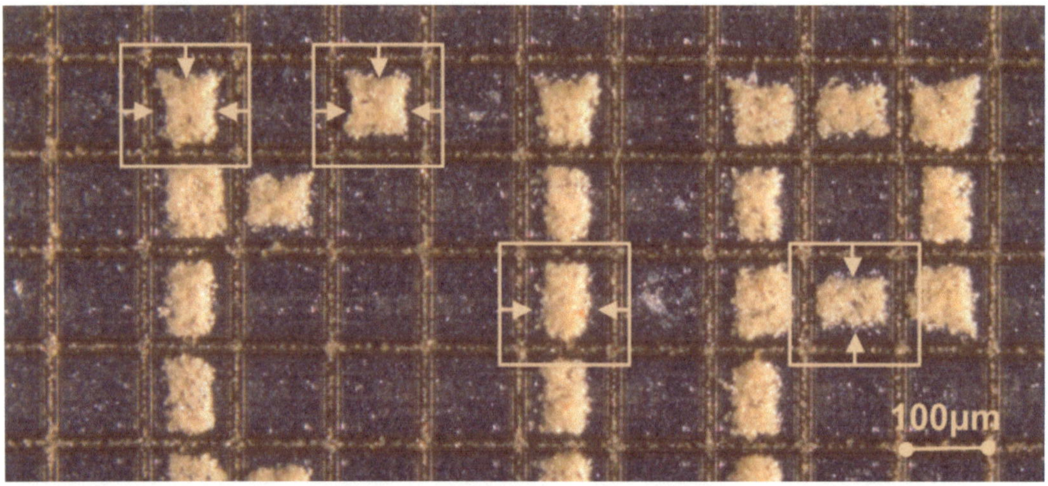

Fig. 3. The quality of the deposition decisively depends on the programmed pattern, the image shows the pincushion effect on the top of the K, the central vertical line-like deposition in the I and the central horizontal line-like deposition in the P

The effects could be explained by modelling the deposition process as a two-phase flow, with air as transport phase that carries the particles, subject to the boundary conditions in the deposition apparatus and the electrical field in front of the chip. Based on this model, particle deposition simulations were performed whose results correlated well with the effects observed in the images of actual depositions Wagner et al. (2011).

As a result, particle deposition patterns were modified such that undesired artefacts like the pincushion effect do not occur. This is achieved by splitting the deposition pattern into several deposition steps for the same kind of amino acids, yielding high quality depositions as shown in Figure 2 on the right.

4.4 Spatially resolved image acquisition and processing of chemical surface analysis

As outlined in Section 3, chemical detection reactions are less precise and on the verge of the detection limit. This is not only the case for the Fmoc detection as described in Section 3, but also for the Bromophenol blue reaction, which is a standard reagent to visualise amino groups.

Hence, surface analysis techniques as listed in Table 1 are considered. The decisive parameters of the methods are the detection range, their analytical spot size and the profile depth. Requiring an analytical spot size in the range of 1 to 10μm, time of flight secondary ion

method	detection range	lateral resolution	profile depth
AES	10^{20} atoms/cm^3	1nm – 10nm	< 10nm
AFM	1 atom/cm^3	100pm – 50pm	uppermost atom layer
TOF-SIMS	10^{15} atoms/cm^3	100nm – 50μm	< 3nm
XPS	10^{19} atoms/cm^3	10μm – 1mm	< 10nm

Table 1. Surface analysis techniques that may be able to resolve the density of amino acids on the chip surface: Auger electron spectroscopy (AES), atomic force microscopy (AFM), time-of-flight secondary ion mass spectrometry (TOF-SIMS), X-ray photoelectron spectroscopy (XPS)

mass spectrometry (TOF-SIMS) seems to be the best option. First of all it can detect down to 10^{15} atoms per cm^3, which should be sufficient to detect amino acids at the coupling sites on the surface because the surface density of coupling sites was determined to be in the range of 10^{16} per cm^2 Schirwitz et al. (2009). Secondly, its profile depth is small enough to analyse the uppermost layer of the surface only. Intruding deeper into the surface, artefacts from the chemical surface activation or even from the chip might obscure the signal actually coming from the amino acids at the top of the growing peptide. This excludes techniques as, for instance, X-ray photoelectron spectroscopy (XPS) or Auger electron spectroscopy (AES). Scanning probe microscopy methods (SPM), as atomic force microscopy (AFM), could also be considered due to their shallow profile depth and their capability of analysing spot sizes far less than 10μm. Yet, inherent to its functional principle, AFM cannot yield a good spatial resolution for the observation of single amino acids coupled to the surface, as the growing peptide is free to move vertically, leading to distorted images. Not shown in Table 1, spatially resolved matrix-assisted laser deposition/ ionisation (MALDI) could also be considered. Yet, this method is excluded again, as the minimum spot size analysable is 20μm.

The TOF-SIMS method is thus selected as method of choice, further encouraged by literature, demonstrating that single molecule detection, especially amino acid detection is possible with this method, for example in Aoyagi et al. (2008) or Hagenhoff (2000). Furthermore, it is possible to chemically characterise self-assembled monolayers (SAMs) by means of TOF-SIMS Graham & Ratner (1994), which can become important for peptide synthesis on CMOS chips as well, since SAMs are currently being established as chemically active surface coating. Knowing the TOF-SIMS fingerprint of the surface, it is easier to filter out the signals from the amino acids thereon.

The imaging of TOF-SIMS measurements works as depicted in Figure 4. The surface of the sample to be analysed is exposed to a pulsed beam of primary ions (usually gallium, bismuth or noble gas ions). The secondary ions that are dissolved from the surface of the sample by the primary ions are accelerated according to their charge and enter a time-of-flight mass spectrometer in which they are separated according to their mass. This procedure is performed as a scan over the entire surface, so that a spatially resolved image of the detected mass distribution is created. The difficulty of recognising the amino acids among all other

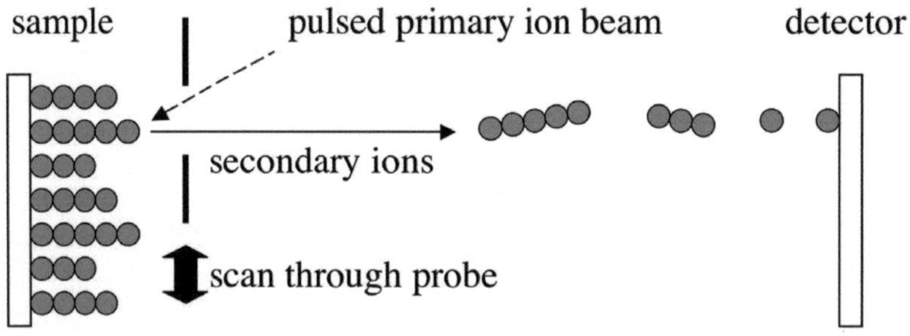

Fig. 4. TOF-SIMS: The sample is exposed to a pulsed beam of primary ions to dissolve secondary ions from the sample surface. The latter enter a time-of-flight mass spectrometer in which they are separated by their mass. Performing the procedure as a scan over the entire surface, a spatially resolved mass distribution is created

signals lies in the fact that, depending on the energy of the primary beam, the fragments ionised out of the sample surface can consist of any sequence of molecules that occurs in the sample.

For the TOF-SIMS imaging, an analysis chip with a test pattern containing three amino acids (proline, tryptophan and arginine) was created. The chip surface was chemically activated with coupling sites, the amino acids were deposited and the chemical washing steps performed, so that the imaging should yield signals from coupled amino acids on the surface. The measurements were then performed, using Bi_3^+ ions, producing images with a resolution of 128×128 pixels, i.e. one pixel corresponds to 3.91μm on a synthesis site.

Figure 5 shows the results: on the left hand side, the total ion rate indicates that all synthesis sites were homogeneously exposed to the ion beam, the centre image shows the most prominent scattered fragment from tryptophan (C_9H_8N), while the potassium signals on the right hand side clearly show the grid that separates the synthesis sites. The latter originates from the fact that the chemical surface activation is broken at the grid and thus confined to the synthesis spots, which was also an important observation discovered in the TOF-SIMS imaging. Hence, as the images show, the signal of the coupled amino acids is clearly visible despite the low signal to noise ratio of 2:1. Furthermore, signals from silicone oils were detected, originating from insufficiencies in the washing process when removing the particle remnants, so that this step could also be improved due to TOF-SIMS imaging results.

4.5 Destruction free quality control

4.5.1 Correlation between particle deposition and TOF-SIMS imaging

Having accomplished the imaging of coupled amino acids, it is possible to test the validity of the following experts' assumptions:

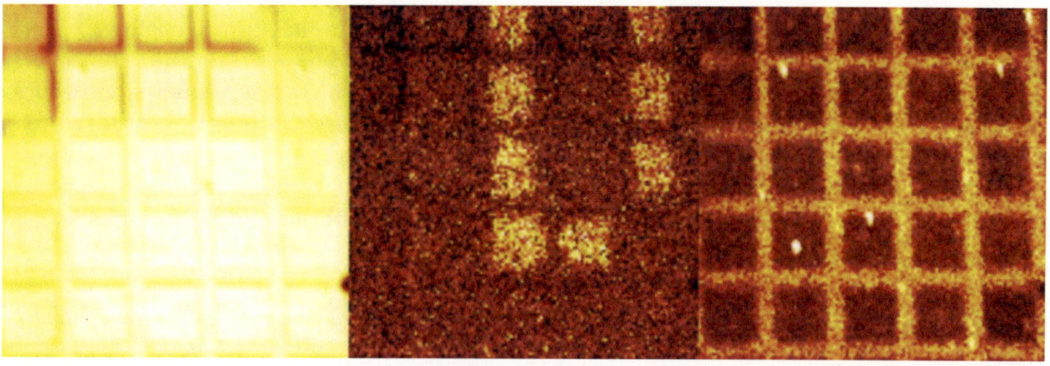

Fig. 5. TOF-SIMS images: Left: total ion image Centre: tryptophan signal with signal to noise ratio 2:1 Right: potassium signal indicating that the surface activation is confined to the spots

- A coverage with particles means that amino acids will couple to the surface underneath, i.e. a particle deposition on the synthesis sites automatically implies the coupling of amino acids there.
- During coupling, the melt of the particles flows isotropically into areas on the spot where no particles were deposited. The amino acids contained therein couple in those areas that the melt reaches.
- The particle depositions for each amino acid per layer must be performed twice to obtain the desired density of coupled amino acids.

To verify these assumptions, the correlation of the particle deposition images obtained with the image acquisition setup described in Section 4.2 with the TOF-SIMS images shown in Section 4.4 is performed by means of image processing.

First, both images are converted to greyscale. Then, the TOF-SIMS images are enlarged by Lanczos-2-kernel for optimal interpolation to match the size of the deposition images.

Subsequently, the two images are manually aligned and matched. Due to the low contrast in the grid regions of the tryptophan image, the image containing the potassium signal is used to match the grid in the TOF-SIMS images with the grid in the deposition images. Another option for alignment could have been to match the chip cell contents of the two images directly by applying a registration and matching algorithm, e.g. finding the largest overlap of the segmented foreground in both images. Yet, as the foreground is the object under investigation, it cannot be used for image alignment. Using the grid for alignment thus enables to detect a systematic shift in deposited particles when melting and coupling. This effect may be caused by unbalanced chip fixation on the circuit board or improper positioning in the oven during coupling, resulting in a unidirectional melt flow instead of a uniform distribution.

Next, both images are segmented by thresholding. The latter is calculated as the average of the maximum mean grey value for an uncovered synthesis site and the minimum mean grey value for a synthesis site covered with particles as this has proven to work well for the unimodal intensity distributions in the images Wagner et al. (2010).

The last step is the correlation of the segmented images, yielding that the first assumption is correct in principle. However, there are areas in which a particle deposition did not lead to a coupling of amino acids. This can be an artefact of the high noise or of the enlargement of the TOF-SIMS image, but could be caused by deficiencies in the surface coating or steric hindrance to coupling as well. Furthermore, the second assumption is also true. The particle melt actually flows isotropically up to 5μm from the location of the deposition and induces coupling of amino acids in those areas. While the first two experts' assumptions were correct, the last one is fortunately not. As the images show contiguous signals from coupled amino acids on the surface, a second deposition step with the same sort of amino acids becomes obsolete, which saves deposition time and reduces the amount of required particles by one half.

4.5.2 Quality control system

Based on these results, a quality analysis was set up that uses the particle deposition image to determine whether the amount of amino acids expected to couple after this deposition is sufficient to continue with the next step or not. The algorithm to evaluate the quality of the synthesis sites on the deposition image was written in MATLAB and consists of the steps shown in Figure 6. Since the size of the synthesis sites has to be known in advance, each image acquisition setup requires a training step to be executed before quality analysis, in which the spot size is determined together with the resolution of the setup and a classification threshold to separate covered from uncovered spots, as well as the segmentation threshold that divides the particles from the background. The latter only has to be determined if the segmentation is performed by thresholding in the first place. Since these parameters only change when the setup is altered, the training step has to be performed once per setup configuration.

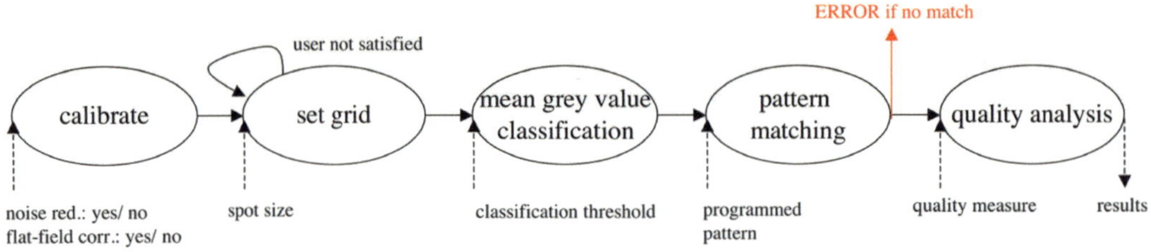

Fig. 6. Quality analysis algorithm: preprocessing is performed when necessary, set grid separates the image into the single synthesis spots, then a consistency check is performed by comparing the actual programming pattern with a rough classification of the spots before quality analysis of each spot starts

In the quality analysis algorithm, preprocessing like noise reduction or flat-field correction is performed when necessary. Subsequently, the image is separated into the single synthesis spots, setting the grid with one mouse click by the user. Later on, this can be performed by the synthesis automaton. Having extracted each single spot, a fast consistency check is performed, comparing the actual programming pattern with a rough classification of the spots. The classification calculates the mean grey value for each synthesis site and uses the trained threshold to classify the spots as uncovered or covered. Comparing the actual deposition pattern with this classification, grave errors like an incorrectly programmed electrode that require a restart in the deposition can be detected very quickly. If the consistency check terminates successfully, the actual quality analysis starts to evaluate each synthesis spot in the image.

As input, the quality analysis step requires a quality measure that decides whether the particle deposition is sufficient to continue the synthesis or not. This measure is set by user input, so that it meets the requirements set by the application the array is produced for. Knowing the correlation between particle deposition and coupling of the amino acids contained therein, the quality measure is defined by determining the degree of particle coverage of two central circles within the synthesis sites, as Table 2 summarises. The large outer circle covers 50% of the spot, while the smaller inner one covers 15%. A distinction is made between covered and uncovered spots because for the ones to be covered, the algorithm is supposed to determine whether the degree of coverage is sufficient to continue, while for the ones to be left uncovered, the amount of incorrectly deposited particles is decisive. Experimental tests using this quality measure

spot type	good	satisfactory	bad
covered	$>$ 90% of inner circle cov. $>$ 50% of outer circle cov.	$>$ 90% of inner circle cov. $>$ 0% of outer circle cov.	other
uncovered	$<$ 10% of inner circle cov. $<$ 20% of outer circle cov.	$<$ 20% of inner circle cov. $<$ 30% of outer circle cov.	other

Table 2. Quality measure based on two central circles for one spot Wagner et al. (2010)

showed that it works well for single particle depositions, as comparisons between human classification and automatic labelling showed high coincidences Wagner et al. (2010). Thus, the algorithm was prepared to cope with an entire peptide synthesis, analysing subsequent particle depositions per layer. This was done by verifying that two images of two subsequent particle depositions are consistent in so far, as the quality classification after the second deposition remains the same as after the first deposition for synthesis spots that were not affected by the second deposition.

Finally, the quality analysis algorithm was tested on a complete peptide synthesis, leading to classifications of 86.3% *good* spots, 5.0% *satisfactory* spots and 8.7% *bad* spots. In order to prove that the quality of the peptide array produced coincides with the prediction of the algorithm, a standard fluorescence detection on the peptides was performed. The image acquisition was performed with fluorescence scanner at a resolution of 5μm. Comparing the average classification label for each spot as shown in Figure 7 with the fluorescence intensity for the correctly assembled peptides, a high coincidence can be observed. The gradients in the left part of the fluorescence image, however, are not correctly predicted by the class labels. Yet, investigations over the entire array revealed that the insufficiencies in coupling at those sites were due to deficiencies in the chemical surface coating that were not subject to the quality control algorithm and hence not predictable.

The successful analysis of the peptide synthesis thus completes the quality analysis algorithm and arises the question how to actively control a peptide synthesis. Using the results shown in Figure 7, the threshold for the repetition of one deposition can be empirically trained, requiring more than 80% of all class labels to be *good* and not more than 20% of the class labels be *bad*. Furthermore, assigning more than 80% of all synthesis spots to the class *satisfactory* should also cause a warning because, in this case, the algorithm is not capable of finding a clear classification, since the *satisfactory* class is the one that is assigned in ambiguous cases.

Taking into account the subsequent particle depositions as well, the quality control algorithm should check the deposition quality of an entire layer by determining the ratio of *good* spots after the first deposition that remain *good* ones in the subsequent steps. The practical

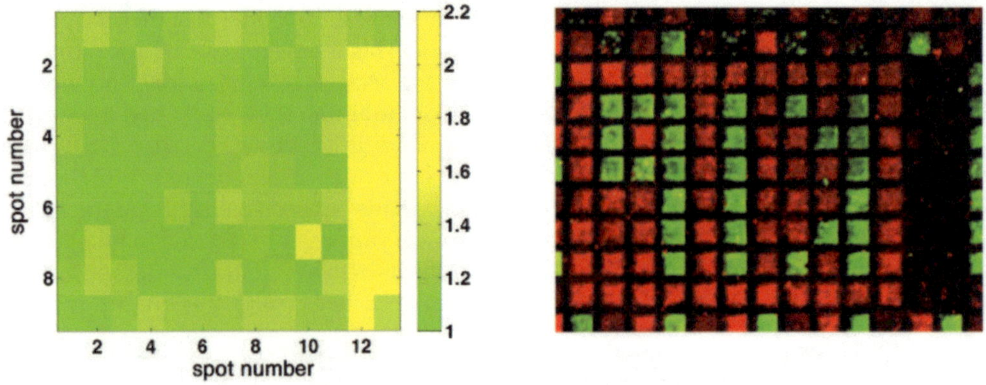

Fig. 7. Comparison of the average quality class with the fluorescence detection of the correctly assembled peptides for an entire peptide synthesis, class label 1 means *good*, class 2 label means *satisfactory* as defined in Table 2

experience of the analysed synthesis favours a threshold of 80% *good* $\rightarrow$ *good* label assignments for two subsequent depositions per layer, below which a repetition of the particle deposition for the entire layer becomes necessary.

4.6 Automation

With the quality control thresholds defined, the algorithm was implemented such that it automatically reads in images coming from the peptide synthesis automaton and outputs the control signals that operate the automaton according to the deposition quality. Since the analysis software is written in MATLAB while the machine control of the automaton still to be constructed is likely to be programmed in LabView, an interface has to be set up for the two programs to communicate with each other. Exchanging command and response files over a shared folder is the simplest method that assures compatibility even in the case when the quality analysis routine is translated to another programming language, e.g. to a C++ program. The LabView process control is supposed to convey the voltage programming files of the chip and the images taken by the camera to the quality analysis program, while the latter sends back responses about the quality to determine the next processing step. Furthermore, the LabView control program is supposed to store the parameter values how to position the chip above the image acquisition setup in order to take optimal pictures. Due to the high positioning accuracy, it is possible to fix the origin of the grid coordinates in the image, so that no user input is required to divide the image into the single synthesis spots before quality analysis.

The state machine shown in Figure 8 depicts the procedure of the automated quality control, i.e. started once, no user interaction is required during normal operation.

First, MATLAB and LabView are started. Before the automated particle deposition begins, LabView exports the chip programming deposition pattern into a folder shared by MATLAB. While LabView controls the particle deposition and takes the image for quality analysis, MATLAB scans that shared folder in previously defined time steps until LabView has exported the image to that folder. During the MATLAB analysis, LabView is in a wait state until it retrieves a response about the quality of the current deposition from MATLAB. The

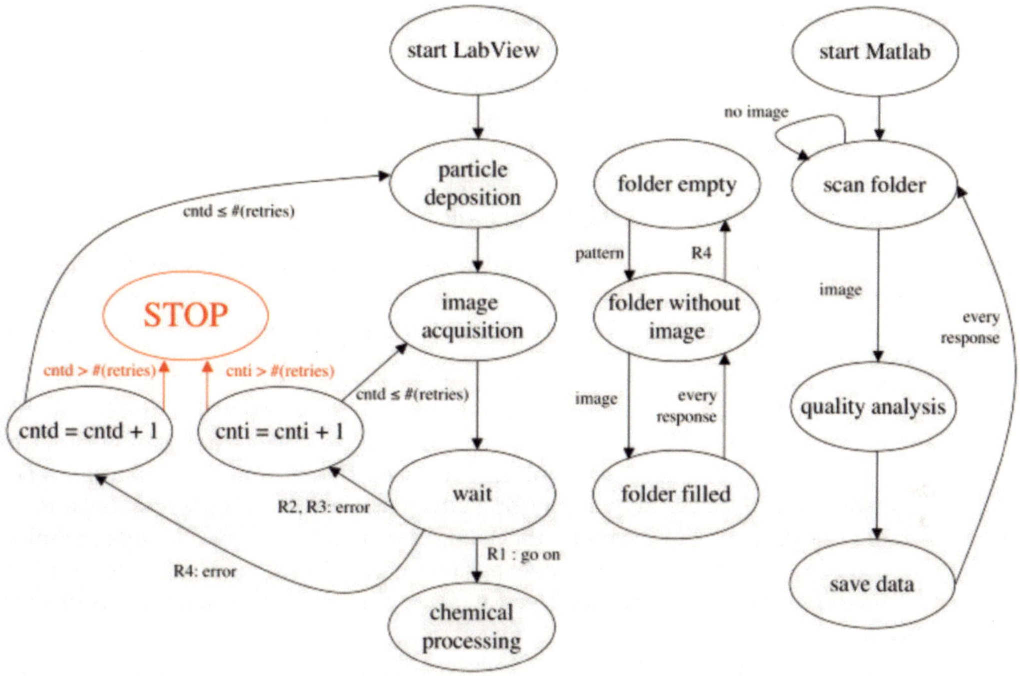

Fig. 8. Finite state machine diagram of automated quality control: after starting LabView, particle deposition, image acquisition, quality analysis and chemical processing can be performed and the respective actions in the image folder and in the MATLAB routine take place as described in the text

chip can already be brought back to the deposition unit of the automaton in the mean time, so that the next step can be immediately started after receiving the response – in the normal case, it is assumed that the quality will be sufficient to continue. The response, together with the analysed data, is saved into another shared folder from where LabView gets one of the four possible responses:

R1 : proceed to next step

R2 : the image data is corrupted so that it cannot be processed

R3 : the image causes a MATLAB intrinsic error

R4 : the image shows that the deposition is not of expected quality

In case of R1, LabView can go on with the next step in the processing queue. For the error messages R2 and R3, the problem could be caused in the image acquisition step. Therefore, this step is repeated once again with a new picture of the same particle deposition on the chip, while the deposition pattern file is kept. Receiving R4, the process has to clean the chip and repeat the steps from particle deposition onwards. In order to assure that no programming error of the chip caused the malfunction, the deposition pattern is also created anew and sent to the shared folder. R4 could also be split into two errors, R4a and R4b, R4a dealing with sparse particle coverage and forcing an additional deposition step and R4b handling the case of too many incorrectly deposited particles requiring the chip to be cleaned prior to a new deposition. If the results do not improve after a previously determined number of retries, LabView stops the processing for human intervention and error inspection. Regardless of the response, MATLAB returns to scanning the shared folder waiting for a new image after termination of the analysis of the previous one.

5. Outlook, improvements and further applications

Integration of the image acquisition setup for quality control into the peptide synthesis automaton still has to be performed, but can easily be achieved replacing the microscope by a suitable objective and illumination device only, so that the optimum conditions defined in Section 4.2 are fulfilled.

The results obtained in Section 4.4 are the first of their kind and demonstrate that it is possible to detect the density of a single layer of coupled amino acids. Nevertheless, the proof of principle experiment should be repeated with an increased signal to noise ratio at a higher resolution so that the TOF-SIMS images can be better correlated to the deposition images that have a higher resolution. Furthermore, they should be performed for all kinds of amino acids used in peptide synthesis. This series of experiments could give insights in the coupling behaviour of the different amino acids and lead to semi-quantitative measurements of their coupling efficiencies.

Additional to that, the quality measure of the control algorithm could be totally based on the results gained in Section 4.4, simulating the coupling of amino acids, taking into account the (estimated areas and amounts of) coupled amino acids in the preceding layer and directly calculating the density of correctly assembled peptides out of this information. Although being more precise, this quality measure would certainly require more processing time for the exact simulation of the coupling and the calculation of the peptide density. Thus, since the time for analysis should be minimised, the current modus of quality analysis probably excels over this precise one, which remains to be checked.

Despite the good results obtained in Wagner et al. (2010) and Section 4.5, the predictive power of the algorithm can be further improved as currently, the assignment of the class labels is too pessimistic, leading to more repeated depositions than actually are necessary. With an increasing number of analysed synthesis, however, the quality measure can be refined, such that the number of unnecessary re-depositions is reduced.

It is also possible to extend the algorithm to evaluate fluorescence images like Figure 7 on the right. For this task, the single colour channels of the image can be evaluated after establishing a quality measure that bases on the intensity signal of the synthesis spots. Exchanging the classification component in the existing system by this one is simple due to its modular structure. The rest of the algorithm can be reused, since the structure of the synthesis sites will also remain the same. Knowing the (integrated) intensities per synthesis spot also enables biological data evaluation like finding the peptide that binds best to a certain test molecule or comparing different peptides with respect to their coupling probability.

Adapting the image acquisition and image processing system for glass slides as solid supports, the quality control can also be used in the peptide synthesis by means of a peptide printer as described in Beyer et al. (2007), another method for automated peptide array production developed by us.

6. Conclusion: Comprehensive imaging based quality control for peptide array production

As shown in this chapter, image acquisition and image processing are vital parts of miniaturised peptide array production, when standard bio-chemical methods reach their detection limit and physical surface analysis techniques destroy the sample. Furthermore, imaging of the sample allows for spatially resolved results while standard quality analysis techniques only yield information about the entire sample.

Four different methods of image acquisition were used to accomplish an automated quality control system for peptide array production: electron microscopy, light microscopy, fluorescence microscopy and time of flight secondary ion mass spectrometry imaging (TOF-SIMS imaging). Figure 9 summarises the design of the quality control system and shows which results were obtained by the individual imaging methods.

To monitor the shape of the micro particles that contain the amino acids electron microscopy was used. It was found out that the majority of the particles has a shape that can be approximated by a sphere, which is an important fact because the size measurement of the particles outputs correct results only if the particles under analysis are approximately spherical. The programming of the chip and the particle deposition are checked by light microscopy. As a result, the comparison of several particle deposition images revealed that the quality of the deposition depends on the pattern programmed. Modelling the deposition and simulating the process, these artefacts could be explained and removed by splitting the deposition pattern into several steps for one kind of amino acid. Then, TOF-SIMS imaging was performed to visualise the density of a single layer of coupled amino acids with an unprecedented resolution of less than $4\mu m$, yielding the first spatially resolved detection of coupled amino acids in such a miniaturised peptide array. As this method destroys the surface, a correlation between the particle deposition and the TOF-SIMS images was established via image processing to obtain a destruction free predictor for the amount of coupled amino acids when analysing the respective particle deposition. The demonstration that this predictor can be applied as quality control in each deposition step was performed by comparing its results with a fluorescence image of the correctly assembled peptides.

Algorithmically, the advantage of the implemented quality control program lies in its flexible structure so that it can analyse any of the images coming from light microscopy, TOF-SIMS imaging or fluorescence microscopy by setting a few parameters only. The training program additionally implemented simplifies the parameter tuning and allows to save standard configurations that can be quickly loaded into the quality control program.

The main future improvements on the system are planned in form of further TOF-SIMS imaging experiments to gain detailed information about the coupling efficiencies of all amino acids and increase the precision of the current correlation between particle deposition and amino acid coupling.

Performing all steps as described in this chapter, the quality control can, in principle, be applied to any kind of peptide array production. Adapting the algorithm to analyse glass slides instead of CMOS chips, and performing the imaging experiments with the arrays

Particle creation	Image acquisition	Quality control
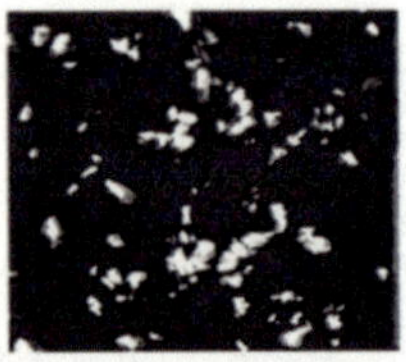	*Electron microscopy* (monitoring the shape of the particles)	Routine checks guarantee reproducible experimental conditions (optimal particles are spheres)
Chip programming 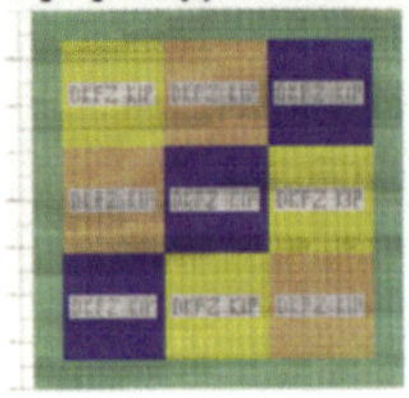	*Light microscopy* (consistency check for the correct deposition pattern)	Correct pattern, particle coverage and contamination can be monitored by light microscopy and image processing. The algorithm that decides to proceed or improve the deposition is based on the particle deposition simulations and the chemical analysis, correlating particle deposition with the density of coupled amino acids
Particle deposition 	*Light microscopy* (controlling the particle coverage and amount of incorrectly deposited particles)	
Chemical processing 	*TOF-SIMS imaging* (visualise density of coupled amino acids)	TOF-SIMS results lead to optimisation in chemical processing and development of the quality measure for the algorithm
Peptide array 	*Fluorescence microscopy* (visualising the density of correctly assembled peptides)	Reusing the algorithm for particle deposition, the number of correctly assembled peptides could be retrieved from the fluorescence image

Fig. 9. Summary of all peptide synthesis steps, the image acquisition methods used and the results obtained that lead to the setup of a quality control system

produced by a peptide printer Beyer et al. (2007), a quality control for another particle based solid phase peptide synthesis can be created. Using liquids as transport medium for the amino acids, the system can still be applied, however, solely as quality analysis because coupling of the amino acids happens immediately when the liquid contacts the surface. Nevertheless, detecting deficiencies at an early synthesis stage saves production time and costs, as non-functional arrays can be discarded just after the step the deficiency occurs in and not at the end of an entire synthesis process.

7. Acknowledgements

We thank Ralf Achenbach, Markus Dorn and the ASIC laboratory for their technical assistance with the microchips, Daniela Rambow, Sebastian Heß, Jürgen Kretschmer, Thomas Felgenhauer and Volker Stadler for their assistance, help and advice concerning particle production and surface activation, Klaus Leibe for his contributions to the design of the deposition apparatus and Jürgen Hesser for stimulating discussions. We gratefully acknowledge the funding of the Baden-Württemberg-Stiftung and the Heidelberg Graduate School of Mathematical and Computational Methods for the Sciences.

8. References

Angulo, J. & Serra, J. (2003). Automatic analysis of DNA microarray images using mathematical morphology, *Bioinformatics* 19(5): 553–562.

Aoyagi, S., Rouleau, A. & Boireau, W. (2008). TOF-SIMS structural charaterization of self-assembly monolayer of cytochrome b5 onto gold substrate, *Applied Surface Science* 255: 1071–1074.

Bajcsy, P. (2005). An overview of DNA microarray image requirements for automated processing, *Computer Vision and Pattern Recognition Workshop* 0: 147.

Beyer, M., Nesterov, A., Block, I., König, K., Felgenhauer, T., Fernandez, S., Leibe, K., Torralba, G., Hausmann, M., Trunk, U., Lindenstruth, V., Bischoff, F. R., Stadler, V. & Breitling, F. (2007). Combinatorial synthesis of peptide arrays onto a microchip, *Science* 381(5858): 1888.

Brown, C. S., Goodwin, P. C. & Sorger, P. K. (2001). Image metrics in the statistical analysis of DNA microarray data, *Proceedings of the National Academy of Sciences* 98(16): 8944–8949.

Chee, M., Yang, R., Hubbell, E., Berno, A., Huang, X. C., Stern, D., Winkler, J., Lockhart, D. J., Morris, M. S. & Fodor, S. P. A. (1996). Accessing genetic information with high-density DNA arrays, *Science* 274(5287): 610–614.

Cretich, M., Damin, F., Pirri, G. & Chiari, M. (2006). Protein and peptide arrays: Recent trends and new directions, *Biomolecular Engineering* 23(2-3): 77–88.

Debouck, C. & Goodfellow, P. N. (1999). DNA microarrays in drug discovery and development., *Nature Genetics* 21(1 Suppl): 48–50.

Fodor, S. P., Read, J. L., Pirrung, M. C., Stryer, L., Lu, A. T. & Solas, D. (1991). Light-directed, spatially addressable parallel chemical synthesis, *Science* 251(4995): 767–773.

Graham, D. J. & Ratner, B. D. (1994). Multivariate analysis of TOF-SIMS spectra from dodecanethiol SAM assembly on gold: Spectral interpretation and TOF-SIMS fragmentation processes, *Science* 264(5157): 399–402.

Gusev, A. I., Wilkinson, W. R., Proctor, A. & Hercules, D. M. (1993). Quantitative analysis of peptides by matrix-assisted laser desorption/ionization time-of-flight mass spectrometry, *Applied Spectroscopy* 47(8): 1091–1092.

Hagenhoff, B. (2000). High resolution surface analysis by TOF-SIMS, *Miicrochimica Acta* 132(2–4): 259–271.

Heller, M. J. (2002). DNA MICROARRAY TECHNOLOGY: Devices, systems, and applications, *Annual Review of Biomedical Engineering* 4(1): 129–153.

König, K., Block, I., Nesterov, A., Torralba, G., Fernandez, S., Felgenhauer, T., Leibe, K., Schirwitz, C., Löffler, F., Painke, F., Wagner, J., Trunk, U., Hausmann, M., Bischoff, F., Breitling, F., Stadler, V. & Lindenstruth, V. (2010). Programmable high-voltage cmos chips for particle-based high-density combinatorial peptide synthesis, *Sensors and Actuators B* 147(418): 418–427.

Löffler, F., Wagner, J., König, K., Märkle, F., Fernandez, S., Schirwitz, C., Torralba, G., Hausmann, M., Lindenstruth, V., Bischoff, F. R., Breitling, F. & Nesterov, A. (2011). High-precision combinatorial deposition of micro particle patterns on a microelectronic chip, *Aerosol Science and Technology* 45: 65–74.

Roepstorff, P. (2000). Maldi-tof mass spectrometry in protein chemistry, *EXS* 88.

Schirwitz, C., Block, I., König, K., Nesterov, A., Fernandez, S., Felgenhauer, T., Leibe, K., Torralba, G., Hausmann, M., Lindenstruth, V. & Stadler, V. (2009). Combinatorial peptide synthesis on a microchip, *Current Protocols in Protein Science* 57: 18.2.1–18.2.13.

Stadler, V., Beyer, M., König, K., Nesterov, A., Torralba, G., Lindenstruth, V., Hausmann, M., Bischoff, F. R. & Breitling, F. (2007). Multifunctional cmos microchip coatings for protein and peptide arrays, *Journal of Proteome Research* 6: 3197–3202.

Templin, M. F., Stoll, D., Schwenk, J. M., Pötz, O., Kramer, S. & Joos, T. O. (2003). Protein microarrays: Promising tools for proteomic research, *PROTEOMICS* 3(11): 2155–2166.

Volkmer, R. (2009). Synthesis and application of peptide arrays: Quo vadis SPOT technology, *ChemBioChem* 10(9): 1431–1442.

Wagner, J., König, K., Förtsch, T., Löffler, F., Fernandez, S., Felgenhauer, T., Painke, F., Torralba, G., Lindenstruth, V., Stadler, V., Bischoff, F., Breitling, F., Hausmann, M. & Nesterov-Müller, A. (2011). Microparticle transfer onto pixel electrodes of 45μm pitch on HV-CMOS chips – simulation and experiment, *Sensors and Actuators A. Physical* 172: 533–545.

Wagner, J., Löffler, F., König, K., Fernandez, S., Nesterov-Müller, A., Breitling, F., Bischoff, F., Stadler, V., Hausmann, M. & Lindenstruth, V. (2010). Quality analysis of selective microparticle deposition on electrically programmable surfaces, *Rev. Sci. Instrum.* 81(7): 073703–1–073703–6.

Wang, X., Ghosh, S. & Guo, S.-W. (2001). Quantitative quality control in microarray image processing and data acquisition, *Nucleic Acids Research* 29(15): e75.

5

Digital Restoration by Denoising and Binarization of Historical Manuscripts Images

Dimitrios Ventzas[1], Nikolaos Ntogas[2] and Maria-Malamo Ventza[3]
[1]*Department of Computer Science and Telecommunications, Technological Educational Institute of Larissa,*
[2]*Computer Science Technology & Telecommunications, TEI of Larisa,*
[3]*University of Western Greece, Dpt of Cultural Resources & New Technologies, Greece*

1. Introduction

This chapter deals with digital restoration, preservation, and data base storage of historical manuscripts images. It focuses on restoration techniques and binarization methods combined with image processing applied on document images for text - background enhancement and discrimination. Sequential image processing procedures are applied for image refinement and enhancement on quality class categorized images. Research results on historical (i.e. Byzantine, old newspapers, etc) manuscripts are presented.

The historical documents images acquisition types / formats are raw data files or JPG, video, i.e. frames at a speed, storage / transfer types / format e.g. lossless / lossy compressed files, standard print formats, reduced by calibration with a flat-field image. Rarely different areas of a large image are shot with overlapping in order to create a panorama; image alignment/stitching include key point detection feature matching , geometric registration and global registration.

Among libraries, and museums, there are old documents preserved in storage areas. Many of these documents are considered as quite important for national heritage, see fig. 1. Their efficient preservation and unconditional exploitation to wider public even through the internet is a trend in modern archaeology.

In image acquisition by digital cameras, see fig. 1, no flash lights are used, since the light could permanently degrade the documents colours and results in poor quality images.

Our work concentrates on two basic techniques used for image enhancement and restoration, denoising and binarization. Denoising refers to the removal of noise on the image and binarization refers to the conversion of a grayscale image to binary. Binarization by thresholding converts the grayscale document image to binary, by changing the foreground pixels (text characters) to black and background pixels to white. Image thresholding obtains a resulting binary image in black and white, easily stored in computer, while retaining all the basic characteristics of the original image.

All algorithms and ideas in this chapter are applied and tested to old pages photographically acquired from historical books and manuscripts called "Codices", from the Holy Monastery of Dousiko, Pylh, near Meteora, Trikala, see Fig. 1.

Fig. 1. Taking photos of Byzantine manuscript from Dousiko Byzantine Holy Monastery, Pylh, Greece

2. Document image acquisition

Document raw image acquisition (sharpness, resolution and transfer function curves) by camera, video or scanner highly depends on machine vision systems (Boyle 1988, Davies, 1990) and the combined effects of viewing distance / angle from the eye, depth of field, optimum aperture, lens sharpness. camera misalignment, aperture, lens characteristics, polarizing filters, diffraction, light and illumination types, focus, zoom, scaling and sharpness control, long exposure noise reduction, optimal intelligence and minimally processing sensors (Adams, 1995).

We acquire old documents images by a digital field camera (a CMOS technology SLR "CANON 1.8II" with a 50 mm lens) with high resolution ratio (4,368 x 2,904 pixels a total of 12,684,672 recorded pixels (12 Mbytes storage space), and stored in computer and compressed for storage minimization and sensors size 24 mm x 36mm (Canon 2007).

Raw images usually have 12 bits colour information per pixel. Image editing software uses 8 bits, or 16 bits. The 12 bits per pixel data from a RAW file is more accurate than the 8 bit format of a .jpg, but the .jpg 8 bits contain various corrections. For textual images published on the web site, enlarged and printed to larger dimensions than 10" x 8" compression may provide inadequate quality. Raw format allows us to correct defects (under/over exposure, colour balance, etc). Raw/.jpg images differ in that we make the adjustment before/after non-linear corrections (γ- correction) i.e. before/after saving it as a .JPG, TIFF, PSD files.

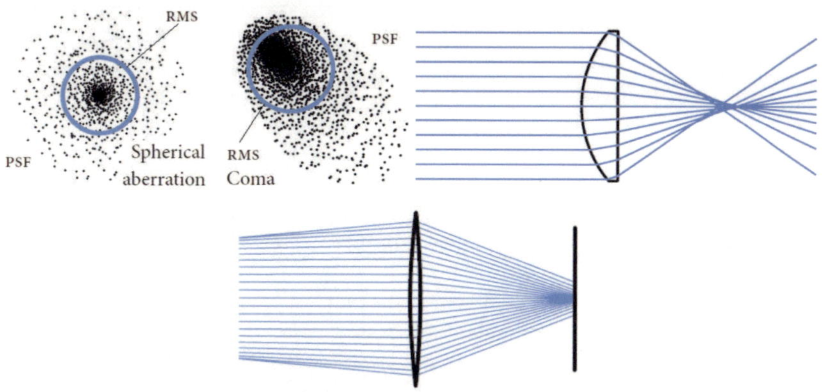

Fig. 2a. Spherical error (lens chromatic aberrations), i.e. optical imperfections (different bending of light at different wavelengths), the inability of spherical surfaces to provide clear images over large fields of view, changes in focus for light rays that don't pass through the center of the lens, etc (Ren, 2006).

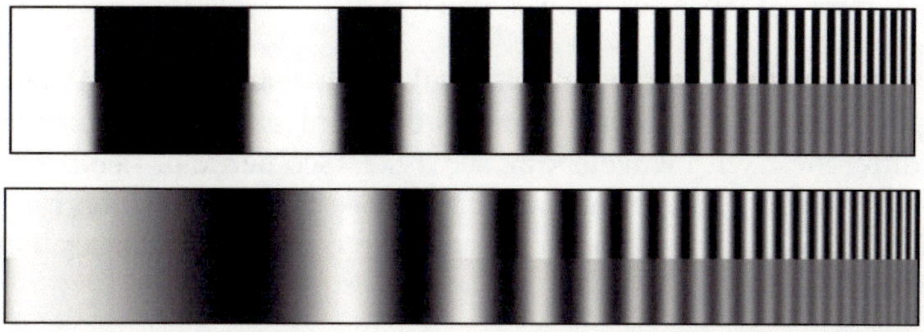

Fig. 2b. Lenses inaccuracies - Sine pattern with lens degradation and low to high spatial frequencies variations. Sharpness boundaries between zones of different tones or colors.

Signal processing varies with image content (feature contrast) and a camera's ability to render fine detail (texture), i.e., low contrast, high spatial frequency image content. Spatial frequency response is related to total image quality resolution and tonal response. Log f-contrast is sensitive to noise. Sensitivity to sharpening decreases and sensitivity to noise reduction increases from top (most contrast) to bottom (least contrast). Tone photos and correct radial exposure and brightness should be calibrated. SQF (subjective quality factor) is a measure of perceived print sharpness that incorporates the contrast sensitivity function (CSF) of the human eye (Legge, 1985). Retouche software filters, focus and control sharpness without edge lines or artifacts, while color correction software, master exposure compensation, white balance corrector that correct miscoloration in photos caused by any light source (Papamarkos, 2001).

Dynamic or exposure range of cameras and scanners is the range of tones over which a camera responds and over which noise remains under a specified level; log exposure is proportional to optical density. Digital cameras output may not follow an exact gamma (exponential) curve (confusion factor), a tone reproduction curve ("S" curve) is superposed on the gamma curve to boost visual contrast without sacrificing dynamic range in middle tones while reducing it in highlights and shadows. Resolution is the ability to resolve fine detail (ppi or dpi).

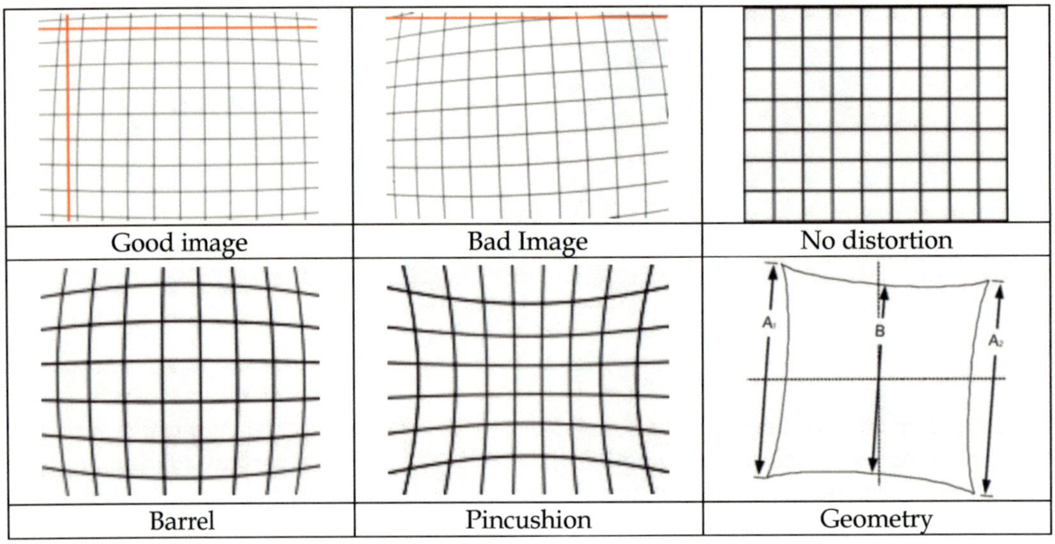

Fig. 3. Geometric errors of lenses or images displays

Aberrations are chromatic (longitudinal / lateral), coma, astigmatism and curvature of field degrade lens performance and cause focus on different image planes, color fringing due magnification differences with wavelength, see fig. 2. Geometric or perspective (radial lens) distortion have two forms, barrel and pincushion, see fig. 3. Distortion can detect vertical and horizontal lines in extreme wide angle, telephoto and zoom lenses. Highly distorted images are a special case.

The ability of the eye to resolve detail is known as visual acuity. The normal human eye can distinguish patterns of alternating black and white lines with a feature size as small as one minute of an arc (1/60 degree or $\pi/(60*180) = 0.000291$ radians). A pattern of higher spatial frequency in larger prints, would appear pure gray, low contrast patterns at the maximum spatial frequency will also appear gray. The human eye and brain have a limited ability to discern tonal values, and to analyze large numbers of images simultaneously; it is more qualitative than quantitative. Wavelength (color) psychophysics influences text vision, especially in low-vision conditions. Photopic / scotopic conditions, photoreceptor disorders, characters near the acuity limit, lower luminance, wavelength effects, spectral sensitivities, light scatter or absorption result in depressed / optimal performance in the red, blue / green, gray regions. Eyes differentiate in vertical and horizontal banding. Eyes are wired to recognize differences in vertical and horizontal banding, while the recorded images appear arranged in diagonal arrays. Noise tends to be most visible at medium spatial (actually angular) frequencies where the eye's Contrast Sensitivity Function is large.

3. Image background - foreground

In foreground / background analysis, the goal is objects separation and cleaning. Poor contrast between foreground and background characters exists in transparent texts.

A text or object within an image viewed dark in color and placed on a light background, exhibits histogram with a good bi-modal distribution, see fig. 4, 5. One peak represents the object pixels, one represents the background (Kapur, 1985) , see fig. 5. Significant incident illumination gradient across the image blurs out the histogram information. The histogram is altered by many image enhancement operators, mainly the contrast stretching and histogram equalization. Contrast stretching improves contrast. High peaks at the end of the histogram, suggest high intensity and contrast colors. Image statistics calculate histogram, mean color values, standard deviation, median, histogram shape matching, histogram based image segmentation, histogram equalization, etc for each color channel in RGB, HSL, YCbCr color space. Vertical - Horizontal Intensity statistics provide information about vertical - horizontal distribution of pixel intensities and is used to locate objects, centers, etc. Picture segmentation maximizes the separability of resultant classes (Yanowitz, 1989).

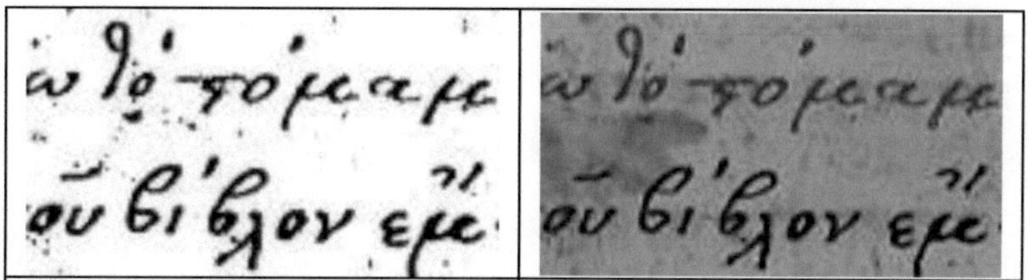

(a) (b)

Fig. 4. Foreground / background analysis

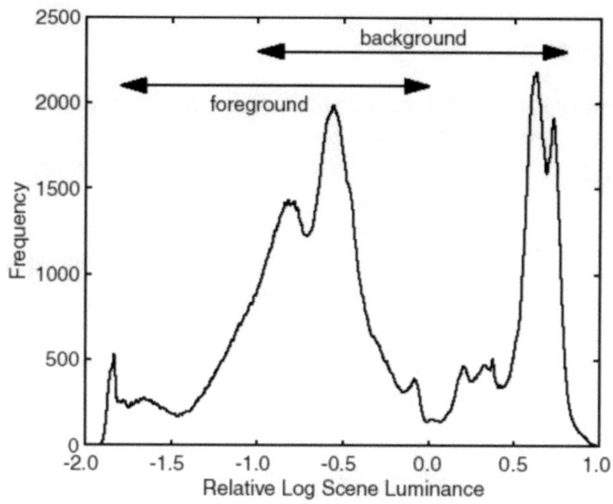

Fig. 5. Histogram of relative log scene luminance range

Because the dynamic range of the original scene is substantially larger than this, a subset of the image data must be selected. Different results are obtained depending on whether the foreground or background region of the image is selected. Background could be complex and inhomogeneous, while segmentation, ratio foreground / background contrast comparison, classification of large background regions optimize results, see fig. 6.

Very low-contrast texts are detrimental to readability and identifiability, because the background may show large variations in luminance (Knoblauch, 1991). While backgrounds (culture, wave, plain) are uniform, the text is not. A common text area contains 23% of text pixels.

Fig. 6. Various quality old paper background textures in old documents, see App. 1.

4. Histogram analysis

Image statistics parameters and transformation include character features, font information, size, mean-square error, position, dimension and shape, area, gravity point, number of work pieces, correlation, clustering, connection characteristics, ROI, min/max, average/deviation/skewness, column / row location, rms pixel values, etc, see fig. 7, 8, 9, 10, 11. Image color spaces offer flexibility on image processing, i.e. the HLS space has advantages since saturation is low for black/white pixels, brightness is independent of the saturation and freedom of choice to brightness, luminance or lightness function; saturation values are easily compared

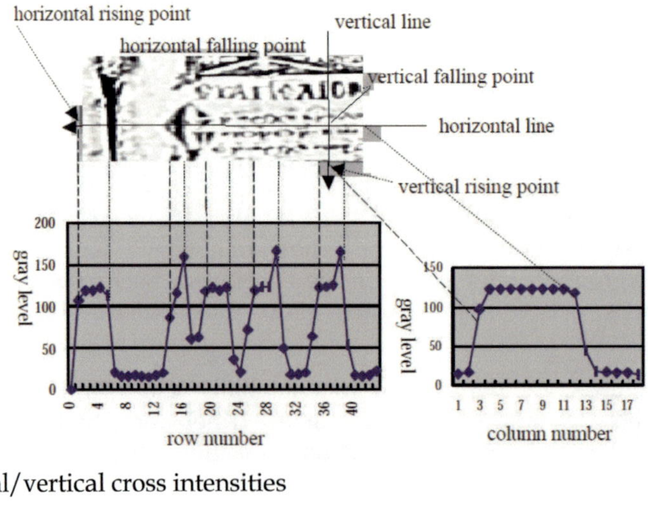

Fig. 7. Horizontal/vertical cross intensities

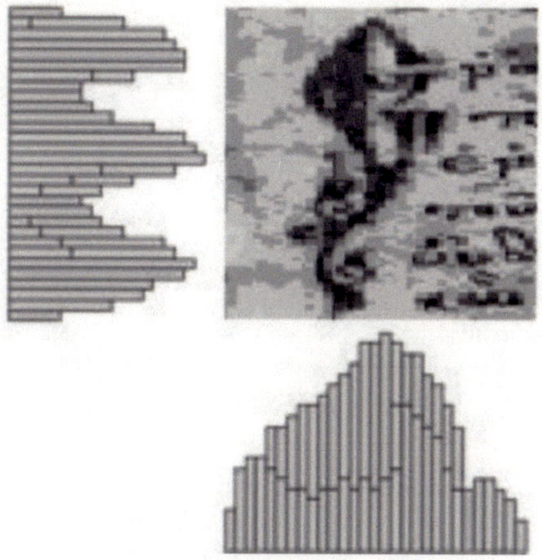

Fig. 8. Horizontal/vertical histogram projections

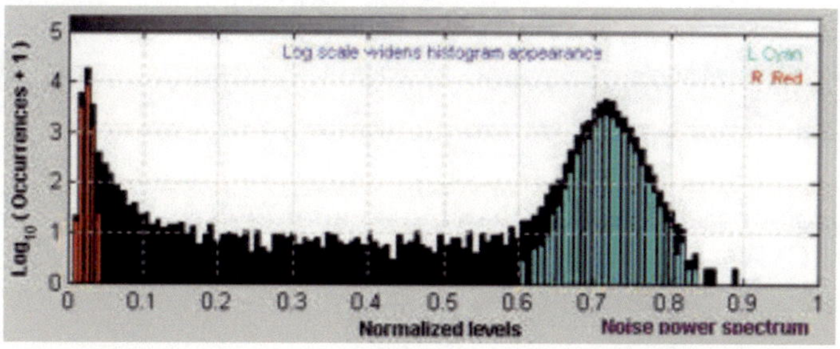

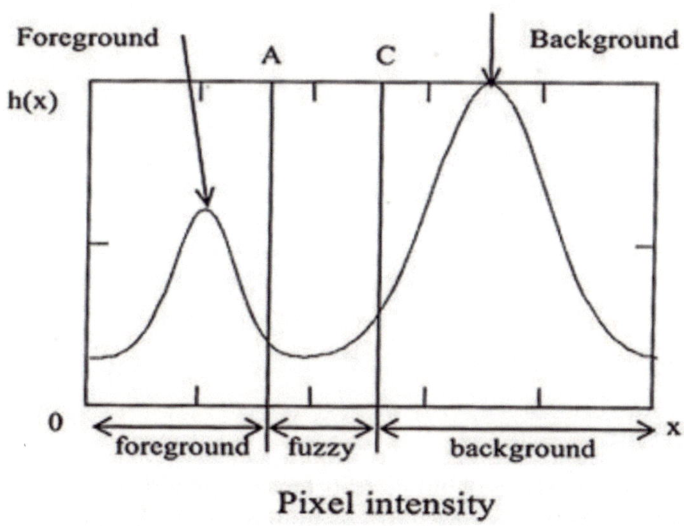

Histograms and noise analysis: The black (background) histogram contains pixel levels for the entire ROI. Sharpening may cause extra bumps to appear in the black histogram. Histogram logarithmic scale improve analysis

Fig. 9. Intensity Histogram with 3 classes of pixels

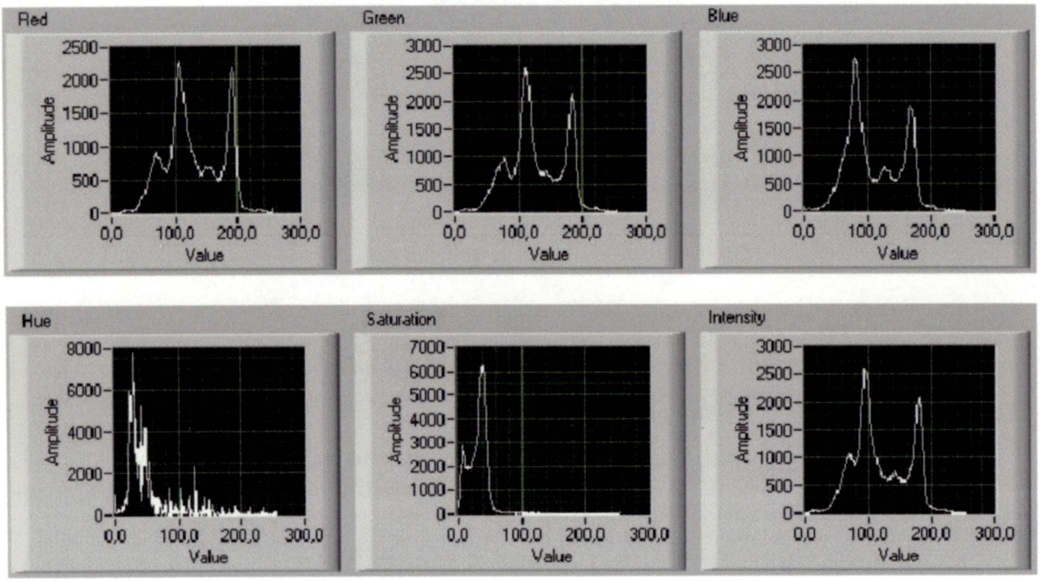

Fig. 10. A CMYK color space is smaller than the monitor RGB color space. Physical display limitations reduce CMYK colors displayed

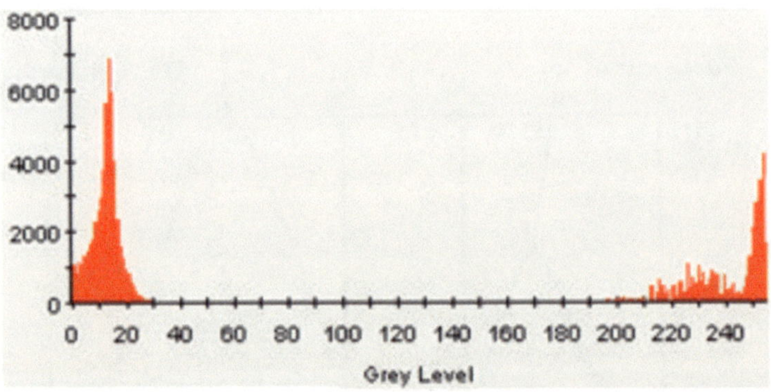

Fig. 11. Hue histogram. The reds and violets are separated by a large discontinuity

5. Color processing

When raw RGB data are used without color balance compensation we get incorrect color result, see fig. 12, 13. Soft proofing process minimizes visible color differences, while PDF/X-4 standard provides a framework that enables colored elements can be reproduced well on different output devices and media. Color (miscoloration) correction software and white balance corrector includes scalar or vectorial processes. The color ratios (R/G) can be especially useful for diagnosing uneven color response.

Original Image

Lightness adjustment

Hue (red = -180)

Saturation

Color balance

Contrast

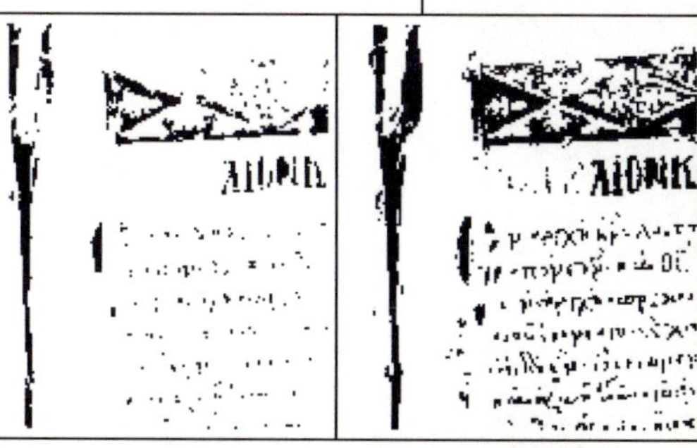

Changing lower Threshold limit

Changing upper Threshold limit

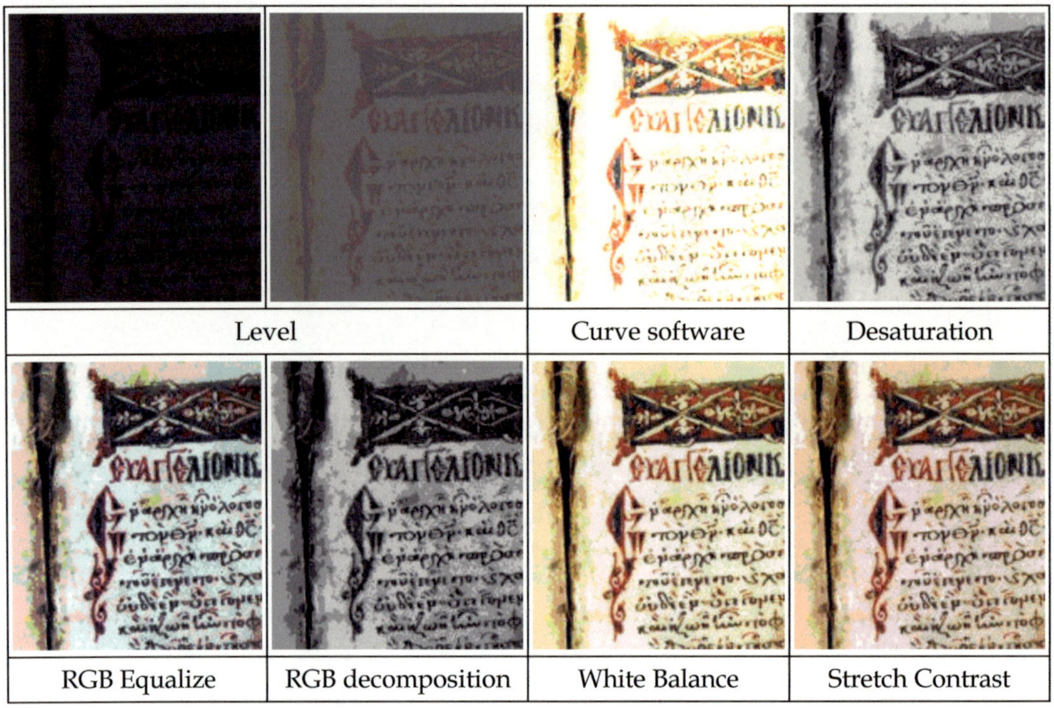

Fig. 12. Signal processing filters

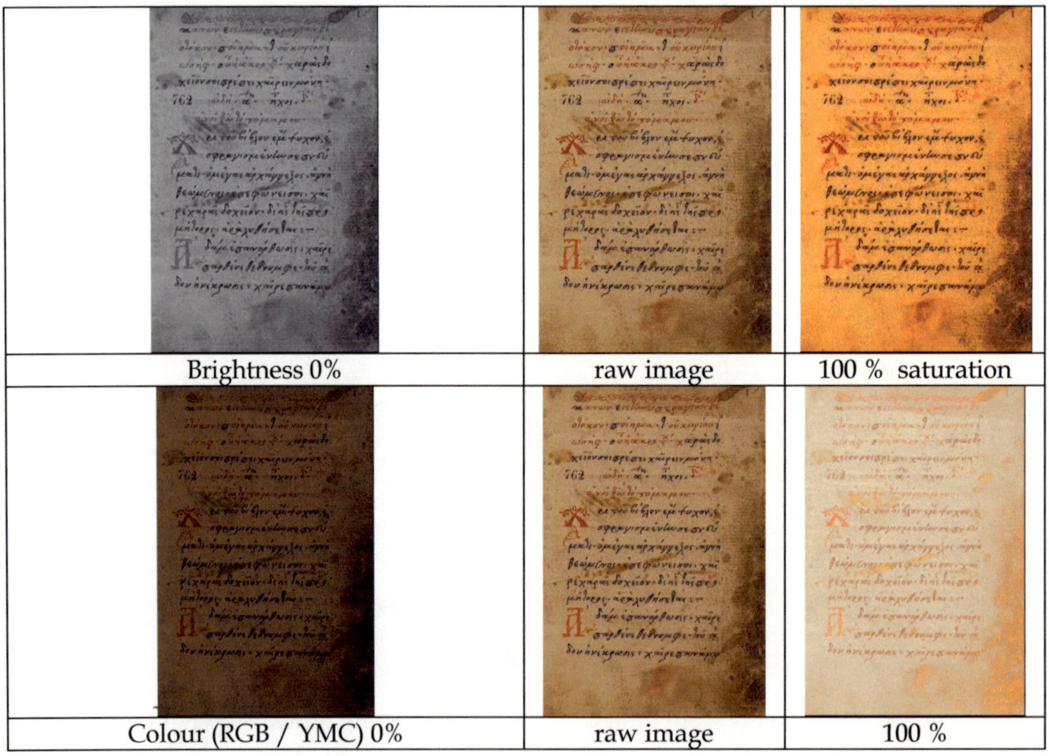

Fig. 13. Saturation enhancement - Text in different color spaces (Hunt, 2001)

All achieved image deformations are artificial but they are used in understanding or inversion restoration of distorted images, e.g. scanned thick bound documents (Zhang, 2001), see fig. 14. Warp occurs in words, location, shape, shade and orientation.

Defocus filter applies a Gaussian blur to the image, making it less clear. Other filters reproduce the effect of aging in old, traditional black-and-white photographs, toned with shades of brown, see fig. 15. To achieve this effect, the filter desaturates the image, reduces brightness and contrast, modifies the color balance and marks the image with spots, see fig. 14.

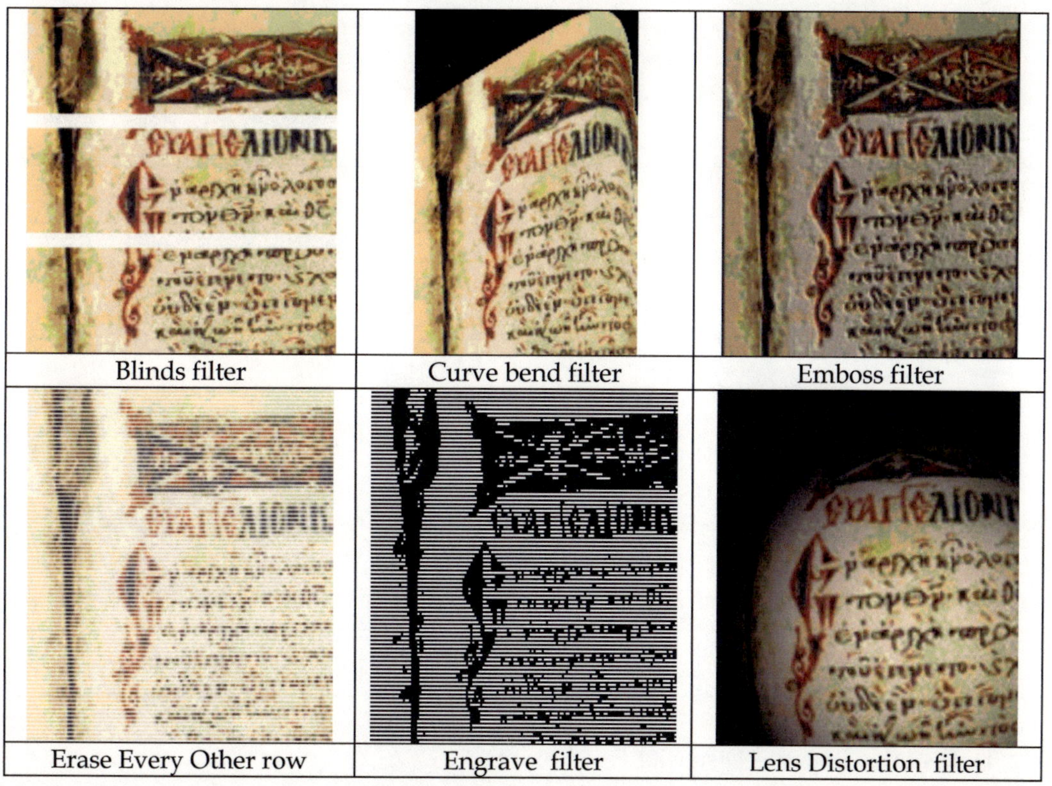

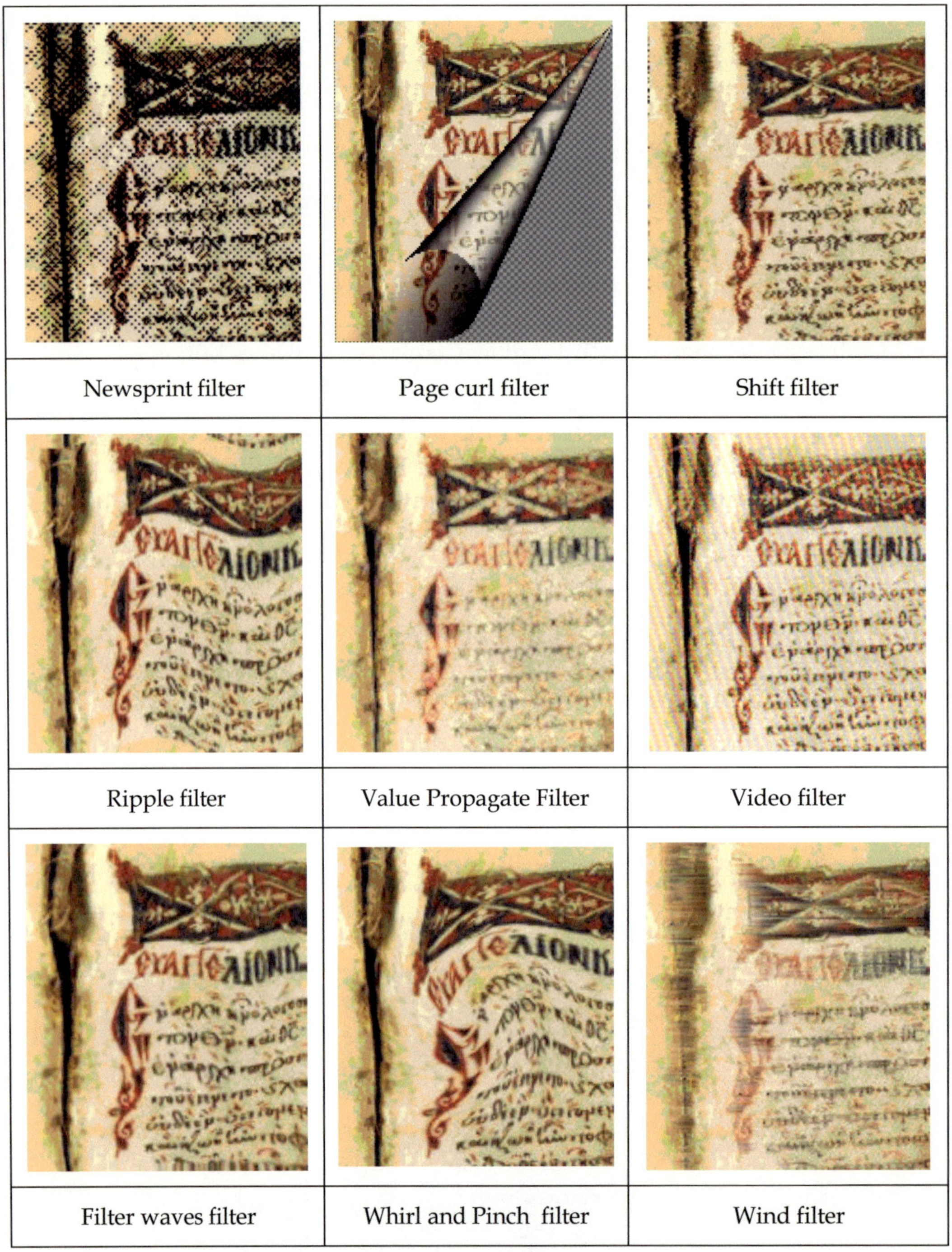

Fig. 14. Distorted images – Distortion

Old photo filter gives an old photo, blurred with brown shade, spots, jagged border	Coffee stain filter adds / subtracts realistic looking stains randomly spread out

Fig. 15. Maturing old images or stains on images

Images sharpen, shifted horizontally / vertically and fused	Images sharpen, shifted horizontally/vertically, rotated and fused

Fig. 16. Images fusion techniques

The apply canvas and the weave filter applies an artist's canvas-like or weave effect with parameters direction, light source, apparent depth. Clothify filter adds a cloth-like texture with parameters azimuth, elevation, depth). Impressionist and Oilify filter include cubism and gives image the look of a painting with parameters overlay, scale, texture, graininess of the texture, relief, brush, luminosity, gamma correction, mid tones brightens/darkens, aspect ratio, directions, color noise, background. The cartoon filter is similar to a black felt pen drawing subsequently shaded with color. This is achieved by darkening areas that are already distinctly darker than their neighbourhood with parameters lines thinner or thicker, darker and sharper. The predator filter effect makes the image/selection look something like a thermogram. This will reduce the image to edges in a few basic (red, green, blue and gray) colors on a dark background. Photocopy filter makes the image like a black and white photocopy. Soft glow filter applied lights the image with a soft glow diffuse effect, see fig. 17.

6. Layers fusion

Certain data fusion techniques of complementary spatial and spectral resolution characteristics produce enhanced observations, see fig. 16. Dual image point processing maps two pixel brightnesses, one from each image, to an output image by the overlay or the composite operation that merges unrelated objects from two images; this is done on a per band basis. The images are identical scenes, but acquired at different times and spectral filters. An alpha channel represents the transparency of the image (D'Zmura, 1997). The Threshold Alpha command converts semi-transparent areas of the active layer into completely transparent or completely opaque areas. It only works on layers of RGB images which have an alpha channel. The transparency transition is abrupt. Composition refers to the merging of two or more distinct objects into a new compound object with new functionality. A single object image is processed to extract object features, modify some of the features, and then merge the modified object back. Image processing techniques include skewed documents correction (Kavallieratou, 1999).

Fig. 17. Artistic effects assist to optimal presentation or understanding of wear and image degradation

7. Image text degradation by noise

Digital camera images with excessive noise reduction will have an unusually rapid falloff of the noise spectrum. The pixel noise is highly visible; it wouldn't be suitable for portraits and other high quality work, but it would be acceptable when a grainy look is tolerated. Temporal noise is the random difference between otherwise identical images: $N_{temporal}$ = Noise($Image_1$-$Image_2$) / $\sqrt{2}$; dividing by the square root of 2 scales temporal noise to be the same as noise measured in an individual image. Noise will be worse for higher contrast cameras, affected by the gamma encoding. Gradual illumination nonuniformities should be removed from the noise results. Noise is largest in the dark areas because of gamma encoding. Noise corrupts the images as additive /multiplicative Gaussian, uniform, speckle noise and complex signal dependent noise, salt and pepper with standard deviations (σ=15.0 ÷ σ =2.5); filters reduce them to σ=2.0 σ=0.5 respectively). Combinations of noise type, amount, etc corrupt images totally, partially or locally.

The documents images are classified into six distinct image categories / conditions, see fig. 18:

1. Acceptable images that are in good condition of camera acquisition and paper
2. Images that present spots, stains, smears, scratches, damages or smudges
3. Images with shadows and wrinkles (Blinn, 1978) caused by:

  3.1 High humidity over the years, fragile paper or
  3.2 Bad / non uniform illumination and background
  3.3 Aging paper colours deterioration and brightness degradation

4. Transparent or oily page or ink wet, seeking / visible from the other side
5. Thin / thick / consistent stroke pen width texts, multiple touching characters
6. Badly blurred or missing ink broken characters with holes or light handwriting
7. Characters with different colours (e.g. red) ink, poor quality of ink

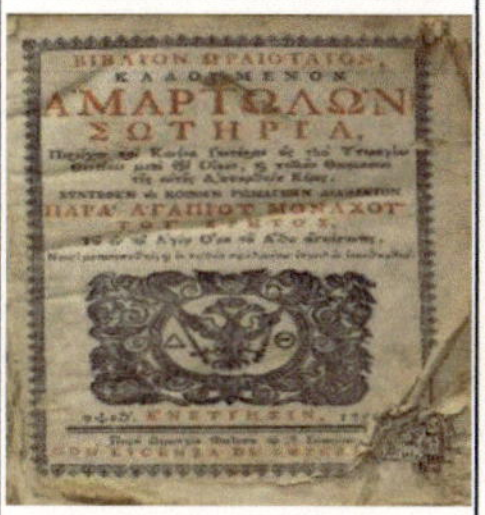	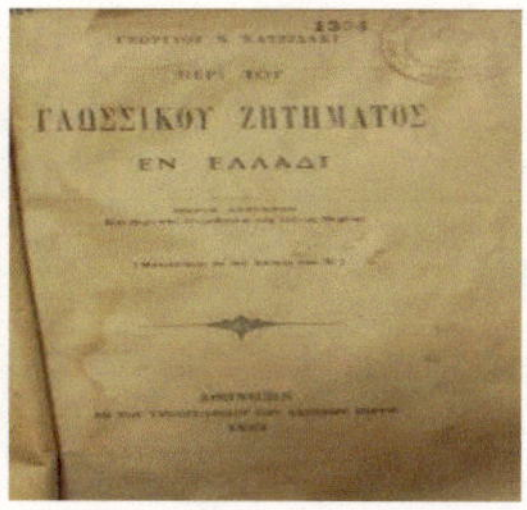	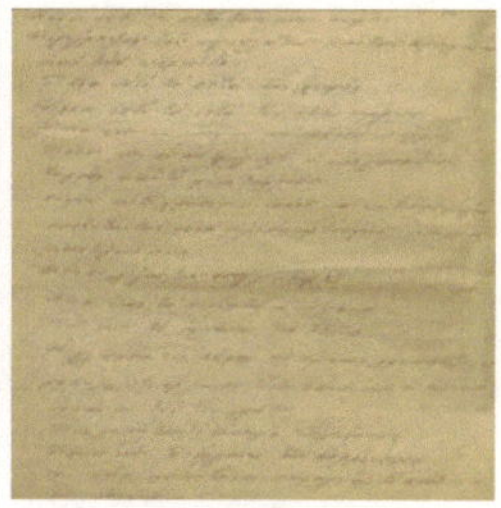	
Documents with poor quality paper, fragile, etc.	The brightness of the aging paper has deteriorated colours over the years.	Poor contrast between foreground and background characters.	Documents condition, poor quality of ink, broken characters, characters with holes or light handwriting.
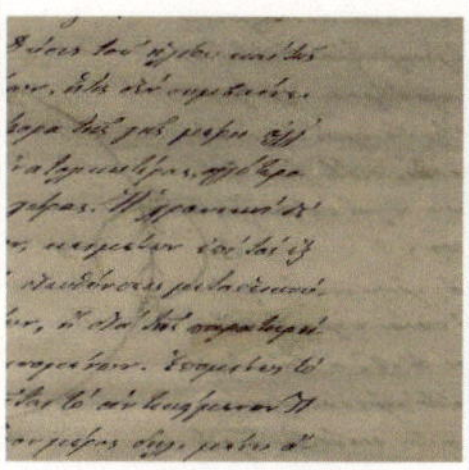	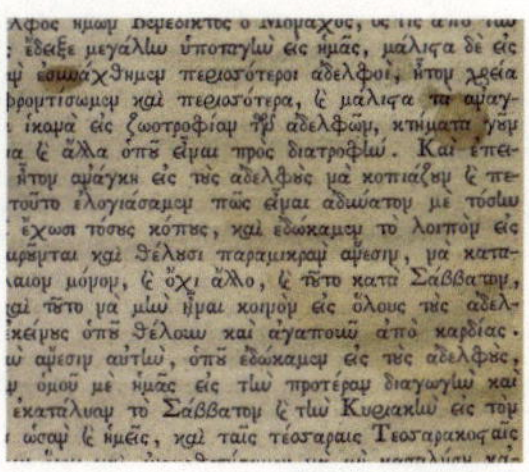		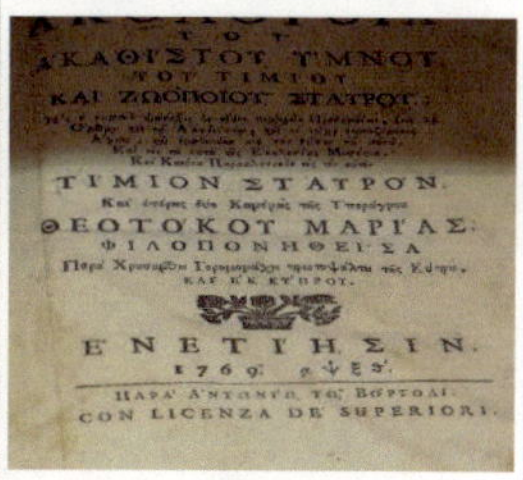
Ink wet paper with characters visible both sides of paper.	Dirty documents with various sizes or colours of spots, stains, smears or smudges.	High humidity over the years cause wrinkles to the paper.	Image acquisition problems illumination, types of light, non uniformity, low contrast, etc.

Fig. 18. Description of problems appeared and examined on Byzantine documents

7.1 Noise on images

Randomization (%) represents the percentage of noise affected pixels. A normal distribution of noise means, that only slight noise is added to the most pixels in the affected area, while less pixels are affected by more extreme values. Noise may be additive (uncorrelated) or multiplicative (correlated - also known as speckle noise), repetitive. For wide band and high-pass noise the summation is quite linear while for low-pass noise no summation needed. Hue noise changes the color (strong /weak hue variation) of the pixels in a random pattern; noise varies by saturation or brightness of scattered pixels.

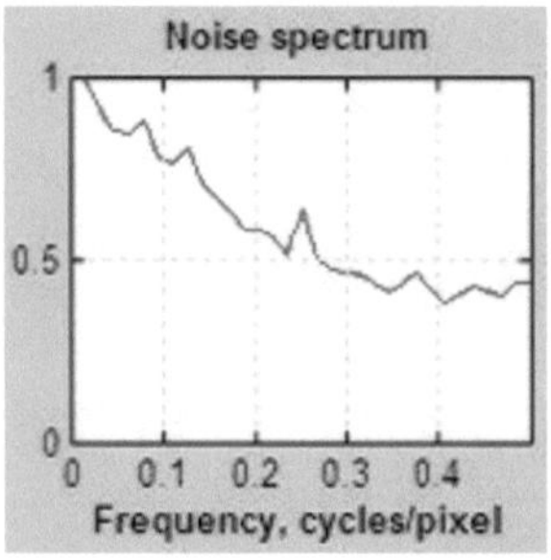

Fig. 19. Noise spectrum

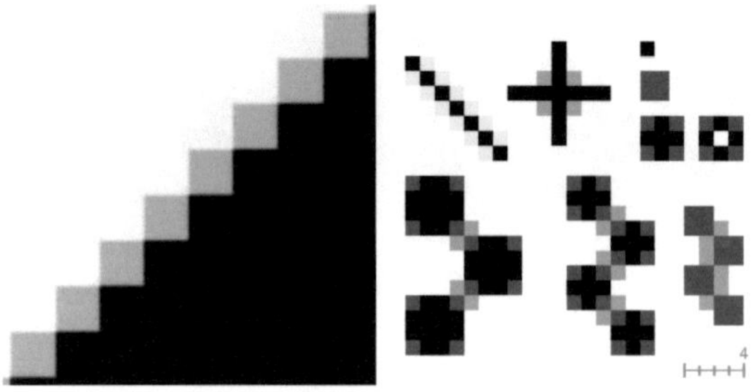

Fig. 20. Antialiased images

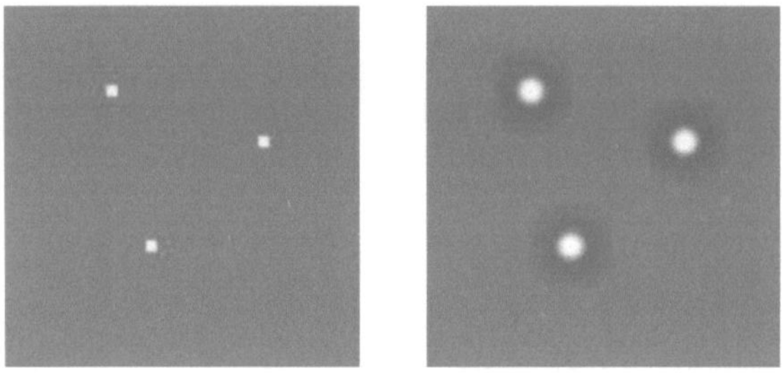

Fig. 21. Sharpened images

Artifacts, noise contamination, see fig. 19, edges, sharp transitions, edge blurring, saturation effect on bright / dark text scenes, high corruption, etc. appear for signal above the Nyquist frequency in the digital sensor. Color aliasing and Moire fringing is a type of aliasing, see fig. 20. Noise in digital sensors tends to have the greatest impact in dark regions. The larger the image (the greater the magnification), the more important noise becomes. Color quantization error cause false colours and contours.

Analog-to-digital image conversion and image sample / capture rate limitations suggest the highest spatial frequency, Nyquist frequency $f_N = 1/(2 * \text{pixel spacing})$; the design of anti-aliasing (lowpass) filters always involves a trade off that compromises sharpness. Antialias filter reduces or reverses alias effects, jaggies. Antialiasing produces smoother curves by adjusting the boundary between the background and the pixel region that is being antialiased; pixel intensities or opacities are changed for a smoother transition to the background. Lateral Chromatic Aberration (LCA), or color fringing, is visible on tangential edge boundaries.

	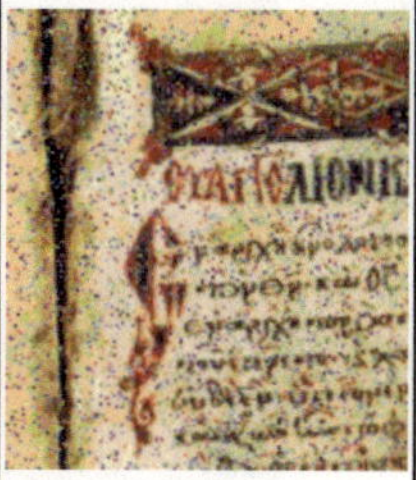			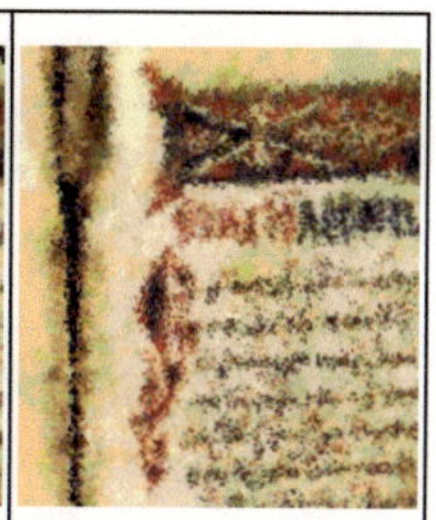
The HSV Noise filter creates noise in the HSV active layer	The Hurl filter changes each affected pixel to a random color	The RGB Noise filter adds noise to a layer normal-ly distributed	Slur Filter effect melts the image downwards	The spread filter swaps each pixel with randomly chosen pixel

Fig. 22. Color spaces filters

Out-of-focus photographs and most digitized images often need a sharpness correction. To prevent color distortion while sharpening, we decompose our image to HSV and work only on value, see fig. 22. So we protect areas of smooth tonal transition from sharpening, see fig. 23, 24. In an image with some blur we sharpen by applying some more blur: the intensity variation will be more gradual. We subtract the blurredness intensity from the intensity of the image and get the red curve, which is more abrupt: contrast and sharpness are increased. If blurring is important, this dip is very deep; the result of the subtraction can be negative, and a complementary color stripe will appear along the contrast, or a black halo around a star on the light background of a nebula (black eye effect) , see fig. 21.

Despeckle removes small isolated defects	Red Eye Removal filter	Sharpen	Unsharp mask filter

Fig. 23. Edges on Images (Ventzas, 1994)

Physical vs image contours are often very different. A physical edge of the image might yield practically no contour, while a shadow casts a clear image virtual contour where there in fact is no physical edge.

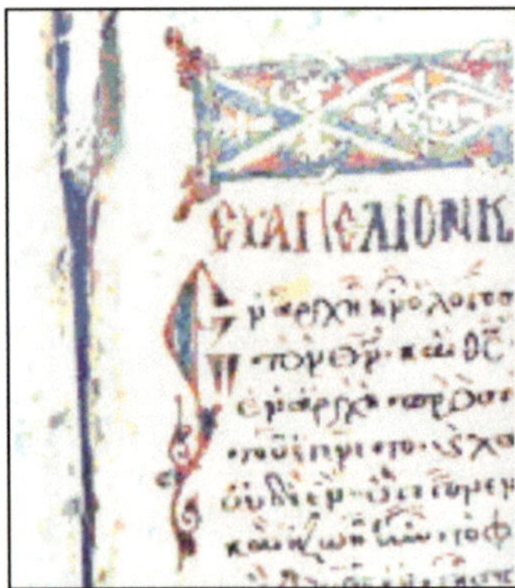	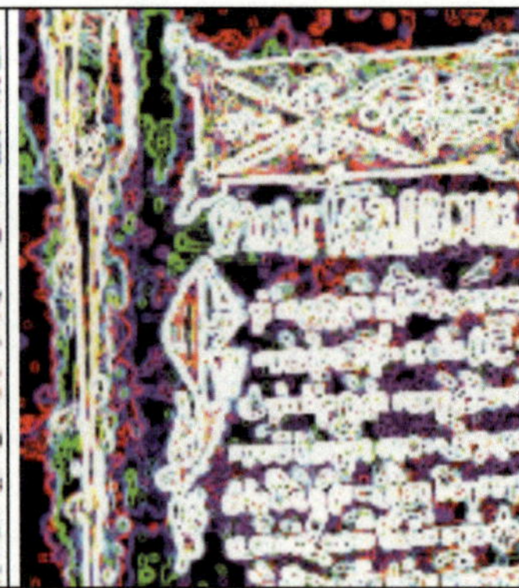	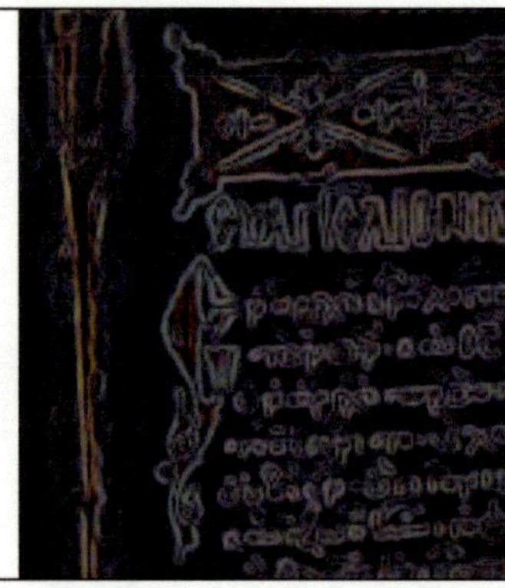
Negative on Difference of Gaussians	Neon filter detects edges and gives them a bright neon effect	Sobel's filter detects horizontal and vertical edges separately on a scaled image

Fig. 24. Grayscale edge detection and preserving algorithms create contours around objects

8. Denoising

Denoising filtering methods are in spatial or in frequency domain (Motwani, 2004). Filters are also subdivided to linear and non-linear filters. Many types of filters exist. We concentrate in three filters in spatial domain (mean, median and wiener) with various windows sizes and two filters in frequency domain (Butterworth and Gaussian), see fig. 28.

8.1 Time domain processing

Mean filter: The intensity of every pixel in the image is replaced with the averaged value of intensity of its neighbour pixels.

$$I(i,j) = \frac{1}{M} \sum_{(x,y)\in N} I(x,y)$$

where M the number of pixels in the neighbourhood N.

Median Filter: This is a non linear filter.

If $A\{a1, a2, a3, ...an\}$

and $a1 \le a2 \le a3 \le ..... \le an \in R$

$$median(A) = \begin{cases} a_{\frac{n+1}{2}}, \text{if n is odd} \\ \frac{1}{2}\left(a_{\frac{n}{2}} + a_{\frac{n}{2}+1}\right), \text{if n is even} \end{cases}$$

Median is a lower rms error filter and remove impulse noise spikes.

Noise - Median - Box filters

Wiener filter: Wiener filter, known as "minimum mean square error filter", is an adaptive linear filter, applied to an image locally, by taking into account the local image variance. When the variance in an image is large the Wiener filter results in light local smoothing, while when the variance is small, it gives an improved local smoothing.

Linear filtering in spatial domain is performed by applying a filter with a weighted sum of neighbouring pixels. Filtering is achieved by convolution or correlation kernel rotated by 180°.

8.2 Blur filter

The motion blur filter creates a movement blur, the simple blur filter produces an out of focus camera effect, the IIR and selective Gaussian blur sets its value to the average of a radius; the blur can be set to act in one direction or above a difference threshold, so contrasts are preserved (blur a background and not foreground) and add depth, see fig. 27. The blur tool is used to soften tile seams in images used in tiled backgrounds. Convolution filtering reduces the effects of noise in images or sharpens the detail in blurred images. The selection of the weights determines the nature of the filtering action (high-pass, low-pass). There are several blurring filter kernel:

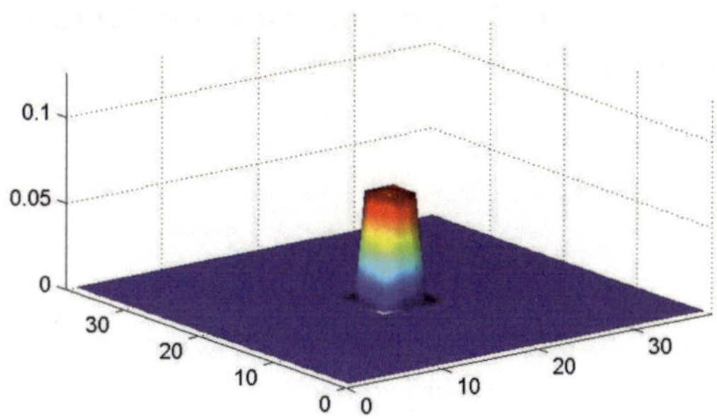

Fig. 25. The Box filter

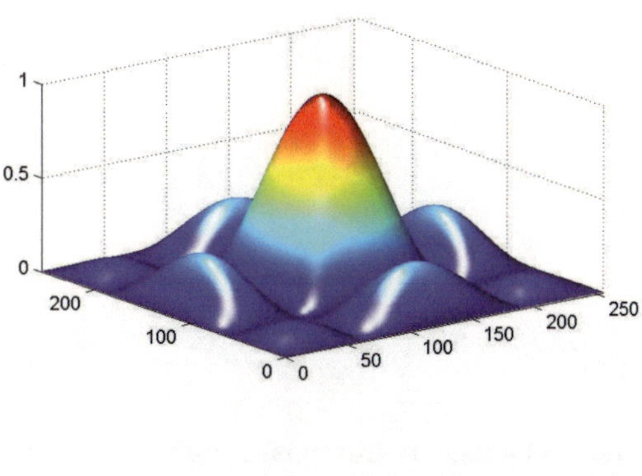

Fig. 26. Bartlett filter

The Box filter is simple, but Bartlett and Gaussian filters produce better blurring, see fig. 25. Bartlett filter pixels to the center are weighted more heavily than pixels away, see fig. 26.

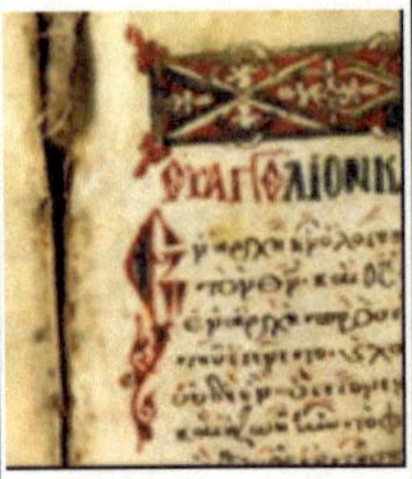				
original	motion blur	IIR Gauss blur	Fractal filter	Rippling filter

Fig. 27. Blur filters

8.3 Frequency domain processing

Image spatial frequency is measured horizontally, vertically or at any diagonal. DCT/IDCT is better at compactly representing very small images (Gonzalez, 2002, Sonka, 1998).

Butterworth Low Pass Filter

$$H(u,v) = \frac{1}{1 + [D(u,v) / D_0]^{2n}}$$

where D_0 is a specific non negative quantity, and $D(u,v)$ it the distance from point (u,v) to the centre of the frequency rectangle, see fig. 28.

Gaussian Low Pass Filter (bell curved kernel).

$$H(u,v) = e^{-D^2(u,v) / 2\sigma^2}$$

where $D(u,v)$ it the distance from the origin of the Fourier transform

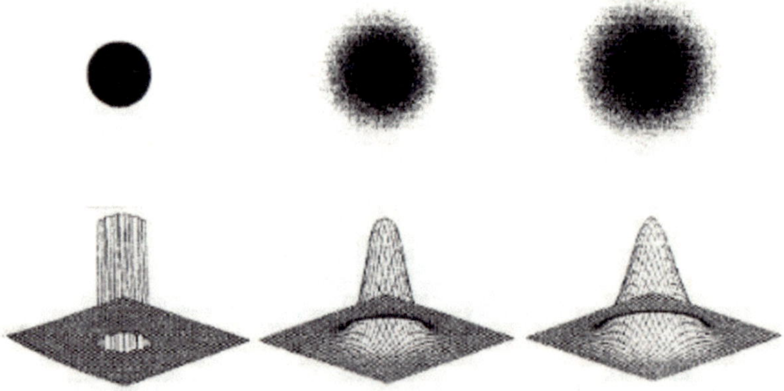

Fig. 28. Ideal, Butterworth and Gaussian low pass filters and corresponding image effects

The Gaussian filter is separable, and can be split into horizontal /vertical passes. We can filter bright portions, downsample, horizontal and vertical blur and accumulate. By skipping the high-pass filter, we soften the entire image (anti-aliasing).

8.4 Non linear filtering

Filters are linear or nonlinear. The linear takes into consideration only the relative position in kernel, and remains constant throughout the whole image filtering. Nonlinear filters are relative to the target pixel and the coefficients are calculated as a function of local variations of the signal. In the linear filter class, average and Gaussian filters are often used. Among the nonlinear filters, the median filter is popular. A selective blurring filter is often used, which emphases the pixels with similar intensity to the target pixel. A bilateral filter is an edge preserving technique being widely used in image processing. Comparing it to the selective blurring filter, it takes into account intensity and spatial similarity with a uniform or Gaussian kernel.

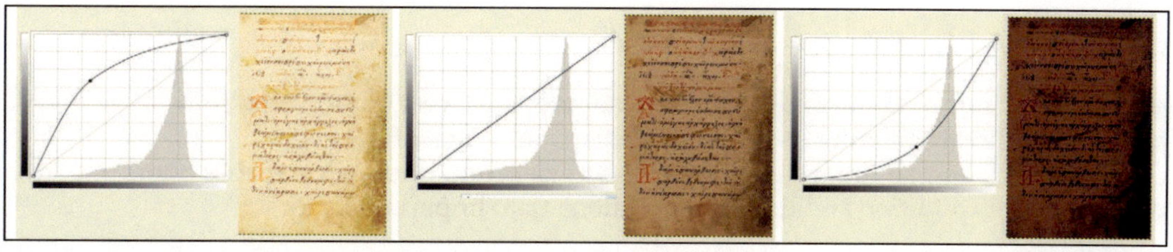

Fig. 29. The image is linearized, the pixel levels are adjusted to remove the camera gamma encoding

Linear image processing assumes linear luminance. Images are frequently gamma encoded, in the sRGB color space, so luminance is not linear. To apply a linear filter, we must gamma decode the values, and if resampling, we must gamma decode, resample, then gamma encode, see fig. 29. The magnitude squared is an enhancement operation, the Phase operation is phase enhancement, quantizing an image on logarithmic rather than linear scale (human eye has a logarithmic intensity response) results in logarithmic enhancement.

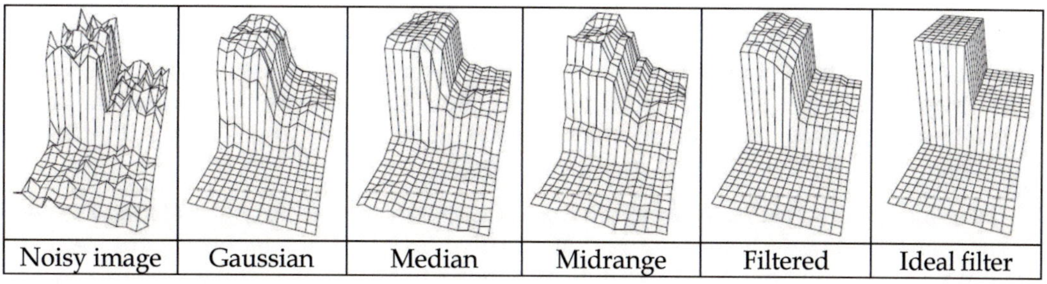

Fig. 30. Filters responses

In low level image processing, for shape and edge detection we differentiate filters performance in cases of high noise compared to small noise conditions, see fig. 30. Nonnegative filters do not introduce overshoot or ringing artifacts. Other temporal/spatial/ frequency averaging filters are the non-liner diffusion, the shock, the inverse scale space filter, reconstruction filter, Brickwall, Tent, BSpline filters. Resampling, decimation, interpolation decreases/increases the sampling rate. In photography, a variety of interpolation filters exist, such as nearest neighbour averaging, bilinear, bicubic interpolation for higher resampling ratios. Reconstruction filters reconstruct an image from a collection of wavelet coefficients.

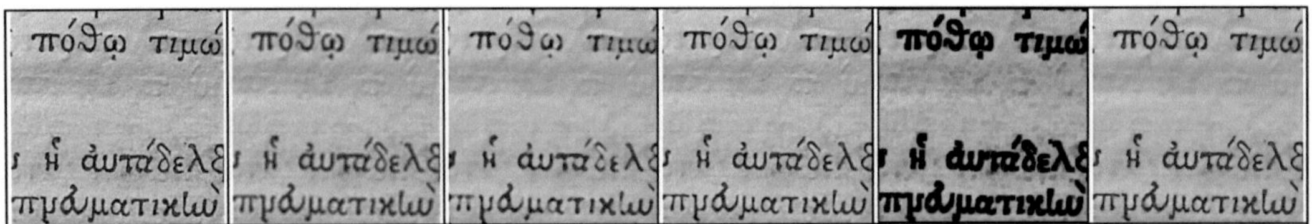

original image grayscale	after mean filter 5-by-5	after median filter 7-by-7	after max filter 5-by-5	after min filter 5-by-5	after wiener filter 7-by-7

Table 1. Filtering on Byzantine documents

9. Denoising results

a. Filtering improves the image quality, and prepares it for binarization
b. Spatial domain filtering uses Mean, Median and Wiener filters
c. Frequency domain filtering uses the Butterworth and Gaussian low pass filters
d. The paper condition and lighting conditions is an important factor

Type of filter	Performance	High Noise	Small Noise
Gaussian	*poor*	*same*	
Median	*good*	*bad*	*good*
		very good and same with Salt & Pepper	
Midrange	*bad*	*bad*	*bad*
Gradient inverse weighed	*good*	*very bad with Salt & Pepper noise*	
K-nearest neighbor	*bad*	*bad*	*bad*

Table 2. Filters performance

Researchers investigated the combined effects of high and low pass filtering on both letters and noise (noise filtered but letters unfiltered, etc). Averaged thresholds showed that for a given noise, unfiltered letters (the sum of the high- and low-pass letters) led to better recognition than either component filtered letter alone. High-pass letters led to better performance than unfiltered letters in low-pass noise.

Cleaning up scanned text pages from old manuscripts is achieved through Dilation Erosion, Opening and Closing techniques of raw or negative images. We look on how to clean up isolated noise dots without removing dots that are part of characters, by using bwareaopen, bwlabel and regionprops to highlight the pixels that were removed and logical operators (logical AND of the dilated characters with the pixels removed or logical OR) to restore the removed pixels. We suggest the use of morphological reconstruction to get all the pixels connected to the overlapping pixels. Thinning and cropping could lead to segmented characters that include parts (remains) of other neighboring print objects, while skeletonization displaces junctions, and short false branches occur. Thinning of thick binary images reduces shape outlines, while different thinning rules optimize edge noise, remove, add or move spurious noise and edges, see fig. 31.

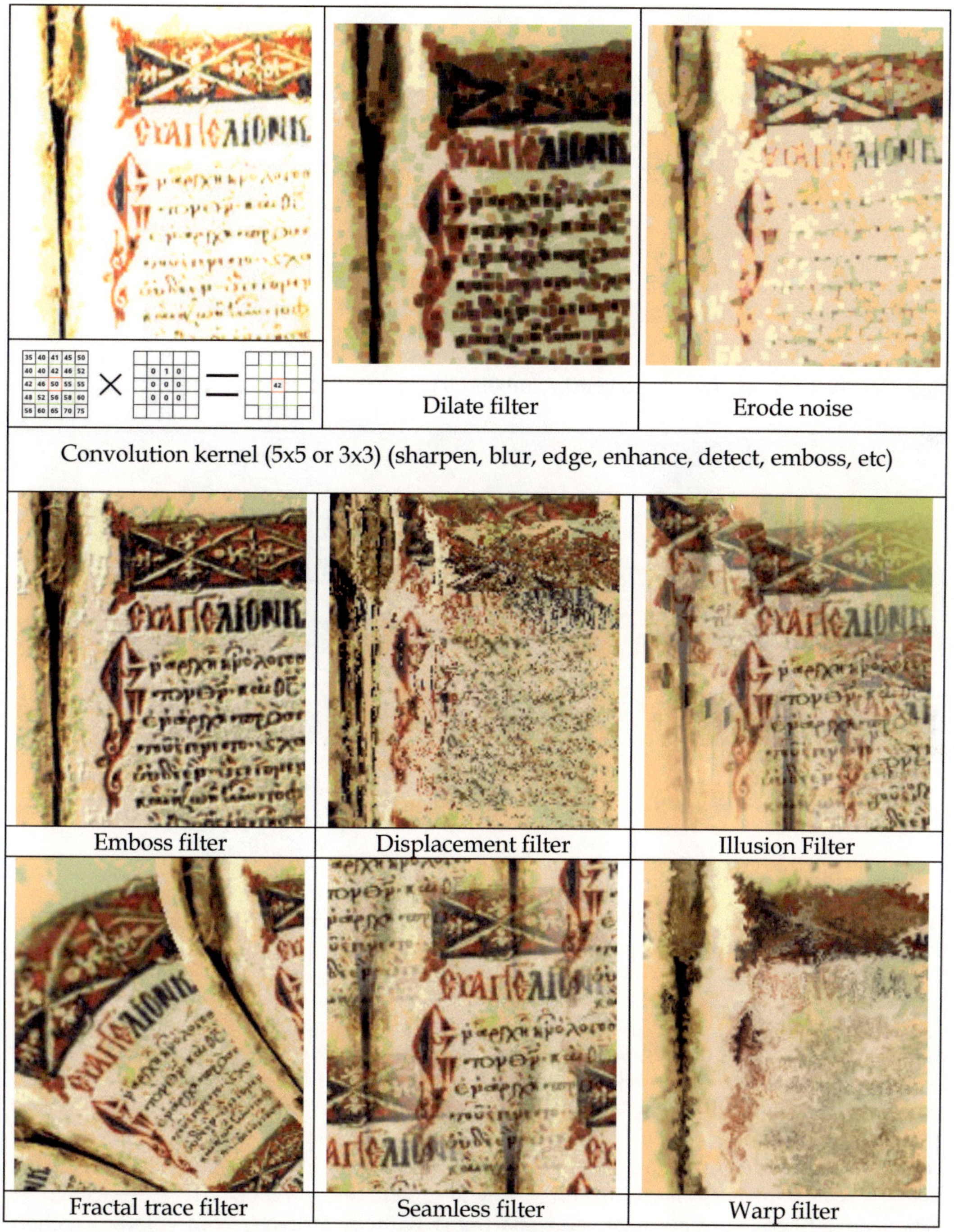

Fig. 31. Convolution filters / Erosion / Dilation on Images

Warp filter masks an image to protect / wrap / unwrap it against filter action (steps, smears, blackens, displaces, dithers, swirls, scatters, etc), see fig. 31.

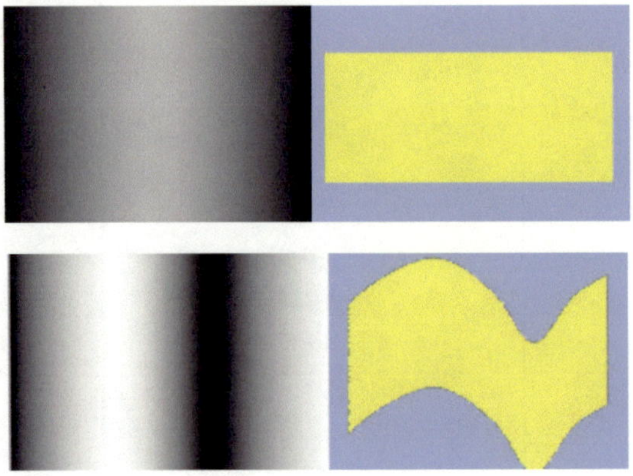

Fig. 32. Whirl: Using gradient to bend / unbend a text

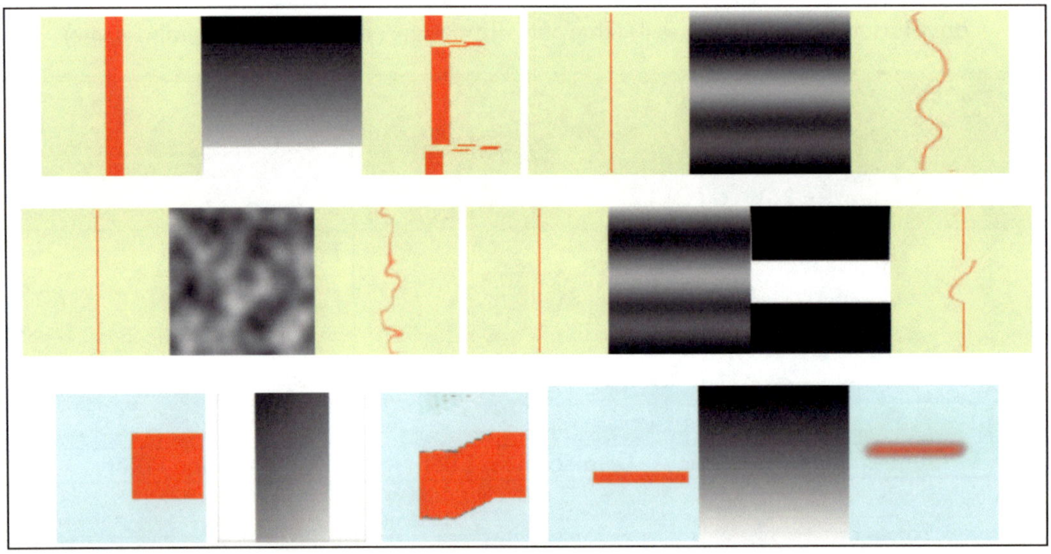

Fig. 33. Convolution filters

9.1 Image enhancement

Image Enhancement of degraded text includes add borders, crop an image, rescale amplitude, equalize / match histogram, modify / apply multi-band (RGB), or color-cube / generic lookup table, dithering, offsets, pixel point processing (pixel inverting), thresholding (binary contrast enhancement), segmentation with / without a priori font information, retouche light, radial exposure and brightness, handwritten characters clarification (Gatos, 2004), texture unsharp masking, edge enhancement, etc (Gupta, 2007) , see fig. 34. Retouching filters, controls focus and sharpness without artifacts, with color correction, exposure compensation, white balance corrector for miscoloration caused by light source, master transparency like GIFs with transparent backgrounds, master contrast, saturation, correct camera lens distortions, master noise filtering, photos tone, etc. Historical manuscripts image processing consists of the following five stages:

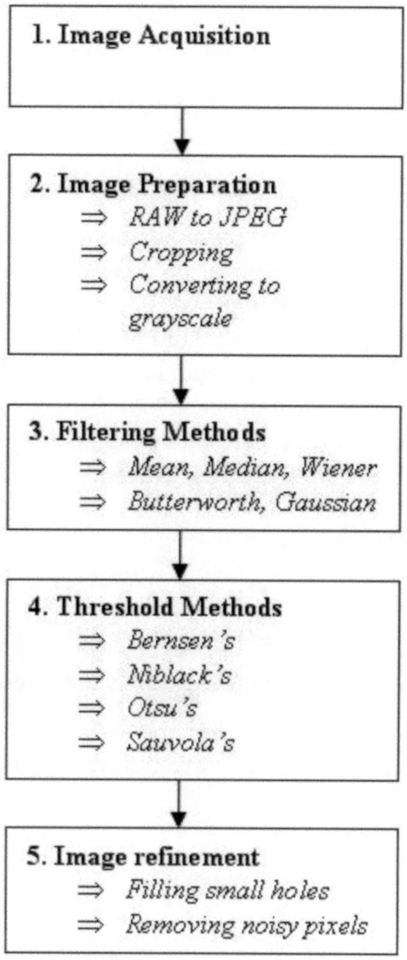

Image acquisition by a digital camera offers inherent advantages, i.e. produces less noise, with high resolution and image prepared for binarization.
Image preparation converts the original raw image format into TIFF /JPEG file format for memory saving and minimal computational effort. Cropping, removing invisible and irrelevant information and converting to grayscale are necessary steps before denoising and binarization.
Denoising is derived by comparing Mean, Median and Wiener filters in spatial domain and Gaussian and Butterworth filters in the frequency domain.
Thresholding is applied by global (Otsu's) and local (Niblack, Sauvola, Bernsen) thresholding techniques to previous stages resulting, filtered images.
Refinement procedure is applied on the binarized image, based on erosion and dilation, such that the obtained image has its characteristics further clarified in the texture and foreground compared with the background area. Cleaning and enhancing stands for visual appearance and beauty while refinement is for reliable, true display.

Fig. 34. Enhancement method stages

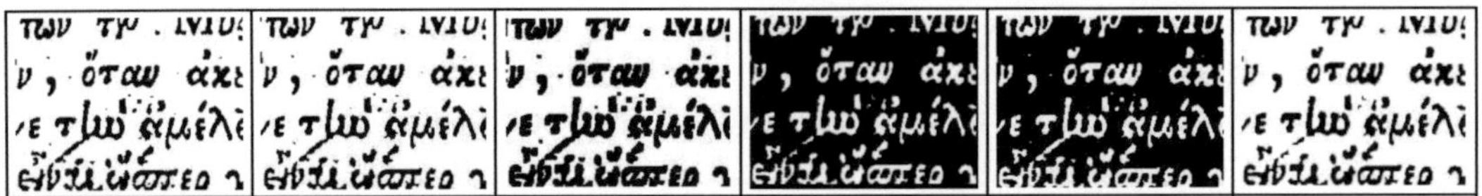

binary	erosion	dilation	negative	opening negative	Final

Table 3. Steps of refinement stage

9.2 Binarization – Thresholding techniques and algorithms

Thresholding, is a binary contrast enhancement technique, that provides a simple means of defining the boundaries of objects that appear on a contrasting background. The threshold range is specified by a low value and a high value (Leedham, 2003, Solihin, 1999) , see fig. 37. For the binarization of images many threshold algorithms, (global, local and adaptive), have been proposed to separate foreground from background objects (Yang, 2000). We have chosen Otsu's (Otsu, 1979), Niblack's (Niblack, 1986), Sauvola's and Bernsen's binarization methods (Sauvola, 2000) are used to compare their results on Byzantine textual images taken from the Holy Monastery of Dousiko, Pylh, near Meteora, Trikala, Thessaly, Greece.

Global thresholding

$$g(x,y)=\begin{cases}1, & if \ \ f(x,y)\geq T \\ 0, & otherwise\end{cases}$$

If T the global threshold of image *f(x,y)* and the *g(x,y)* is the thresholding result.

Otsu's optimal threshold method minimizes the class variance of the two classes of pixels.Threshold selection is absolute, conventional, optimal, automatic, adaptive, nonparametric, parametric, etc.

9.3 Lighting conditions

Light text is harder to read than dark text. Responses to light text are slower and less accurate for a given contrast. Letters recognition is based on component features. Optical density is the amount of light reflected or transmitted on a logarithmic scale. Vectorial processing depends on the exposure light conditions. (sun, daylight, lamp, cool white fluorescent lighting, incandescent lamp, flash, candle, etc), illumination, non uniformity, low contrast, degradation, shadows etc. The camera and lighting should be calibrated, each channel is processed separately, stray light reduce the measured dynamic range while lighting should be even, aligned, glare-free with variation less than ±5%, with gray surround and no light behind the camera and stable background intensity to flatten image tones; two lamps at least with incident angle of 20-40° and auto-exposure cameras compensate glare in the dark zones.

Sparkle filter adds sparkles to our image, Lens flare filter gives the impression that sun hit the shot object and creates reflection effect. 3D Effect filter highlights perspective, Drop shadow filter adds a drop-shadow to the image, see fig. 35.

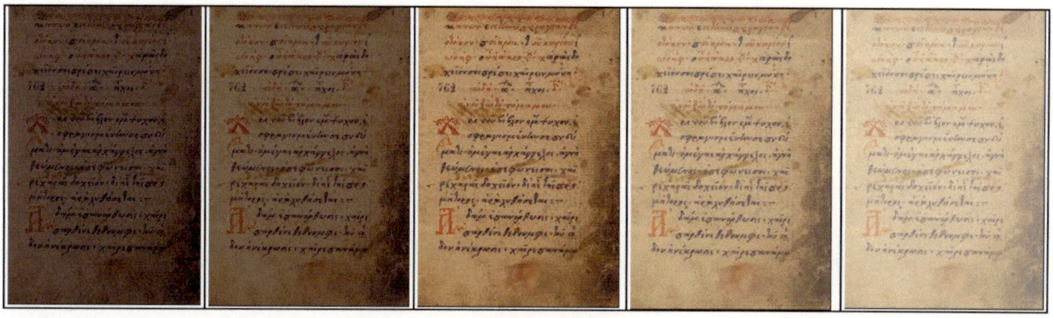

Table 4. Lighting conditions and effects on a Byzantine page

Gradient flare or supernova filter creates random glow, rays, opacity

Lighting effects filter simulates the light up of a spot, with no shadows and details in dark zones, transparency, background, direction, color, intensity, position, reflections by objects.

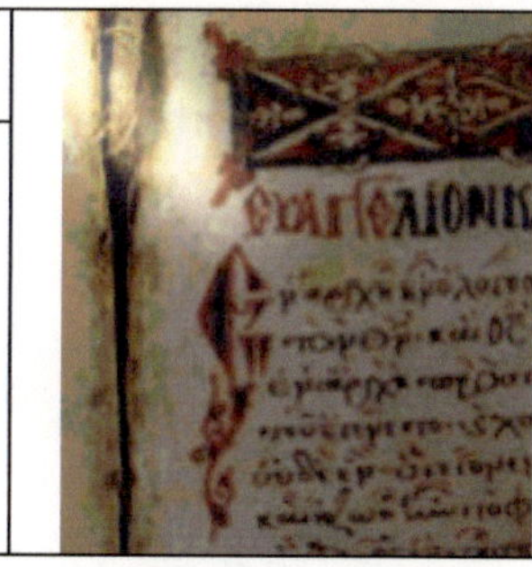

Fig. 35. Lighting effects filter

Changes in illumination, or local shadows do not provide global threshold, see fig. 36.

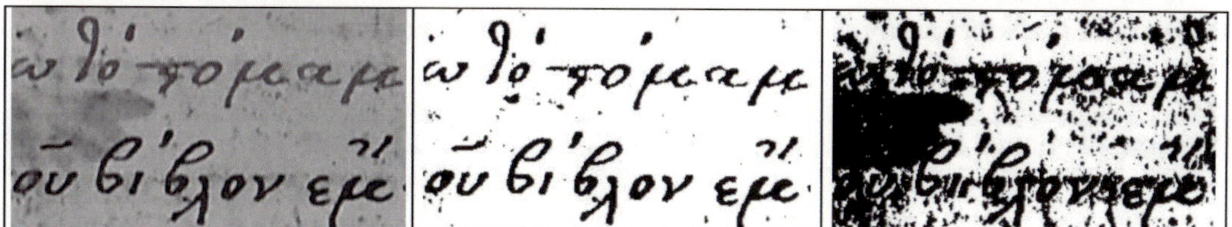

(a)	(b)	(c)

Fig. 36. Global threshold (a) grayscale image (b) T=100 (c) T=150

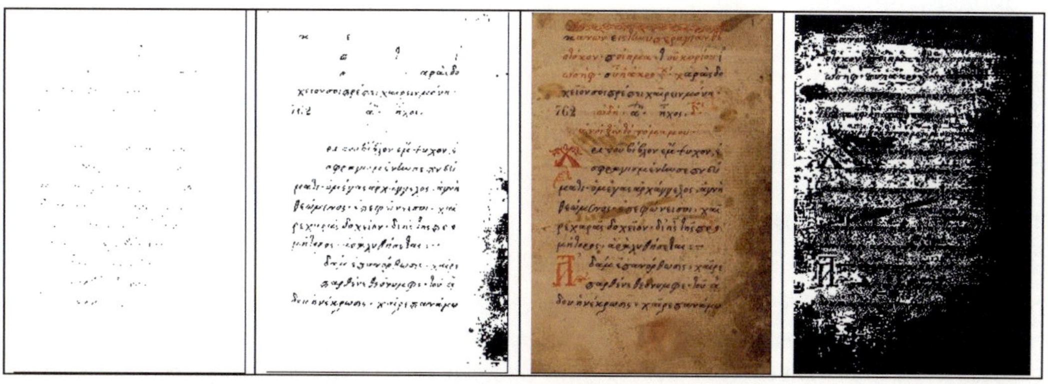

Fig. 37. Levels of thresholding and quality of results

Local thresholding

Niblack's method

$$T(x,y)=m(x,y)+k*s(x,y) \quad k=-0.2$$

where m(x,y) and $s(x,y)$ are the average of a local area and the standard deviation. . A window size 15-by-15 suppresses the noise in the image, but preserves local details

Sauvola's method is an adaptive threshold method, with $k=0.1$ and $R=128$.

$$T(x,y) = m(x,y)\left[1 + k\left(1 - \frac{s(x,y)}{R}\right)\right]$$

Bernsen's method where Z_{max} and Z_{min} are maximum/minimum intensity and works in high contrast $C(x,y)$ dependent on k and on the window size n. Threshold produces ghosts.

$$T(x,y) = \frac{Z_{\max} + Z_{\min}}{2}$$

$$C(x,y) = Z_{\max} - Z_{\min}$$

9.4 Thresholding results

Binarization is applied to all document image categories. Image focusing, sharpness and clarification on the handwritten characters (Kavallieratou, 2002), and texture was compared with the original ones, see Table 5. The binarization, based on adaptive global /local thresholding, is efficient in image digitalisation and works best on high resolution images. JPEG file formats need the least computational effort to be processed.

Documents Image Category / Binarization	Bernsen	Niblack	Otsu	Sauvola
GOOD CONDITION	***BEST***	***BEST***	***BEST***	***BEST***
SPOTS and STAINS	*BAD*	*GOOD*	*BAD*	***BEST***
SHADOWS or WRINKLES	*BAD*	***BEST***	*BAD*	***BEST***
INK SEEKING from other SIDE	*BAD*	*GOOD*	*BAD*	***BEST***
THIN STROKES of PEN	*BAD*	*BAD*	*GOOD*	*BAD*
RED coloured CHARACTERS	***BEST***	*GOOD*	*GOOD*	*GOOD*

Table 5. Results from combination of Wiener filter 5x5 with binarization methods for image category

Thresholding techniques applied to classified byzantine documental images reveal the comparative effect of combined filtering and binarization.

Niblack's and Sauvola's methods produce efficient results in almost all categories except the category of thin strokes of pen in which global Otsu's method has the best results on the produced binary images (Niblack, 1993). Bernsen's method produced best results in manuscripts with characters with "spots and stains" and "red coloured characters". Our post-binarization refinement improves the image quality, the appearance of the binary images and text readability, clarifies the background area, especially in documents with red ink characters and line gaps or holes. Refinement consists of the successive erosion followed by dilation operation, and opening on the negative image, see fig. 38, 39.

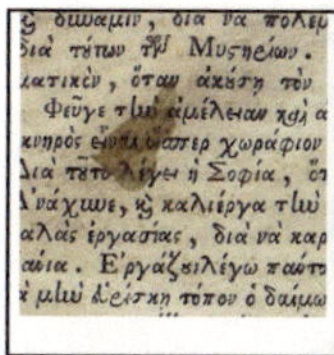	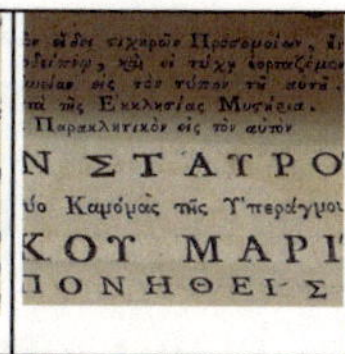	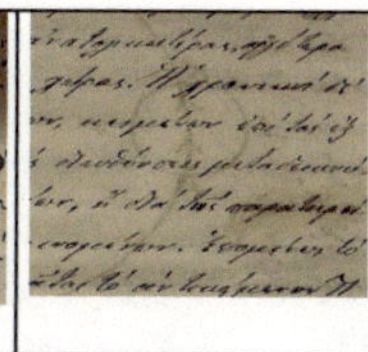	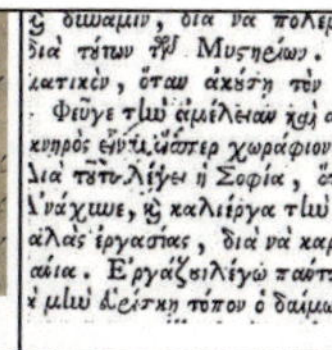		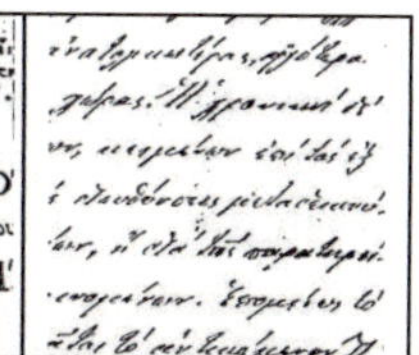
original document image with spot	original document image with illumination shadow	with ink seeking from other side, transparent background	binary image with Sauvola's method after 5x5Wiener filter	binary image with Sauvola's method after 5x5Wiener filter	Sauvola method binary image after Wiener filter 5-by-5
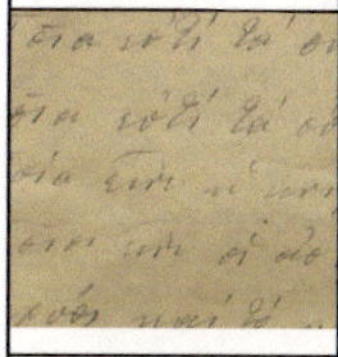	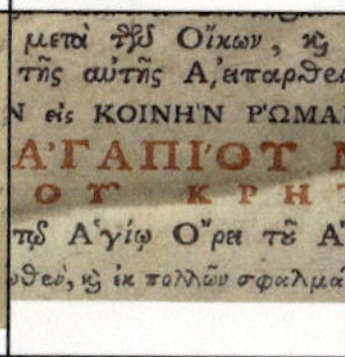	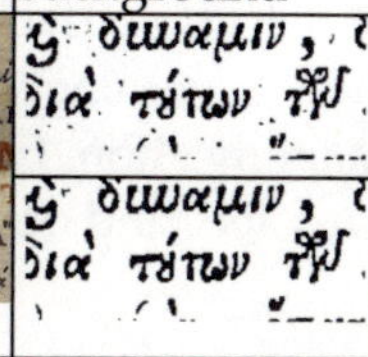	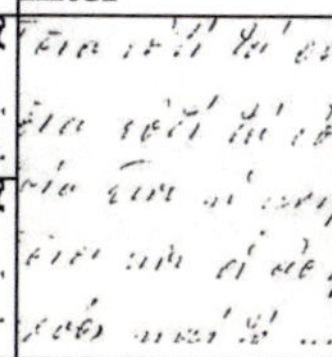	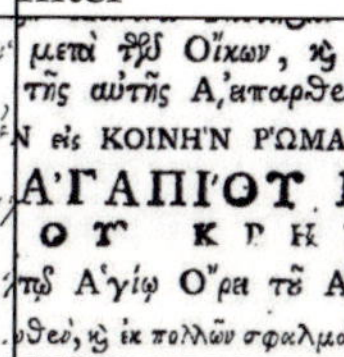	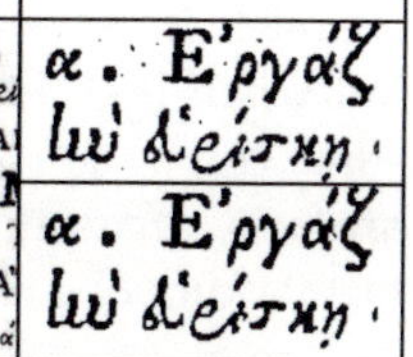
original Document image with thin strokes of pen	original Document image with characters with red ink	detail of image with black dots before / after refinement step	binary image with Sauvola's method after 5x5Wiener filter	binary image with Otsu's method after Wiener filter 5x5	image with holes on characters before/after refinement step

Table 6. Document image before and after binarization

Fig. 38. Equalize and Negative or Invert Value and White balance for thresholding

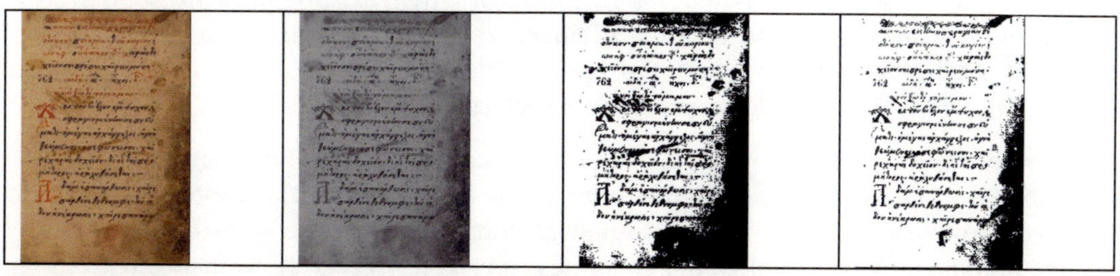

Fig. 39. Colorify / Color enhance and threshold

10. Compression

Byzantine images are saved as RAW file, TIFF, or high quality JPEG. Raw images can be converted to JPEG (maximum quality), TIFF (without LZW compression), or PNG and removes redundancy. TIFF is the standard print industry format. We crop the images to minimize edge effects. RAW to TIFF, JPEG, etc converters perform additional functions such as add gamma curve and an additional tonal response curve, they reduce noise and sharpen the image. Compression tools (lossless and lossy) for images are included, depending on streaming (capture, store, and transfer (via a network) images) vs relative CPU, memory usage, channel demands, and storage requirements. Different compression algorithms are available such as whitespace compression, Run-Length Encoding (RLE), Huffman Encoding, Lempel Ziv-Compression, etc. A special quality of word-based Huffman compressed text is that it does not needs to undergo decompression to be searched by standard searching algorithms, so would lose none of the algorithm searchability. Compression problems include nonlinear quantization, colour channels, etc. JPEGs compress the file or the colour channels in ways that the eye is unable to easily detect, i.e. the structural detail is preserved, but when high levels of compression are applied increasingly fine detail is sacrificed, and some corruption will be detectable at higher magnification. Compression that gives rise to artifacts, corruption of the image, is lossy compression, and once the clarity of your image is lost it cannot be restored.

10.1 Database

Organizing valuable or impossible to access fragile images from Byzantine sources in a database, (Gatos, 2004) is a powerful way to communicate and distribute them on the web by handling a massive quantity of images. Content-Based searching (texture/pattern, shape, color, orientation, and layout or a combination) of Large Image Databases is impractical and time consuming (Date, 2002). The relational database organize and manage such information, create virtual classifications, virtual folders, and interact with images, and metadata. Most frequently requested and computationally intensive jobs should be pre-processed, so that will be quickly hit, while others at the time of request. Utilities and software tools (middleware) facilitate organization for efficient access (searching, browsing, and retrieval), manipulate, enhance, and annotate existing information. Multimedia information contains an enormous amount of embedded information. An abstract function operation is edge detection or thresholding. The semi-compressed domain is convenient since it is an intermediate form that compressed video frames and images must pass through during decompression. A Byzantine manuscript consists of hundreds of pages of high fidelity images where each image is 12÷21 MB or larger; existing tools are not designed to display / search / browse massive digitized documents. Multimedia information is stored at multiple resolutions, and the appropriate level of resolution is selected and transferred automatically based on parameters such as the speed of the link.

It is increasingly difficult to ask a spreadsheet combined questions and we need to normalize the database rows/columns referred to as attributes. Database normalization iteratively divides large tables into smaller, enhances database consistency, reduces redundant data and ensures data dependencies, speeds up server performance with faster sorting and indexing (Date, 1999, Picard, 1993).

SFR_lwph.xls

	A	B	C	D	E	F	G	H	I	J
1	File	Date/time	PH	Ch	H/V	10-90U	10-90C	Over-	Over-	MTF!
2						/PH	/PH	shoot%	sharp%	LW/I
3	canon_eos10d_sfr.jp	3/19/2004 22:21	2048	Y	H	1422	1447	19.5	-0.7	1:
4	canon_g5_sfr.jpg	3/19/2004 22:24	1955	Y	H	1973	1301	48	21.3	1.
5	sigma_sd9_sfr.jpg	3/19/2004 22:27	1504	Y	H	1432	1676	2.4	-7.7	1.
6	sigma_sd10_sfr.jpg	3/19/2004 22:28	1504	Y	H	1563	1628	11.9	-2	1!
7										

Fig. 40. Spreadsheet images acquisition classification scheme

10.1.1 Classification

We classified byzantine images according to their content, i.e. old handwriting, (Greek) manuscript (varying in types, size, color, format and level of noise, capital /lower case letters), document images and photos, byzantine music symbols, etc. Historical documents are high / low contrast, colour / grayscale, totally/partially degraded or damaged, paper image condition, with red ink characters and line gaps or holes, transparent, with transparent objects, transparent background, simple / complex, text / graphics highly mixed, etc (Foley, 1990). Text mining is not information retrieval, extraction, categorization, because they do not generate new information but it involve new discoveries through analysis of a text, i.e. uncover a new relationship. There is always a risk of missing, or misclassifying. We wish to optimize subjective impression and readability perception. Text readability increases by text contrast, background contrast, and relative text contrast (text contrast divided by background contrast). A software classifier can automate processing per document class assisted by a training database for the sorting system composed of images that have distinct differences.

10.2 Suggestions for further work

Documents image restoration, binarization, filtering and processing is an issue of continuous researching. Most of the historical documents images, in libraries and museums, can be acquired and stored dynamically in computers, in digital format for preservation, storage, computation, reproduction, visualization, interpretation and recognition. The proposed technique investigated for optimal methods for every image type, among the existing methods, the image noise and the paper conditions. We investigated for a universally efficient method for all the images categories by focusing on best thresholding value for every pixel area in the image, i.e. a combination of global and local methods structured into processing levels.

Potential application fields include the automation of the combined binarization-filtering procedure and the extension of the method to a wider area of documental and similar or non-documental images.

An image typically goes through a series of transformations that extract information from the image or compute new information based on the image; this sequence can be monitored and automated through an Expert System.

11. Conclusion

Although excellent image processing tools and techniques exist we either do not use them efficiently in application fields, or in an intelligent way (GIMP, 2011, Mathworks, 2011). Errors classification in old documents background, text, stamps and images, image processing by experts or an expert system assisted by image segmentation techniques could reveal lost details.

The purpose of our work on denoising and binarization was to introduce an innovative sequential procedure for digital image acquisition of historical documents including image preparation, image type classification according to their condition and their spatial structure, global and local features or both, including document image data mining.

Image processing pixel alterations, allow one-pass iterations only by near neighborhood of alteration reprocessing algorithms. Algorithm complexity analysis is O(N3), while computational effort and execution time needed is overcome by parallel computational machines. In handwritten documents text orientation, skew, skew detection time and skew reconstruction time are critical parameters.

The estimated results for each class of images and each method are further enhanced by an innovative image refinement technique and a formulation of a class proper method. Our work tends to focus mostly on Images Digital Restoration rather than on Binarization. Due to the dynamic research on the field, comparison of methods and techniques is continuous. Method efficiency, universality, versatility, flexibility and robustness is straightforward on any historical document and other cases, but selection or combination of appropriate algorithm (no single algorithm works well for all types of images) is needed. Compared to the image enhancement method, the image classification method is more text / image characteristic-oriented. It highly depends on the images to be processed, or saying in another way, the historical document to be investigated. There is no ideal method working for every case. There is not a single suitable method that can be applied to all types of images.

12. Appendix I. Properties of paper

Property	Comment	Meaning	Range	Standard
Print quality	*appearance properties*	*roughness, gloss, ink absorption, whiteness, brightness*		
Printability	*dot reproduction/gain, print gloss, hue shift and print uniformity*	*true reproduction of original artwork*		
	Good printability, compressibility, absorbency and ink hold out give good printing and hand writing.			
Readability	*ink to paper contrast*			
Basis Weight or Grammage:	*most fundamental property of paper*	*weight of paper per unit area*		*TAPPI T 410, SCAN P6, DIN53104 & ISO: BSENISO536*

Bulk	*(cubic centimetre/g) = Thickness (mm)* Basis Weight (g/m²) * 1000*	*volume or thickness in relation to weigh reciprocal of density*		*TAPPI T 500, SCAN P7 DIN53105, ISO534, BS: ENISO20534*
Decrease in bulk/ increase in density makes the sheet smoother, glossier, less opaque, darker, lower in strength for printing bible				
Caliper or Thickness		*how bulky or dense paper is*	*range from 70 GSM onwards*	*TAPPI T 411*
Curl	*Stresses that are introduced into the sheet during manufacture and use*	*Paper curl is a deviation of a sheet from flat form*		*TAPPI T 466 & T520*
There are three basic types of curl, mechanical, structural and moisture curl; one side of the sheet pick up more moisture				
Dimensional Stability		*dimensional changes cause undesirable cockling and curling*		
	All papers expand with increased moisture content and contract with decreased moisture content, but the rate and extent of changes vary with different papers.			
Moisture			*2 - 12%*	*ISO 287*
	Moisture varies depending on relative humidity, type of pulp used, degree of refining and chemical used. Most properties change as a with moisture content. Very low porosity or coated on one side or wax pick gives resistance to grease and moisture.			
Porosity	*total connecting air voids both vertical and horizontal,*	*ability of fluids, to penetrate the paper structure*	*Paper is highly porous, contains up to 70% air*	
	Porosity is an indication of absorptivity, the ability to accept ink or water			
Smoothness	*roughness, levelness, compressibility, finish, appearance, pattern*	*surface contour of paper*		
Smoothness for writing, ease of travel of the pen over the paper, gives eye appeal as a rough paper is unattractive.				
Permanence	*degree to which paper resists deterioration over time.*			
Optical properties				
Brightness	*for readability and opacity*	*% reflectance of blue light at a wavelength*		*TAPPI/GE and ISO 11475.*
Whiteness	*Balanced white sheets have a yellowish cast but we perceive sheet with a bluish to be whiter*		*Whiter sheets reflect equally red, green, blue light, the visual spectrum*	

Color:	*quality of light, viewed under a different light source*	*hue, saturation, darkness or lightness).*	*aesthetic value*	
Gloss	*Gloss and smoothness*	*diffusely reflected light*		*TAPPI T 480*
Opacity	*sheet light absorbed, both sides printed*	*light not passing through a sheet*		*ISO 2471 and TAPPI T425.*
Sizing / Cobb	*the ability of fluids, , to penetrate the structure of pap*	*the writing ink go into the paper instantly and dry*	*water-repellent materials (rosin, wax, gelatinous)*	
Dirt Content	*visible to the eye such as bark, undigested wood, pitch, rust, plastic, etc*	*dirt specks, unwanted foreign particle*	*change reflected or transmitted light*	
Pin Holes	*Imperfections*	*looking through*		
Other properties are Temperature and Humidity, Conditioning of Paper, Wire side and Felt side, Strength Properties, Surface Strength, Compressibility, Resiliency, Stiffness, etc. Certain properties such as smoothness, texture and ink absorbency differ between wire and felt side.				
Paper types include alkaline paper, antique paper, art paper, Bible paper, General Writing paper, etc.				

13. Acknowledgements

We would like to thank:

1. The Department of Computer Science Technology & Telecommunications, TEI Larisa
2. Holy Monastery Dousiko, Pylh near Meteora, Greece for Codices 1611 AD
3. Professor N.Papamarkos for software, http://ipml.ee.duth.gr/~papamark/demos.htm

14. References

[1] Adams, A, The Camera. Bulfinch Press, 1995

[2] Blinn, James F. "Simulation of Wrinkled Surfaces", Computer Graphics, Vol. 12 (3), pp. 286-292 SIGGRAPH-ACM, August 1978

[3] Boyle R. and R. Thomas Computer Vision: A First Course, Blackwell Scientific Publications, 1988, Chap. 4.

[4] Canon Europa N.V. and Canon Europe Ltd, Digital SRL Camera "5D", 2002-2007, http://www.canon-europe.com/For_Home/Product_Finder/Cameras/Digital_SLR/EOS_5D/index.asp.

[5] Date C.J., Hugh Darwen, Nikos Lorentzos. Temporal Data and the Relational Model. Morgan Kaufmann (2002), p. 176

[6] Date C.J. An Introduction to Database Systems. Addison-Wesley (1999), p. 290

[7] Davies E. Machine Vision: Theory, Algorithms and Practicalities, Academic Press, 1990, Chap. 4.

[8] D'Zmura M., Colantoni P., Knoblauch K., Laget B. (1997). Color transparency. *Perception*, 26, 471–492.

[9] [GIMP] GIMP - The Gnu Image Manipulation Program. http://gimp.org, 2011

[10] Foley and van Dam, et al, Computer Graphics, Principles and Practice, Copyright © 1990 Addison Wesley. Addison Wesley. 2nd Ed. (Addison Wesley, 1990)
[11] B. Gatos, K. Ntzios, I. Pratikakis, S. Petridis, T. Konidaris and S. J. Perantonis, A segmentation free recognition technique to assist old Greek handwritten manuscript OCR, IAPR Workshop on Document Analysis systems (DAS'2004), Lecture Notes in Computer Science (3163), Florence, Italy, September 2004, pp. 63-74
[12] B. Gatos, I. Pratikakis, S. J. Perantonis, Locating Text in Historical Collection Manuscripts, Lecture Notes on AI, SETN 2004, pp. 476-485
[13] Gonzalez, C.R. and E.R. Woods, "Digital Image Processing", 2nd ed, 2002, Prentice-Hall Inc, pp 75-278.
[14] Gupta A. et al, Enhancement of Old Manuscript Images, Proceeding ICDAR '07 Proceedings of the Ninth International Conference on Document Analysis and Recognition - Vol 2 IEEE Computer Society, Washington, USA 2007, ISBN:0-7695-2822-8
[15] Hunt R.W.G, The Reproduction of Colour in Photography, Printing and Television, Fountain Press, Tolworth, England, 5th edition, 2001
[16] Kapur, J., P.K. Sahoo, and A.K.C. Wong, "A new method for gray-level picture. Thresholding using the Entropy of the Histogram", Computer Vision Graphics and Image Processing, 1985, pp. 273-285
[17] E. Kavallieratou, N. Fakotakis, G. Kokkinakis, Handwritten character recognition based on structural characteristics, 16th International Conference on Pattern Recognition, 2002, pp.139-142.
[18] E. Kavallieratou N.Fakotakis G Kokkinakis, New algorithms for skewing correction and slant removal on word-level, Proc. IEEE, 1999, pp 1159-1162.
[19] Knoblauch K., Arditi A., Szlyk J. (1991). Effects of chromatic and luminance contrast on reading. *Journal of the Optical Society of America* A, 8, 428–439.
[20] Leedham, CG, et al. "Comparison of some Thresholding Algorithms for Text /Background Segmentation in Difficult Document Images", Proceedings of 7th International Conference on Document Analysis & Recognition, 2003, IEEE
[21] Legge G., Pelli D., Rubin G., Schleske M, 1985, Psychophysics of reading. I. Normal vision. *Vision Research*, 25, 239–252
[22] MathWorks Inc., "Image Processing Toolbox - User Guide", 2011
[23] Motwani, M., C., et al. "Survey of Image Denoising Techniques", in Proceedings of GSPx, 2004, Santa Clara Convention Center, Santa Clara, CA
[24] Niblack, W., "An Introduction to Digital Image Processing" 1986, Prentice Hall, pp.115-116.
[25] Niblack, W. et al. 1993. The QBIC project: querying images by content using color, texture, and shape. SPIE 1908:173-81, February
[26] Otsu, N., "A threshold selection method from gray-level histograms", IEEE Trans. Systems, Man, and Cybernetics, 1979. vol. 9 (no. 1), pp 62-66
[27] Papamarkos, N., "Digital Processing and Image Analysis", 2001, Athens, Giourdas
[28] Picard, R. W. and Kabir, T. 1993. Finding similar patterns in large image databases.
[29] Ren Ng, Digital Light Field Photography, a dissertation submitted to the department of computer science of Stanford University, in partial fulfilment of the requirements for the degree of Doctor of Philosophy, July 2006

[30] Sauvola, J. and M. Pietikainen, "Adaptive document image binarization", Pattern Recognition 33, 2000, pp. 225-236
[31] Solihin, Y. and C.G. Leedham, "Integral Ratio: A New Class of Global Thresholding Techniques for Handwriting images", IEEE Trans. on PAMI, 1999, vol 21 (no 8), pp. 761-768
[32] Sonka, M., V. Hlavac, and R. Boyle, "Image Processing, Analysis and Machine Vision", 1998.
[33] Ventzas, D., "Edge Detection Techniques in the Industry", Advances in Modelling & Analysis, Series B, vol. 29, No. 2, pp. 57-64, Winter 1993-1994, AMSE, 1994.
[34] Yang, Y. and H. Yan, "An Adaptive logical method for binarization of degraded document images", Pattern recognition 33, 2000, pp. 787-807.
[35] Yanowitz, D.L. and A.M. Bruckstein, "A new Method for image segmentation", Computer Vision Graphics and Image Processing, 1989, vol.46 (no 1), pp.82-95.
[36] Zhang, Z. and C. Tan, "Restoration of images scanned from thick bound documents", in proceedings of International Conference on Image Processing 2001, Vol 1, 2001, pp. 1074-1077
[37] http://www.imatest.com/docs/sfrplus_instructions3.html
[38] http://www.dii.unisi.it/~nencini/datafusion.html. Data fusion web, Nov 2007
[39] http://ipml.ee.duth.gr/~papamark/demos.htm

6

Applications of Image Processing Technique in Porous Material Characterization

Ming Gan[1] and Jianhua Wang[2]
[1]*School of Aeronautics & Astronautics Engineering, Purdue University, IN,*
[2]*Department of Thermal Science & Energy Engineering,*
University of Science & Technology of China, Hefei,
[1]*USA*
[2]*P.R. China*

1. Introduction

Nondestructive testing (NDT) provides safe operation to engineering components – it eliminates the risk of damage during operation, and does not require specific sample preparation. It has been widely used to detect and evaluate defects, or measure properties of different types of materials and engineering structures. Examples of NDT techniques include ultrasonic, radiography, infrared thermography, electromagnetic techniques and visible optical methods. The imaging principles and imaging facilities used by these techniques can be very different, but almost all the techniques listed above require image processing to some extent. In this chapter, instead of extensively exploring all the NDT techniques and corresponding image processing methods, we will focus on optical measurement technique and related image processing methods, and use porous materials as specimens.

Optical microscopy and digital camera imaging are two examples of optical measurement technique, where optical microscopy is the conventional one. Based on how the light transfers from the sample to the objective, it can be categorized to two different modes – transparent mode and reflected mode. Digital camera imaging appeared with the development of semiconductor industry. Digital images bring convenience for image storage, image transferring, and subsequent image processing. Actually, digital image acquisition facilities, e.g. Complementary Metal Oxide Semiconductors (CMOS) and Charge Coupled Device (CCD), can be combined with the traditional microscope to form digital microscopes. As a convenient way of measurement, optical microscope and digital camera imaging system has been extensively used in the area of microelectronics, nanophysics, biotechnology, pharmaceutical research, mineralogy, and material science.

Typical image processing procedures include image acquisition, image alignment/stitching, image contrast enhancement, grey scale thresholding, and/or image subtraction. The characteristic of the specimens determines which image processing techniques to be used. For example, for the images with background noise, image subtraction can be applied when the background can be evaluated; otherwise thresholding might be applied to eliminate the background influence.

In this chapter, the image processing techniques will be reviewed. Their applications in characterizing porous materials will be explored.

2. Overview of image processing techniques

2.1 Image acquisition

Image acquisition is the first step of optical characterization techniques. It is also the first place where noise can be introduced. The characteristic of the noise introduced in the image acquisition process dominates the following image processing techniques. In order to understand the cause of noise, the principles of image acquisition devices will be discussed first.

For digital image acquisition, CMOS and CCD are the most commonly used devices. The first solid-state imager presented in the 1960's. The CMOS image sensors appeared in 1967 [1], and the first CCD sensor appeared in 1970 [1]. In early 1970's MOS diodes were used as light sensitive elements [2]. However, at that time, CMOS image sensors had poor performance and large pixel size, compared to CCD. CCD has been the major imaging device owing to their superior dynamic range, lower fixed-pattern noise, higher fill factor, and higher sensitivity to light [3]. However, during the last decade, CMOS sensor implementing buffer per pixel has been developed, which is known as active pixel sensors (APS). APS provides high speed readout, which makes it suitable for high speed imaging [4]. Table 1 is the comparison of CCD and CMOS image sensors.

Features	CCD	CMOS
Sensitivity	Higher, especially for still images	Lower
Noise level	Lower	Higher
Dark current	Lower	Magnitudes higher than the CCD [5]
High speed performance	-	Good
Power consumption	Higher	Lower
Compatibility	-	Higher integration capability with chip circuits

Table 1. Comparison of CCD and CMOS

Right now, CMOS is being used in the area of security surveillance, automotive, imaging phones, etc., owing to the properties of lower power consumption, lower operation voltage, high compatibility and high speed readout rate. CCD has application in the area of medical imaging, astronomy, professional cameras, etc., because of its high performance and image quality [6].

In the material characterization area, CCD is the dominating digital imager. CCD device consists of arrays of capacitors, which accumulate electric charge proportional to the light intensity at the location. In an ideal case, every photon striking the CCD sensor will be converted to one electron. Then the intensity of the incoming light can be quantified by counting the corresponding electrons. Unfortunately, noise always exists in this process. Noise in CCD images appears in multiple ways, including dark background areas, faint horizontal or vertical lines, blotchy gradients, and low contrast images. A brief overview of noise sources in CCD is listed below.

Dark current

All CCD sensors generate a dark signal to some degree. CCD builds up dark current whether the CCD is being exposed to light or not. Dark current arises from thermal energy within the silicon lattice in the CCD [7]. Electrons dependent of the incoming light are collected over time by the CCD potential wells and counted as signal electrons. This signal also carries a statistical fluctuation known as dark current noise. The rate of dark current accumulation depends on the temperature of the CCD, but will eventually fill every pixel in a CCD. The pixels in the CCD will be cleared and reset before imaging. However, dark current accumulates again when exposure starts. In the case of long integration time usage of CCD systems, e.g. in astrophotography and spectroscopy, more input signal is collected, as well as more dark current noise. Ideally, the dark current noise should be reduced to a point where its contribution is negligible over a typical exposure time. The rate of dark current can be reduced by a factor of 100 or more by cooling the CCD [7]. CCDs can be cooled either with thermoelectric coolers (TECs) or liquid nitrogen. The amount of dark current noise highly depends on the temperature, with half value of dark current for every $5^oC \sim 9^oC$ cooling down of the system [8]. Therefore, cooling system is integrated to high sensitivity CCDs, e.g. the CCD used in spectroscopy area, to increase the signal-to-noise ratio. However, running the CCD cooler than necessary can also lead to extra noise, which appears as a 'ghost' image.

Besides eliminating the dark noise in the hardware level, methodological ways are also necessary. In intensity-oriented measurements, in order to further eliminate the effect of dark signals, sub-exposure of dark frames is usually applied for calibration of the image acquisition system. When acquiring the dark frames, all the other conditions are kept the same. The acquired dark frame is the background of the measurement, which will be subtracted from the measurement images in the following process.

Pixel non-uniformity

CCD pixels are made to be uniform. Unfortunately, in really practice, they are slightly different to each other. The sensitivity to light of the pixels is typically within 1% to 2% fluctuation of the average. This non-uniform sensitivity brings error to the image. Pixel non-uniformity can be reduced by calibration with a flat-field image [9].

One way to take account the dark current noise and pixel non-uniformity is to normalize them using the following equation (Eqn. 2.1) [10].

$$I_n = \frac{I_o - I_{dark}}{I_{flat} - I_{dark}} \tag{2.1}$$

where I_o is the acquired image; I_{dark} is the dark current frame; I_{flat} is the flat-field image; I_n is the normalized image.

Shot noise

The random arrival of photons to the CCD surface introduces shot noise. The probability of the photon arrival follows Poisson distribution. Shot noise becomes obvious when collecting a small amount of photons. Shot noise can be eliminated by collecting more photons, either with a longer exposure time or by combining multiple frames [9].

2.2 Image alignment/stitching

Image alignment discovers correspondence among images with a certain degree of overlap. It is essential for image stabilization in computer vision. In material characterization area, it is required when comparing images of the same place of interest, but taken with different shoots. It is the former step of image subtraction. Image alignment techniques include pixel-based alignment [11], feature-based alignment [12-14], Fourier-based alignment [15, 16] and incremental refinement [17, 18].

Image stitching combines multiple images of different areas with overlapping to create a panorama. It is useful for obtaining high resolution overview of an object from multiple microscopic images. Image stitching techniques include key point detection [19, 20], feature matching [21], geometric registration [22, 23] and global registration [24, 25]. In material characterization area, feature matching is the commonly applied technique. Detailed description of image alignment algorithms and image stitching methods can be found in the technical report written by R. Szeliski [26].

2.3 Image contrast enhancement

Electronically acquired images often have grey scale distortion and require contrast enhancement to restore their quality. Image contrast enhancement makes it easier for object detection, edge detection, and image segmentation. However, this technique is only applied when image intensity is not related to the parameter to be measured. The enhancement algorithm is highly affected by the properties of material to be measured. The contrast enhancement algorithms can be classified as histogram-based [27-29] or frequency domain-based [30-32]. Among these algorithms, histogram equalization is the basis of many derivatives. It includes block-based histogram equalization methods such as contrast limited adaptive histogram equalization [27-30, 32-34]. Traditional histogram equalization modifies the histogram of the entire image to obtain a contrast-enhanced image with a more uniform histogram. Although it enhances the contrast to a large extent to produce a better visualization effect, it still cannot discriminate details in homogeneous regions in the image. Chang et al proposed a block-based histogram equalization method, called collaborative learning method for image enhancement, which works well for images with homogeneous regions [35].

2.4 Thresholding

Thresholding is one of the traditional image processing methods. It is also the simplest method of image segmentation. In the thresholding process, individual pixels are treated as object pixels if their values are greater or smaller than a threshold value. Thresholding a grey image results in a binary image, which can be used to perform measurement of interest, e.g. area fraction, and spatial distribution. Choosing threshold value is essential in image processing. In fraction measurement or porosity detection, slightly different threshold values can lead to dramatic difference in the final results. In practice, the threshold value is affected by measuring conditions also, e.g. illuminatiing intensity.

The thresholding algorithm can be categorized to four groups - histogram shape-based methods [36, 37], entropy-based methods [38], locally adaptive methods [39, 40] and spatial methods[41]. In the histogram shape-based methods, the aim is to find an optimal threshold value that separates two major peaks in the histogram. This is performed by applying smoothing filters to the histogram, followed by applying a difference filter or fitting the histogram. The drawback of the histogram shape-based method is the lack of spatial information of images. The entropy-based methods use the entropy of the image as a constraint for selecting thresholds. There are two ways to conduct this process - maximizing the entropy of the thresholded image or minimizing the cross entropy between input image and the output image [42]. The disadvantage of this method is the complexity and low image quality. Locally adaptive thresholding method calculates threshold at every pixel. The threshold value is determined by local parameters, e.g. mean, variance, surface fitting parameters or their combinations. Due to the algorithm of this method, the calculation of threshold is usually time-consuming. Spatial methods use higher-order probability distribution and/or correlation between pixels for thresholding.

Recently, wavelet transformation fuzzy set theory [43], and Parzen window estimate [44] technique are applied to create multi-level thresholing methods. More details on image thresholding methods can be found in the article written by Sezgin and Sankur [45].

2.5 Subtraction

Image subtraction is the process in which one reference/background image is 'subtracted' from measurement images, to record changes in luminosity or to remove the effect of the background. In the case of subtracting reference image, the images were focused on the same measurement place, but taken at different time slots. The change in luminosity may be from object movement or property change of the area to be measured. It is applicable in the area of particle image velocimetry, star movement detection in astronomy, angiography of blood vessels and porosity detection of porous materials. The key point of reference image subtraction technique is to create localized luminosity change of particles or areas to be measured, while keeping the luminosity of the other areas with minimum change. The methods to illuminate the particles or areas include visible light illumination, laser (UV, visible, IR) illumination, and fluorescence effect. In the case of star movement detection, no artificial illumination needed. However, the objects to be measured usually do not possess such optical properties. Therefore, assistant illumination additives are applied to reveal the properties of interest. In particle image velocimetry, seeding particles are added to the fluid and illuminated with external light source; in angiography of blood vessels, fluorescence effect is applied to reveal the blood flow; in porosity detection of porous materials, purified water is used to reveal the location of penetrating pores by reflecting visible light. The reference images are taken at the same conditions but before the property (e.g. position, velocity) changes. In order to keep the conditions unchanged during taking reference and measurement images, vibration control, temperature control, and shooting parameter control are necessary. To further maintain consistency between different images, calibration of dark noise, image alignment, image thresholding techniques would also be useful.

2.6 3-D reconstitution

3-D reconstitution of images usually requires several image processing steps. It includes image reconstruction, image enhancement, image classification, and structure clustering. The techniques involved here are similar to the ones we discussed previously, but with focus on 3-D image processing.

3-D images are obtained by stacking sequence of 2-D slice images, which are tomographic reconstructions from projection images. The commonly used algorithm for image reconstruction is filtered back-projection algorithm [46, 47]. This algorithm filters the images and then back-projects them to the 3-D image volume [10].

In the image enhancement process, smoothing filters, e.g. Box filters and Gauss filters [47, 48], are usually applied to images to eliminate the influence of noise. Median filters are also used when there are outliers in the images. All the filters listed above have low-pass characteristics and are spatially invariant [10]. The smoothing filters have negative effect on the sharp edges in the image. Research has been carried out to find a low-pass filter which suppresses the noise without sacrificing the edge sharpness. The solutions involve numerically solving partial differential equations (PDEs). They are the non-liner diffusion filter [49, 50], the shock filter [51] and the inverse scale space filter [52]. More details on different type of filters can be found in the book written by Aubert and Kornprobst [53]. These filters were designed for 2-D image processing. Since 3-D reconstruction is based on sequence of 2-D images, the filters described above can be applied to 3-D image processing.

Compared to the image enhancement method, the image classification method is more material characteristic-oriented. It highly depends on the images to be processed, or saying in another way, the property of the material to be investigated. There is no ideal method working for every case. The generally applied classification methods include histogram-based thresholding [36, 37], region growing [54, 55], iterative class property minimization [56, 57] and segmentation [58].

Structure clustering is the process to perform interested measurement, e.g. the grain size distribution, and area fraction, etc. one example of segmentation algorithm is the watershed algorithm, which is based on the principle of a landscape flooded by water [59].

3. Application of image processing in porous material characterization

As a non-destructive test method, image processing-based method can perform repeated tests of the same sample. The properties of the sample can be monitored both spatially and temporally. Furthermore, with proper imaging techniques, image processing-based method can provide 3-D scanning of the sample, to obtain an in-depth view of material. This is very useful in the area of porous materials, where the 3-D structure plays an important role to the functioning. The major image processing techniques involved in characterizing porous materials include noise reduction, image enhancement, image subtraction, pixel classification and pixel clustering.

3.1 Porous material

Porous material is a material with irregular pores (or voids) and solid skeletons. One simple example is the sponge. Many materials are considered as porous materials, such as rocks, soil, wood, paper, catalysts, biological tissues (bone), cements, and some ceramics. Some important properties of these materials can only be rationalized when they are treated as porous media. The application area of porous materials is so wide that it includes from rock mechanics, petroleum engineering, to filtration, acoustics, biology and material science. The featured properties of porous materials include density, porosity, pore size, permeability and mechanical strength. The structure of porous materials has been modeled in three different ways - networks of capillaries, arrays of solid particles and trimodal.

The complicated structures of porous materials bring significant challenge to characterization techniques. Owing to the aspect of non-destructive and deep investigating capability, image processing-based techniques have been applied to characterize porous materials in many different ways. The properties can be detected include the 2-D properties of porosity [60], pore diameter [60, 61] and 3-D structure [62-64], as well as flow behavior inside the porous media [10].

3.2 Surface porosity and pore diameter

Surface porosity and pore diameter are the fundamental properties of porous materials. The detection of these two properties starts with imaging techniques to differentiate the pores from the frame of the porous materials. One way to do that is filling the pores with resins. After that the sample will be cut and polished for subsequent imaging [65]. The spatial resolution of this technique not only depends on the imaging hardware, but also the image processing algorithm. Due to the limitation of image segmentation and mathematic morphology filters, the pores can only be detected when they span more than five pixels. Prado et al obtained a resolution of 50 μm using this method [65].

Wang et al. investigated the surface porosity of a sintered porous material using a different imaging technique [60]. The penetrating pores were indicated by water coming out from the bottom through them. Images of the top surface were taken before and after the water reaching the top surface but not flowing out. In this process, all the test conditions remained the same except for the water flow. In these two images, the brightness of the pixels at the place where the penetrating pores locate was different, because the penetrating pores reflect more light when filled by water. Image subtraction was applied to these images subsequently, resulting in an image with the information of the penetrating pores. The porosity and pore diameter can be measured by analyzing the subtracted image, using thresholding, edge detection, etc. The typical images are shown in Fig. 1. The usage of water flooding and visible light illumination make the detection of penetrating pores safe and convenient. The image subtraction method applied here eliminated the influence of hardware noise, e.g. dark current noise and pixel non-uniformity noise. The optical measurement and image processing showed their property of non-destructive here. However, limited by the imaging technique, this measurement only applies to specimens with a flat surface.

(a) (b) (c)

Fig. 1. (a) Digital camera image of the porous surface; open pores fully filled with water but not to overflowing. (b) Water level has receded from the penetrating pores. (c) Binary image containing information of the penetrating pores; white pixels indicate pores [60].

3.3 3-D structure

3-D structures of porous materials and fluid flow inside them have attracted more and more interest recently. For example, in the porous materials used for transpiration cooling, the distribution of the penetrating pores and how the coolant flows through them significantly affect the cooling efficiency of this material. The protocol to obtain 3-D geometric information of porous material is based on stacking 2-D image slices. There are several imaging techniques available to obtain these 2-D images and scan in the third dimension. One major imaging technique is computed tomography (CT). Based on the facility used, it can be further categorized to X-ray-based and neutron-based method [10]. These two methods are based on observing the scattered intensity of X-ray and neutron, which represents the difference in density, polarization, or scattered angle of the sample. The resolution of the X-ray microtomography can be as low as $0.1\,\mu m$. Another imaging technique is Magnetic Resonance Imaging (MRI) [66], which has the resolution of tens of nanometers. For even higher resolution, a dual-beam Focused Ion Beam (FIB) imaging method has been proposed to investigate the 3-D geometry of porous materials [67]. The voxel resolution of this method is $15\,nm$.

The examples of 3-D geometric investigation of porous materials range from soil to biological tissues. A. Kaestner et al. measured the hydraulic properties of soil aggregate packing using both neutron radiography and X-ray tomography [10]. The neutron radiography has the ability to show water distribution within a sample, while X-ray tomography shows the structures at higher resolution. L. Pothuaud et al. investigated the microarchitecture of trabecular bone using MRI [66]. In the image processing part, they interpreted the graphs in terms of vertices and branches. A six-connection algorithm was applied to form 3-D structure. Fig. 2 shows the procedure of 3-D reconstruction of an Al foam using 2-D images [68]. The Al foam was sectioned physically, and then images of each slice were taken consequently. However, the image processing technique remained the same as that for other 3-D imaging methods, e.g. MRI.

More research work on 3-D reconstitution of porous media from image processing can be found in the area of soil [69-74], ceramics [75, 76], polyethylene [77], bone [78], metal [79, 80] and general porous media [81, 82].

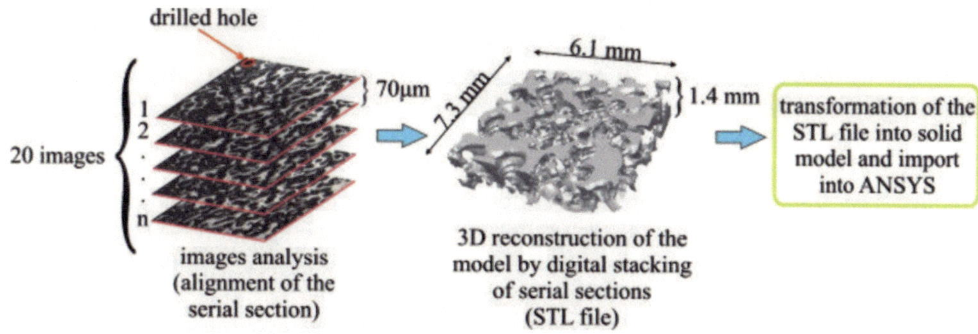

Fig. 2. Schematic diagram accounting for the image processing to obtain the 3D model of the Al-foam [68].

3.4 Fluid behavior

As discussed before, fluid behavior inside the porous material has significant effect on its performance. Not only for the sintered porous media used for transpiration cooling, but also for the porous material used as catalyst carrier, the fluid flow and diffusion inside the pore network is doomed to be important. Simulation work of fluid flow in a porous medium has been conducted for decades, which usually involves solving transportation equations for an unsteady state. Speaking of the experimental work, during the last two decades, the nuclear magnetic resonance (NMR) technique has been proven to be a successful imaging technique [83]. This technique measures the Fourier transform of self-diffusion propagator of the inside fluid [84]. Fig. 3 shows multiphase fluid core saturation through sodium NMR signal measurement [85]. In the mixture of water and oil, sodium only present in the water phase. Therefore, those two fluid can be distinguished by imaging the sodium component. This research has application in the area of rock content analysis and petroleum industry.

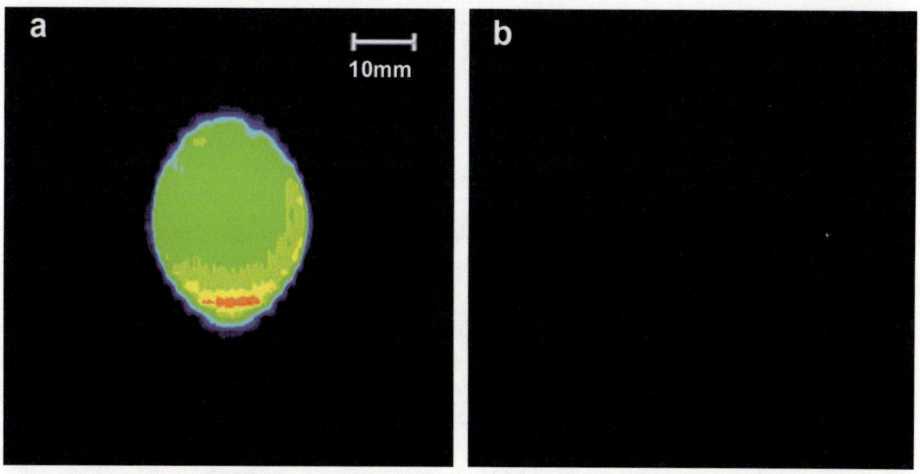

Fig. 3. 2D axial images of a Bentheimer core (a) fully saturated with 100 kppm brine (b) fully saturated with Isopar L [85].

Research work on fluid behavior in porous material has also been performed to the material of polyethylene [77], rocks [86-88] and general porous materials [87, 89].

4. Conclusion

In conclusion, image processing-based measurement techniques have the advantages of being non-destructive, easy operation, in-depth 3-D view capability and considerably high resolution. It has wide applications in material characterization area, especially the area of porous materials. The application area can be further extended with proper imaging technique. The image processing techniques involved include image alignment, image stitching, contrast enhancement, thresholding, image substraction, and 3-D reconstruction etc. Corresponding image processing techniques to be applied are highly affected by the properties of materials to be measured. The image processing methods can be migrated to other areas with similar image characteristics. For achieving accurate results, the image processing-based measurement should be improved from the image acquisition hardware, experimental setup and image processing algorithms aspects of view.

5. References

[1] W. S. Boyle and G. Smith, *Charge-coupled semiconductor devices.* Bell System Techanics of Journal, 1970. 49: p. 587-593.

[2] E. R. Fossum, *CMOS image sensors: Electronic camera-on-a-chip.* IEEE Transactions on Electron Devices, 1997. 44(10): p. 1689-1698.

[3] Stephen Kempainen, *CMOS image sensors: Eclipsing CCDs in visual information?* EDN, 1997. 42(21): p. 101-102.

[4] J. Zarnowski, M. Pace, and M. Joyner, *Active-pixel CMOS sensors improve their image.* Laser Focus World, 1999. 35(7): p. 111-114.

[5] Zurich Nicolas Blanc, *CCD versus CMOS - has CCD imaging come to an end?*, in *Photogrammetic Week 01.* 2001: Wichmann Verlag, Heidelberg.

[6] M. Bigas, E. Cabruja, J. Forest, and J. Salvi, *Review of CMOS image sensors.* Microelectronics Journal, 2006. 37(5): p. 433-451.

[7] R. Widenhorn, M. M. Blouke, A. Weber, A. Rest, and E. Bodegom, *Temperature dependence of dark current in a CCD*, in *Sensors and Camera Systems for Scientific, Industrial, and Digital Photography Applications III.* 2002, Spie-Int Soc Optical Engineering: Bellingham. p. 193-201.

[8] K. Miyaguchi, H. Suzuki, J. Dezaki, and K. Yamamoto, *CCD developed for scientific application by Hamamatsu.* Nuclear Instruments and Methods in Physics Research Section A: Accelerators, Spectrometers, Detectors and Associated Equipment, 1999. 436(1-2): p. 24-31.

[9] G. E. Healey and R. Kondepudy, *Radiometric CCD camera calibration and noise estimation.* IEEE Transactions on Pattern Analysis and Machine Intelligence, 1994. 16(3): p. 267-276.

[10] A. Kaestner, E. Lehmann, and M. Stampanoni, *Imaging and image processing in porous media research.* Advances in Water Resources, 2008. 31(9): p. 1174-1187.

[11] Michael J. Black and Anand Rangarajan, *On the unification of line processes, outlier rejection, and robust statistics with applications in early vision.* Int. J. Comput. Vision, 1996. 19(1): p. 57-91.

[12] M. J. Hannah, *Computer Matching of Areas in Stereo Images*. 1974, Stanford University.

[13] M. J. Hannah, *Test results from SRI's stereo system*, in *Image Understanding Workshop*. 1988, Morgan Kaufmann Publishers: Cambridge, Massachusetts. p. 740-744.

[14] H. P. Moravec, *The Stanford Cart and the CMU Rover.* Proceedings of the IEEE, 1983. 71(7): p. 872-884.

[15] D. S. Zhang and G. J. Lu, *A comparative study of curvature scale space and Fourier descriptors for shape-based image retrieval.* Journal of Visual Communication and Image Representation, 2003. 14(1): p. 41-60.

[16] Iivari Kunttu, Leena Lepisto, Juhani Rauhamaa, and Ari Visa, *Fourier-based object description in defect image retrieval.* Machine Vision and Applications, 2006. 17(4): p. 211-218.

[17] Bruce D. Lucas and Takeo Kanade, *An iterative image registration technique with an application to stereo vision*, in *Proceedings of the 7th international joint conference on Artificial intelligence - Volume 2*. 1981, Morgan Kaufmann Publishers Inc.: Vancouver, BC, Canada. p. 674-679.

[18] Qi Tian and Michael N. Huhns, *Algorithms for subpixel registration.* Computer Vision, Graphics, and Image Processing, 1986. 35(2): p. 220-233.

[19] W. Forstner, *A feature-based correspondence algorithm for image matching.* . Intl. Arch. Photogrammetry & Remote Sensing, 1986. 26(3): p. 150-166.

[20] C. Harris and M. Stephens. *A Combined Corner and Edge Detection.* in *Proceedings of The Fourth Alvey Vision Conference*. 1988.

[21] Jianbo Shi and Tomasi. *Good features to track.* in *Computer Vision and Pattern Recognition, 1994. Proceedings CVPR '94., 1994 IEEE Computer Society Conference on*. 1994. Seattle, WA, USA.

[22] Richard Szeliski, *Video Mosaics for Virtual Environments.* IEEE Comput. Graph. Appl., 1996. 16(2): p. 22-30.

[23] Richard Szeliski and Heung-Yeung Shum. *Creating full view panoramic image mosaics and texture-mapped models.* in *Computer Graphics*. 1997. SIGGRAPH'97, Los Angeles: Association for Computing Machinery, Inc.

[24] H. Y. Shum and R. Szeliski, *Construction of panoramic image mosaics with global and local alignment (vol 36, pg 101, 2000).* International Journal of Computer Vision, 2002. 48(2): p. 151-152.

[25] Satyan Coorg and Seth Teller, *Spherical Mosaics with Quaternions and Dense Correlation.* Int. J. Comput. Vision, 2000. 37(3): p. 259-273.

[26] Richard Szeliski, *Image Alignment and Stitching: A Tutorial.* 2006, Microsoft Corporation.

[27] Stephen M. Pizer, E. Philip Amburn, John D. Austin, Robert Cromartie, Ari Geselowitz, Trey Greer, Bart ter Haar Romeny, John B. Zimmerman, and Karel Zuiderveld, *Adaptive histogram equalization and its variations.* Computer Vision, Graphics, and Image Processing, 1987. 39(3): p. 355-368.

[28] Tae Kim, Joon Paik, and Bong Kang, *Contrast enhancement system using spatially adaptive histogram equalization with temporal filtering.* IEEE Transactions on Consumer Electronics, 1998. 44(1): p. 82-87.

[29] D. Coltuc, P. Bolon, and J. M. Chassery, *Exact histogram specification.* IEEE Transactions on Image Processing, 2006. 15(5): p. 1143-1152.

[30] J. L. Starck, F. Murtagh, E. J. Candes, and D. L. Donoho, *Gray and color image contrast enhancement by the curvelet transform.* IEEE Transactions on Image Processing on, 2003. 12(6): p. 706-717.

[31] S. Dippel, M. Stahl, R. Wiemker, and T. Blaffert, *Multiscale contrast enhancement for radiographies: Laplacian pyramid versus fast wavelet transform.* IEEE Transactions on Medical Imaging, 2002. 21(4): p. 343-353.

[32] Wan Yi and Shi Dongbin, *Joint Exact Histogram Specification and Image Enhancement Through the Wavelet Transform.* IEEE Transactions on Image Processing, 2007. 16(9): p. 2245-2250.

[33] D. T. Cobra, *Image histogram modification based on a new model of the visual system nonlinearity.* Journal of Electronic Imaging, 1998. 7(4): p. 807-815.

[34] H. Liu and C. F. Nodine, *Generalized image contrast enhancement technique based on the Heinemann contrast discrimination model.* Journal of Electronic Imaging, 1996. 5(3): p. 388-395.

[35] Chang Yuchou, Lee Dah-Jye, J. Archibald, and Hong Yi. *Using collaborative learning for image contrast enhancement.* in *Pattern Recognition, 2008. ICPR 2008. 19th International Conference on.* 2008.

[36] N. Otsu, *A threshold selection method from gray-level histograms.* IEEE Transactions on Systems, Man and Cybernetics, 1979. 9(1): p. 62-66.

[37] Steven M. Kay, *Fundamentals of Statistical Signal Processing, Volume 2: Detection Theory.* 1998: Prentice Hall.

[38] J.N. Kapur, P.K. Sahoo, and A.K.C. Wong, *A new method for gray-level picture thresholding using the entropy of the histogram.* Computer Vision, Graphics, and Image Processing, 1985: p. 273-285.

[39] S. Hemachander, A. Verma, S. Arora, and Prasanta K. Panigrahi, *Locally adaptive block thresholding method with continuity constraint.* Pattern Recognition Letters, 2007. 28(1): p. 119-124.

[40] J. M. White and G. D. Rohrer, *Image thresholding for optical character-recognition and other applications requiring character image extraction.* IBM Journal of Research and Development, 1983. 27(4): p. 400-411.

[41] K. V. Mardia and T. J. Hainsworth, *A Spatial Thresholding Method for Image Segmentation.* IEEE Trans. Pattern Anal. Mach. Intell., 1988. 10(6): p. 919-927.

[42] C. H. Li and C. K. Lee, *Minimum cross entropy thresholding.* Pattern Recognition, 1993. 26(4): p. 617-625.

[43] Jamal Saeedi, Mohammad Hassan Moradi, and Karim Faez, *A new wavelet-based fuzzy single and multi-channel image denoising.* Image and Vision Computing, 2010. 28(12): p. 1611-1623.

[44] Shitong Wang, Fu-lai Chung, and Fusong Xiong, *A novel image thresholding method based on Parzen window estimate.* Pattern Recognition, 2008. 41(1): p. 117-129.

[45] M. Sezgin and B. Sankur, *Survey over image thresholding techniques and quantitative performance evaluation.* Journal of Electronic Imaging, 2004. 13(1): p. 146-168.

[46] Avinash C. Kak and Malcolm Slaney, *Principles of Computerized Tomographic Imaging.* 1988: IEEE Press.

[47] Anil K. Jain, *Fundamentals of Digital Image Processing*. 1988: Prentice Hall.

[48] Jahne B., *Digital Image Processing*. 2 ed. 2002: Springer-Verlag.

[49] P. Perona and J. Malik, *Scale-space and edge detection using anisotropic diffusion.* IEEE Transactions on Pattern Analysis and Machine Intelligence, 1990. 12(7): p. 629-639.

[50] F. Catte, P. L. Lions, J. M. Morel, and T. Coll, *Image selective smoothing and edge detection by nonlinear diffusion.* SIAM J. Numer. Anal., 1992. 29(1): p. 182-193.

[51] Stanley Osher and Leonid Rudin, *Feature-oriented image enhancement using shock filters.* SIAM J. Numer. Anal., 1990. 27(4): p. 919-940.

[52] L. I. Rudin, S. Osher, and E. Fatemi, *Nonlinear total variation based noise removal algorithms.* Physica D, 1992. 60(1-4): p. 259-268.

[53] Gilles Aubert and Pierre Kornprobst, *Mathematical problems in image processing: Partial Differential Equations and the Calculus of Variations.* , in *Applied Mathematical Sciences.* 2002, Springer-Verlag.

[54] R. Adams and L. Bischof, *Seeded region growing.* IEEE Transactions on Pattern Analysis and Machine Intelligence, 1994. 16(6): p. 641-647.

[55] Jianping Fan, Guihua Zeng, Mathurin Body, and Mohand-Said Hacid, *Seeded region growing: an extensive and comparative study.* Pattern Recognition Letters, 2005. 26(8): p. 1139-1156.
[56] Wonho Oh and W. Brent Lindquist, *Image Thresholding by Indicator Kriging.* IEEE Trans. Pattern Anal. Mach. Intell., 1999. 21(7): p. 590-602.
[57] Riyadh I. Al-Raoush and Clinton S. Willson, *A pore-scale investigation of a multiphase porous media system.* Journal of Contaminant Hydrology, 2005. 77(1-2): p. 67-89.
[58] Peter J. Burt, Tsai-Hong Hong, and Azriel Rosenfeld, *Segmentation and Estimation of Image Region Properties through Cooperative Hierarchial Computation.* IEEE Transactions on Systems, Man and Cybernetics, 1981. 11(12): p. 802-809.
[59] Pierre Soille, *Morphological Image Analysis: Principles and Applications.* 2 ed. 2004: Springer.
[60] Jianhua Wang, Ming Gan, and Junxiang Shi, *Detection and characterization of penetrating pores in porous materials.* Materials Characterization, 2007. 58(1): p. 8-12.
[61] F. H. She, K. L. Tung, and L. X. Kong, *Calculation of effective pore diameters in porous filtration membranes with image analysis.* Robotics and Computer-Integrated Manufacturing, 2008. 24(3): p. 427-434.
[62] J. F. Daian, C. P. Fernandes, P. C. Philippi, and J. A. Bellini da Cunha Neto, *3D reconstitution of porous media from image processing data using a multiscale percolation system.* Journal of Petroleum Science and Engineering, 2004. 42(1): p. 15-28.
[63] S. Blacher, V. Maquet, F. Schils, D. Martin, J. Schoenen, G. Moonen, R. Jerome, and J. P. Pirard, *Image analysis of the axonal ingrowth into poly(,-lactide) porous scaffolds in relation to the 3-D porous structure.* Biomaterials, 2003. 24(6): p. 1033-1040.
[64] Elena Sevostianova, Bernd Leinauer, and Igor Sevostianov, *Quantitative characterization of the microstructure of a porous material in the context of tortuosity.* International Journal of Engineering Science, 2010. 48(12): p. 1693-1701.
[65] B. Prado, C. Duwig, J. Marquez, P. Delmas, P. Morales, J. James, and J. Etchevers, *Image processing-based study of soil porosity and its effect on water movement through Andosol intact columns.* Agricultural Water Management, 2009. 96(10): p. 1377-1386.
[66] L. Pothuaud, P. Porion, E. Lespessailles, C. L. Benhamou, and P. Levitz, *A new method for three-dimensional skeleton graph analysis of porous media: application to trabecular bone microarchitecture.* Journal of Microscopy, 2000. 199(2): p. 149-161.
[67] L. Holzer, F. Indutnyi, P. H. Gasser, B. MÜNch, and M. Wegmann, *Three-dimensional analysis of porous BaTiO3 ceramics using FIB nanotomography.* Journal of Microscopy, 2004. 216(1): p. 84-95.
[68] N. Michailidis, F. Stergioudi, H. Omar, and D. N. Tsipas, *An image-based reconstruction of the 3D geometry of an Al open-cell foam and FEM modeling of the material response.* Mechanics of Materials, 2010. 42(2): p. 142-147.
[69] J. F. Daïan, C. P. Fernandes, P. C. Philippi, and J. A. Bellini da Cunha Neto, *3D reconstitution of porous media from image processing data using a multiscale percolation system.* Journal of Petroleum Science and Engineering, 2004. 42(1): p. 15-28.
[70] Erwan Plougonven and Dominique Bernard, *Optimal removal of topological artefacts in microtomographic images of porous materials.* Advances in Water Resources, 2011. 34(6): p. 731-736.
[71] Riyadh Al-Raoush and Khalid A. Alshibli, *Distribution of local void ratio in porous media systems from 3D X-ray microtomography images.* Physica A: Statistical Mechanics and its Applications, 2006. 361(2): p. 441-456.
[72] Olivier Monga, *Defining and computing stable representations of volume shapes from discrete trace using volume primitives: Application to 3D image analysis in soil science.* Image and Vision Computing, 2007. 25(7): p. 1134-1153.

[73] W. Wang, A. N. Kravchenko, A. J. M. Smucker, and M. L. Rivers, *Comparison of image segmentation methods in simulated 2D and 3D microtomographic images of soil aggregates.* Geoderma, 2011. 162(3-4): p. 231-241.

[74] Jean-François Delerue and Edith Perrier, *DXSoil, a library for 3D image analysis in soil science.* Computers & Geosciences, 2002. 28(9): p. 1041-1050.

[75] Eric Maire, Paolo Colombo, Jerome Adrien, Laurent Babout, and Lisa Biasetto, *Characterization of the morphology of cellular ceramics by 3D image processing of X-ray tomography.* Journal of the European Ceramic Society, 2007. 27(4): p. 1973-1981.

[76] T. Wiederkehr, B. Klusemann, D. Gies, H. Müller, and B. Svendsen, *An image morphing method for 3D reconstruction and FE-analysis of pore networks in thermal spray coatings.* Computational Materials Science, 2010. 47(4): p. 881-889.

[77] M. Prodanovic, W. B. Lindquist, and R. S. Seright, *Porous structure and fluid partitioning in polyethylene cores from 3D X-ray microtomographic imaging.* Journal of Colloid and Interface Science, 2006. 298(1): p. 282-297.

[78] Eduard Vergés, Dolors Ayala, Sergi Grau, and Dani Tost, *3D reconstruction and quantification of porous structures.* Computers & Graphics, 2008. 32(4): p. 438-444.

[79] Bungo Otsuki, Mitsuru Takemoto, Shunsuke Fujibayashi, Masashi Neo, Tadashi Kokubo, and Takashi Nakamura, *Pore throat size and connectivity determine bone and tissue ingrowth into porous implants: Three-dimensional micro-CT based structural analyses of porous bioactive titanium implants.* Biomaterials, 2006. 27(35): p. 5892-5900.

[80] T. Kujime, M. Tane, S. K. Hyun, and H. Nakajima, *Three-dimensional image-based modeling of lotus-type porous carbon steel and simulation of its mechanical behavior by finite element method.* Materials Science and Engineering: A, 2007. 460-461: p. 220-226.

[81] Z. R. Liang, C. P. Fernandes, F. S. Magnani, and P. C. Philippi, *A reconstruction technique for three-dimensional porous media using image analysis and Fourier transforms.* Journal of Petroleum Science and Engineering, 1998. 21(3-4): p. 273-283.

[82] J. T. Fredrich, *3D imaging of porous media using laser scanning confocal microscopy with application to microscale transport processes.* Physics and Chemistry of the Earth, Part A: Solid Earth and Geodesy, 1999. 24(7): p. 551-561.

[83] P. T. Callaghan, A. Coy, D. MacGowan, K. J. Packer, and F. O. Zelaya, *Diffraction-like effects in NMR diffusion studies of fluids in porous solids.* Nature, 1991. 351(6326): p. 467-469.

[84] P. Levitz, *Toolbox for 3D imaging and modeling of porous media: Relationship with transport properties.* Cement and Concrete Research, 2007. 37(3): p. 351-359.

[85] Kathryn E. Washburn and Guillaume Madelin, *Imaging of multiphase fluid saturation within a porous material via sodium NMR.* Journal of Magnetic Resonance. 202(1): p. 122-126.

[86] S. Galaup, R. Burlot, A. Cerepi, L. Wang, and M. Dai, *Modelisation and circulation of fluids in geological porous systems. Images analyzing and mercury porosimetry,* in *Studies in Surface Science and Catalysis*, F.R.-R.J.R. P.L. Llewellyn and N. Seaton, Editors. 2007, Elsevier. p. 705-712.

[87] Yannick Anguy, Robert Ehrlich, Azita Ahmadi, and Michel Quintard, *On the ability of a class of random models to portray the structural features of real, observed, porous media in relation to fluid flow.* Cement and Concrete Composites, 2001. 23(2-3): p. 313-330.

[88] Tetsuro Hirono, Manabu Takahashi, and Satoru Nakashima, *In situ visualization of fluid flow image within deformed rock by X-ray CT.* Engineering Geology, 2003. 70(1-2): p. 37-46.

[89] Nejib Smaoui and Ridha B. Gharbi, *Using Karhunen-Loéve decomposition and artificial neural network to model miscible fluid displacement in porous media.* Applied Mathematical Modelling, 2000. 24(8-9): p. 657-675.

7

Accurate Spectral Measurements and Color Infrared Imagery of Excised Leaves Exhibiting Gaussian Curvature from Healthy and Stressed Plants

Christopher R. Little[1] and Kenneth R. Summy[2]
[1]*Kansas State University*
[2]*The University of Texas - Pan American*
USA

1. Introduction

The interactions of light with a leaf are determined by the three-dimensional internal and external leaf structure as well as photosynthetic pigment content within the cells (Gamon and Surfus, 1999). The three-dimensional structure and pigment content of a leaf is determined by a number of factors including plant species and varieties within species (genetics), leaf age, and growth conditions including abiotic and biotic stress factors, hormonal activity, and light history (Gamon and Surfus, 1999; Nath et al., 2003). Stresses such as water loss, suboptimal temperatures, high soil salinity, disease, arthropod feeding damage, nutrient deficiency, chemical pollution, and micronutrient toxicities may alter the internal structure of leaves (Gausman, 1985).

During the past fifty years, remote sensing applications in agriculture have proven their effectiveness as non-destructive, rapid, and relatively inexpensive techniques for obtaining information about plants and crop status (Johannsen et al., 1999). Successful use of remote sensing in agriculture has been predicated on knowledge regarding the nature of electromagnetic radiation (EMR) and its interactions with vegetation. EMR is characterized by both electrical and magnetic properties and by both particles and waves, which are most commonly measured in micrometers (μm) or nanometers (nm). The totality of EMR emitted by the sun forms the electromagnetic spectrum, which extends from short-wavelength high-energy gamma and x-rays (< 300 nm) to long-wavelength low-energy microwaves and radio waves (> 1 mm) (Figure 1). Reflected EMR of greatest value in remote sensing of vegetation includes the visible spectrum (400 to 700 nm), which constitutes the basis for conventional photography, and the near- and mid-infrared regions (700 to 3,000 nm), which are not detectable by the human visual system. Extensive reviews of the theory and use of color-infrared (CIR) imagery to detect visible and invisible wavebands are provided in Avery and Berlin (1992), Campbell (2002), Jensen (2004, 2006), Lillesand et al. (2007), and Wilke and Finn (1996).

It has long been known that the degree to which incident EMR is absorbed, transmitted, or reflected by vegetation is governed by the presence of phototsynthetic pigments (chlorophyll *a*, *b*; carotenes; xanthophylls; phaeophytin *a*, *b*) and the structure of cells within the spongy mesophyll layer of leaves (Gates et al., 1965; Gausman et al., 1969; Myers, 1970). A typical "spectral profile" of healthy foliage usually indicates a relatively low reflectance of blue and red wavelengths (400 to 500 nm and 600 to 700 nm, respectively), a slight increase in reflectance of green wavelengths (500 to 600 nm), and a substantial increase in reflectance of near-infrared (700 to 1,300 nm) and mid-infrared (1,300 to 3,000 nm) wavelengths (Figure 1). Reflectance of blue and red wavelengths (both of which are used to drive photosynthesis) is largely an effect of chlorophyll absorption, while reflectance of near-infrared (NIR) wavelengths is largely determined by the configuration and condition of air spaces within the spongy mesophyll layer of leaves (Lillesand et al., 2007). Water content of leaves appears to be the principal determinant of mid-infrared (MIR) reflectance. EMR in the green region of the spectrum is not absorbed to any extent by most plant species and is thus transmitted or reflected in relatively large quantities, hence the slight increase in reflectance of EMR near the center portion of the visible spectrum (Figure 1).

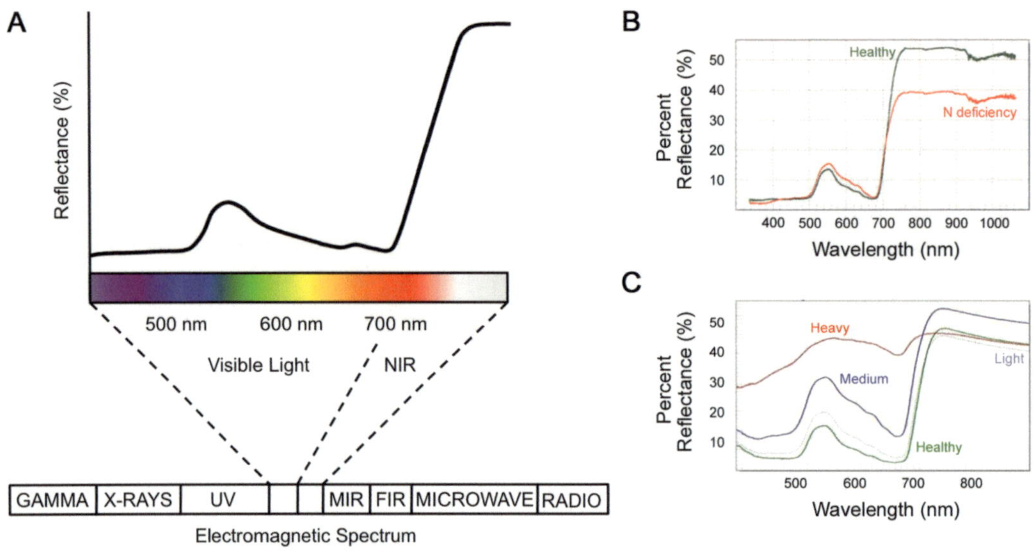

Fig. 1. The electromagnetic spectrum and a typical spectral reflectance curve for healthy plant tissues (A). Spectral reflectance curves for foliage of healthy and nitrogen deficient cucumber (*Cucumis sativus*) plants (B). Spectral reflectance curves for healthy foliage of *C. sativus* plants and those with "light", "medium", and "heavy" feeding damage by carmine spider mites (*Tetranychus cinnabarinus*) (C). Figure adapted from Summy et al. (2003) (A, B,) and Summy et al. (2007) (C), respectively.

Physiological stress in plants is commonly characterized by significant changes in reflectance of EMR in one or more regions of the spectrum. In subtle forms of stress in which leaf structure or water content has been altered without adversely affecting photosynthesis, changes in reflectance may be restricted to wavelengths in the NIR and/or MIR regions, neither of which is detectable by the human eye (Figure 2). Senescence, nutrient stress, pathogens, and insect predation have been shown to result in significant reductions of NIR reflectance by affected foliage (Wiegand et al., 1972; Murtha, 1978). In more advanced or severe forms of stress in which absorption by photosynthetic pigments has been seriously impeded or halted, increases in reflectance of photosynthetically active EMR (blue and red wavelengths) are inevitable and are responsible for many of the visible symptoms of plant stress, e.g., *chlorosis*. This classic symptom of plant stress occurs when reflectance of red wavelengths increases to levels equivalent to those of green wavelengths and is perceived by the human visual system as yellow.

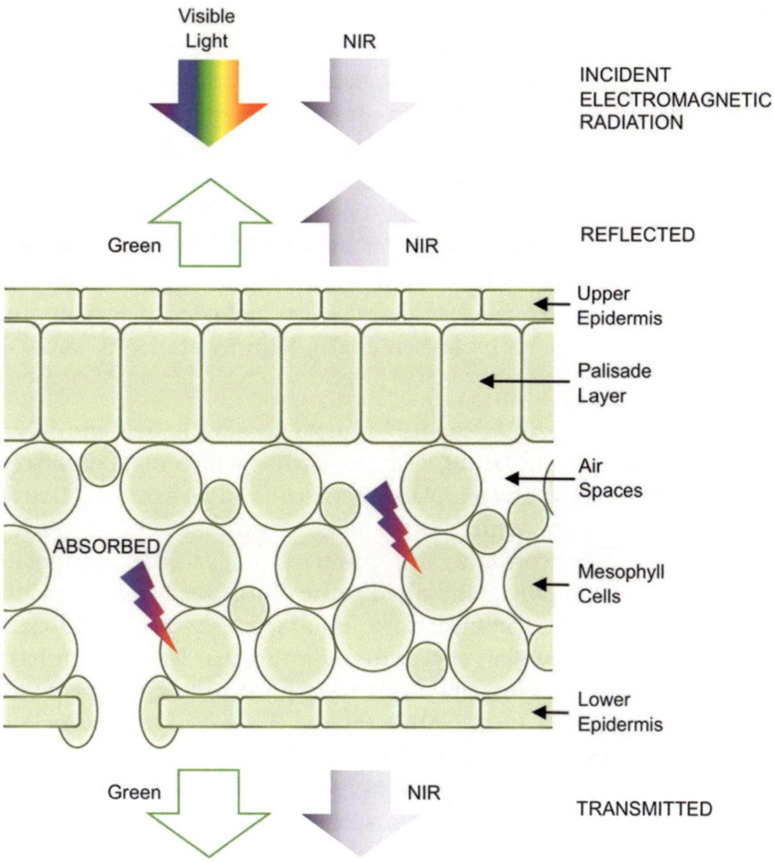

Fig. 2. Structure of a typical plant leaf showing patterns of transmission (green and NIR), absorption (blue and red), and reflectance (green and NIR) of incident electromagnetic radiation in various regions of the spectrum.

Use of remote sensing technology for detection and monitoring of plant stress caused by diseases and other factors has traditionally involved one or both of the following approaches: 1) *in situ* collection of spectral measurements using field spectroradiometers at ground level, and/or 2) acquisition of various types of imagery using sensors (e.g., cameras or scanners) mounted in aircraft or satellite platforms (see reviews in Avery and Berlin, 1992; Jensen, 2006; Lillesand et al., 2007; Cracknell and Hayes, 2007). This manner of data acquisition is conducted "at a distance" from the target and involves reflectance from either whole plants or plant canopies under natural lighting conditions. This conventional approach has yielded a wealth of information relating to characteristics of and temporal changes occurring in the earth's land and water surfaces, but is subject to one major constraint, i.e., a requirement for suitable weather conditions (e.g., clear sunny skies) for the acquisition of most types of imagery (Gandy et al., 2011).

In certain types of studies, however, the use of leaf samples (rather than whole plants or canopies) and artificial lighting sources (rather than sunlight) may be required to obtain spectral data required to analyze certain variables or parameters. For example, Gandy (2010) evaluated the relationship between foliar reflectance by common sunflower (*Helianthus annuus* L.) and arsenic content of individual leaves. The experimental design of this particular study involved the acquisition of spectral measurements for excised individual leaves under an artificial lighting source in the laboratory followed by the immediate preservation of sample leaves for subsequent chemical analyses. Studies of this type, which involve "close-up" remote sensing under laboratory conditions require prior knowledge of several effects including: 1) the spectral properties of a suitable artificial lighting source in relation to sunlight, 2) the spectral effect(s) of various background materials and 3) the effects of leaf excision and handling methods on leaf tissues to ensure that spectral measurements obtained from excised leaf samples are biologically meaningful (for recent studies on these factors, see articles by Jensen (2007), Summy et al. (2003a, 2004, 2011), and Gandy et al. (2011)).

One factor of major importance in "close-up" remote sensing is the naturally wrinkled or curved surfaces (e.g. Gaussian curvature) of plant leaves, which may adversely impact the ability to obtain consistent data between plant species and plant samples. Gaussian surfaces are represented universally in nature. In general, simple structures, such as spheres, cylinders, and cones, exhibit constant and positive, or *synclastic*, Gaussian curvature. However, plant leaves are complex, paraboloid or free-form surfaces that exhibit synclastic and negative, or *anticlastic*, Gaussian curvature simultaneously at both "global" and "local" levels. In general, synclastic Gaussian curvature indicates that leaf growth has occurred in the center, where the edges have remained relatively fixed producing a convex, or cupped structure (Nath et al., 2003; Liu et al., 2010) (Figure 3). A leaf with synclastic Gaussian curvature exhibits increased scattering of reflected light. Light scattering (Figure 3) occurs when reflected light (θ_r) deviates significantly from its incident angle ($\theta_i \neq \theta_r$). This is type of curvature is exhibited by leaves of *Cucumis sativus* L. (cucumber) and *Glycine max* (L.) Merrill (soybean). Anticlastic Gaussian curvature is characterized by slower growth of the central portion of the leaf structure relative to the edges, e.g. the leaf may be either slightly concave, yet the edges take on a wavy or uneven appearance (Nath et al., 2003). This type of curvature may also be seen in *C. sativus* and *G. max*, but is more often observed in elongated leaf types as seed in *Lycopersicon esculentum*, *Citrus* spp., and *Ficus* spp., and monocots, including *Sorghum bicolor* (L.) Moench and *Zea mays* L. Stressors may increase synclastic and anticlastic Gaussian leaf curvature, thus increasing the need to compress the reflective Gaussian surface so as to measure treatment differences in imagery as opposed to reflectance artifacts due to curvature of the leaf. Although a typical plant canopy may contain many different leaf surfaces each existing at different angles and exhibiting different levels of Gaussian curvature, we have not attempted to address that level of complexity in this chapter. In order to assess the contributions of individual leaves to whole plant remote-sensing data, these should be reliably mounted using an *in situ* image acquisition system (Figure 4) in which (1) significant turgor loss is not observed (after leaf excision) and (2) light scattering (defined herein as variability in angles of reflectance) is reduced after flattening. Both factors (1) and (2) could potentially influence the interpretation of remotely sensed data (Daughtry and Biehl, 1985). The purpose of the studies described in this chapter was to design and evaluate an image acquisition system where individual leaves can be remotely sensed under artificial lighting while mitigating turgor loss and leaf curvature.

2. Previous work

One of the principle advantages of CIR imagery is its ability to capture NIR wavelengths not visible by the human visual system. CIR photographs and digital CIR images consist of three broadband layers sensitive to EMR in the green, red and NIR regions of the spectrum. A ratio of NIR and red wavebands (a *simple vegetation index*) can be used to enhance acquired CIR imagery and facilitate quantitative comparison of images obtained from different treatments. This capability has been used to detect and monitor a variety of stress factors in agricultural crops, including damage caused by excess salt and moisture (Myers et al., 1963; Everitt et al., 1981; Yousef et al., 2011), nutrient deficiencies (Thomas and Oerther, 1977; Summy et al., 2003b; Yousef et al., 2011), and a variety of agricultural pests and plant diseases (Colwell, 1956; Brenchley, 1964; Norman and Fritz, 1965; Hart and Myers, 1968; Hart et al., 1973; Blazquez et al., 1979; Blazquez and Horn, 1980; Blazquez et al., 1988; Payne et al., 1971; Toler et al., 1981; Everitt et al., 1994; Everitt et al., 1996; Summy et al., 2003a Summy and Little, 2008; Summy et al., 2010).

Fungal pathogens of glasshouse plants represent a major constraint for optimum production and product quality. Significant changes in the reflected wavelengths of the near-infrared portion of the electromagnetic spectrum occur when reflectance measurements are obtained from plants infected by fungal pathogens and also from plants covered with sooty mold. Summy and Little (2008) collected data from several species of citrus seedlings (*Citrus sinensis, C. aurantium, C. paradisi* and *Poncirus trifoliata*), Bo seedlings (*Ficus religiosa*), and cantaloupe (*Cucumis melo reticulata*) propagated under natural lighting conditions in the glasshouse. Spectroradiometric measurements and color infrared (CIR) images of control, honeydew only, and sooty molded leaves from *F. religiosa, C. sinensis, C. aurantium,* and *P. trifoliata* were obtained. *C. paradisi* infected with the greasy spot fungus (*Mycosphaerella citri*) was also imaged under glasshouse lighting. Similar data was obtained from healthy foliage of *C. melo reticulata* and foliage with various levels of powdery mildew (*Sphaerotheca fuliginea*) infection.

Summy and Little (2008) assessed the relative levels of visible and near-infrared (NIR) reflectance from plants infested with sooty mold (coated with insect honeydew) and infected with fungal pathogens versus respective controls, under glasshouse conditions. Both "control" and "treated" whole plants and single leaves were imaged using conventional color and color infrared (CIR) photography

Although differences were observed when looking at leaves that were coated in honeydew only, accumulations of honeydew on leaf surfaces generally presented the same trends between plant species and different depositors. For example, NIR/red ratio images showed a significant decrease in reflectance when comparing sooty-molded plants versus "clean" controls. This relationship was sustained in three of the citrus species tested (*P. trifoliata, C. aurantium,* and *C. sinensis*) as well as "bo" tree seedlings (*F. religiosa*). This trend is accentuated when observing the individual contributions of particular leaves with varying levels of sooty mold after being mounted on the *in situ* image acquisition system. The reason for the decrease in NIR reflectance is due to the growth of dematiaceous (dark) fungal hyphae on the honeydew substrate. The resulting "mat" of fungal hyphae absorbed NIR light as opposed to reflecting it. Dematiaceous hyphae, which characterize the Capnodiaceae (including *Capnodium* spp.), contain significant amounts of melanin giving the sooty mold its dark color. Melanin is a polymer of indoles and tyrosine conversion intermediates that function in fungi and animals to absorb light and protect against irradiative damage (Riley, 1998). Therefore, it is not surprising that reflectance should decrease significantly from sooty-mold infested plant leaves. In fact, the absorption maxima of melanins derived from several dematiaceous ascomycetes and deuteromycetes have been shown to absorb red (400 to 500 nm), infrared (> 700 nm), and UV-B (280 to 315 nm) wavelengths (Bell and Wheeler, 1986; Babitskaya and Shcherba, 2002).

Summy and Little (2008) also tested leaves of varying ages from trifoliate orange (*P. trifoliata*) and sour orange (*C. aurantium*). In the case of trifoliate orange, there was no difference between NIR/red ratio images of 20 d or 35 d old leaves. However, sour orange differed in that the greatest NIR/red ratios were seen in 20 d old leaves and differed significantly from the 10 d and 35 d leaves.

A number of studies have demonstrated the ability to detect the red and NIR reflectance changes of plant tissues associated with fungal pathogens in the field (Colwell, 1956; Brenchley, 1964; Norman and Fritz, 1965). However, there is very little information concerning pathogen detection using CIR imagery and analysis in the glasshouse setting. Summy and Little (2008) considered two examples of foliar diseases: (1) powdery mildew of cucurbits (*Sphaerotheca fuliginea*) and (2) greasy spot of citrus (*Mycosphaerella citri*).

The powdery mildew diseases are characterized by extensive white fungal growth on the upper surface of the plant leaf. The "powdery" appearance is due to the production of numerous conidia and conidiophores. It is hypothesized that incident radiation that comes in contact with the fungal structures is both scattered *and* absorbed. Scattering may be due to the random placement of conidiophores on the leaf surface leading to an infinite number of angles at which light may be reflected. Absorption may occur due to small water droplets that are trapped between the fungal hyphae and the conidiophores. Summy and Little (2008) showed a significantly reduced NIR/red ratio and lower NIR reflectance in leaves infected with powdery mildew. This is an area requiring further study.

Decreases in NIR/red ratios in the case of leaf chlorosis appear to be quite common whether the stress is abiotic or biotic in nature. Chlorosis (see above) is a primary symptom that accompanies pseudothecium (fungal sexual fruiting structure) development in the greasy spot disease of citrus. Summy and Little (2008) indicated that red reflectance increases as greasy spot severity increased, whereas NIR reflectance did not appear to change appreciably, thus the NIR/red ratios decreased.

Color infrared (CIR) and multispectral imagery have been used for many years to assess damage caused by insect and mite infestations in conventional (outdoor) agricultural crops, but have not been used for this purpose to any extent within the commercial glasshouse environment or to evaluate individual leaves. In an effort to evaluate the potential of CIR imagery for detection and monitoring of arthropod infestations on glasshouse plants,

Summy et al. (2010) assessed spectral changes in foliage occurring in response to damage caused by three common glasshouse pests: 1) citrus mealybug, *Planococcus citri* (Pseudococcidae), 2) California red scale, *Aonidiella aurantii* (Diaspididae) and 3) carmine mite, *Tetranychus cinnabarinus* (Tetranychidae). Damage caused by each of these representative pest species resulted in distinct spectral signatures that were distinguishable from those of healthy foliage in both spectroradiometer measurements and CIR imagery (see examples in Figure 1). Potential applications of CIR imagery for the detection and monitoring of insect and mite infestations on glasshouse are discussed below.

Ornamental plants and vegetable crops produced commercially under glasshouse conditions are subject to infestation by most, if not all, of the insect and mite pests that are associated with these same crops in conventional (outdoor) plantings. Pest infestations developing on glasshouse crops commonly occur under near-optimal environmental conditions, which may include an absence of natural enemies (predators, parasites and pathogens) that provide a measurable degree of control in field infestations. As a result, insect and mite infestations developing within the protected glasshouse environment commonly exhibit relatively high rates of increase that provide a potential to cause levels of damage equivalent to or greater than those occurring in conventional field situations. Thus, effective management of such pests is predicated, in part, on the availability of efficient survey methodology designed to provide the glasshouse manager with timely and accurate information regarding the occurrence and current status of pest infestations, and the need (or lack thereof) for suppression measures. In order to be feasible, any such survey methodology must provide accurate information in near real-time and must be usable under all weather and lighting conditions. In addition, such methodology should be relatively inexpensive and simple to use.

Citrus mealybug, *Planococcus citri* (Hemiptera: Pseudococcidae), is one of the most serious insect pests associated with citrus and numerous ornamentals grown under glasshouse conditions. Damage results from the combined effects feeding activities (i.e., extraction of sap via sucking mouthparts) and excretion of copious quantities of honeydew (a sugary waste product), which accumulate on leaves and serve as a medium for sooty mold fungus. Dense deposits of sooty mold fungi may attenuate a significant portion of the electromagnetic radiation (EMR) incident on leaves. This is an effect that tends to severely retard photosynthesis. Field populations of *P. citri* on citrus in southern Texas and other areas are normally regulated at subeconomic densities by a complex of predators and parasites (Ancisco et al., 2002), although these are typically lacking in glasshouse infestations.

Summy and Little (2008) provided a comprehensive discussion of the spectral changes in foliage associated with the accumulation of honeydew and development of sooty mold deposits on foliage of citrus and other plants. One particularly important trend reported in that study relates to the observation that honeydew accumulations on foliage tend to increase NIR reflectance (with little or no apparent effects in reflectance in the visible region), whereas sooty mold deposits tend to decrease NIR reflectance and increase reflectance of wavelengths in the blue and red regions of the spectrum. Leaves contaminated with honeydew and sooty mold deposits were distinguishable from undamaged leaves in CIR imagery, and their presence on foliage was particularly evident in ratio (NIR/R) images. The capability of CIR and derivative imagery to detect honeydew deposits on foliage should be particularly useful in detection of incipient (low-density) infestations of *P.*

citri and other "honeydew excretors," including the soft scales (Coccidae), aphids (Aphididae), and whiteflies (Aleyrodidae).

Summy et al. (2010) found that although uninfested mature and immature *Citrus sinensis* leaves were distinguishable in the conventional color (RGB) image, no differences in coloration were evident among a series of mature leaves exhibiting a range of scale insect (A. *aurantii*) densities. These observations were consistent with spectroradiometer measurements, which detected no significant differences in reflectance of visible wavelengths among the series of infested mature leaves. In the CIR composite image, the presence of scale armor on infested foliage was indicated by a distinct speckling pattern. Although spectral curves for infested leaves indicated a significant reduction in NIR reflectance with increases in scale densities, only subtle differences in coloration of infested foliage were evident in the CIR composite image. However, evidence of physiological stress in infested leaves was evident in a ratio image which indicated high ratios of NIR:R in uninfested leaves and low ratios in infested leaves. Similar trends were evident in imagery of a Valencia orange tree acquired at a distance of 2.5 m under natural lighting conditions. The presence of scale armor on leaves was detectable in the conventional color image and was very conspicuous in the CIR composite image. Although differences in leaf coloration were very subtle in both RGB and CIR images, a ratio image indicated high NIR:R ratios for uninfested or lightly-infested leaves, and lower ratios for heavily infested leaves, many of which exhibited ratios similar to those of background reflection.

Spider mites (Acari: Tetranychidae) rank among the most chronic and potentially destructive pests of vegetable crops and ornamentals grown in commercial glasshouses. Damage results from the destruction of leaf epidermal tissue, which produces a distinctive "mottled" appearance of infested foliage. As a result of their short developmental times and high fecundities, spider mite infestations tend to increase rapidly to damaging levels, which may result in substantial damage and/or defoliation of glasshouse plants. A number of predaceous mites, e.g., *Phytoseiulus persimilis* (Acari: Phytoseiidae), have been shown to be effective in spider mite control and are produced commercially for this purpose (Yepsen, 1984), although these typically require introduction into the glasshouse environment.

Summy et al. (2010) found that differences in coloration between undamaged *Cucumis sativus* leaves and those exhibiting a slight degree of carmine spider mite (*T. cinnabarinus*) damage were very subtle and difficult to distinguish in RGB imagery, while leaves exhibiting moderate and intense damage were distinguishable. Similar trends were evident in the CIR composite image. These observations were consistent with spectroradiometer measurements, which indicated significantly higher levels of reflectance of visible wavelengths from the damaged leaf relative to the undamaged control, and a substantial and progressive increase in reflectance of visible wavelengths as the extent of tissue damage increased. Although an analysis of variance detected one significant difference in reflectance at 850 nm, the similarity of NIR reflectance among the remaining groups (i.e., undamaged controls and those exhibiting slight and intense damage) suggests that mite feeding injury did not influence this parameter.

Summy et al. (2010) showed that the rapidity at which mite damage increased between two late sampling dates exemplifies the destructive potential of spider mites in the glasshouse environment and the need to detect such infestations while they are still at the incipient stage, i.e., have not increased to damaging levels. Such infestations exhibit an aggregated distribution and may occur at densities too low to produce symptoms that are readily detectable through visual inspection or use of conventional photographic techniques. Leaves exhibiting a low intensity of spider mite damage were difficult to distinguish from undamaged foliage using either conventional RGB or CIR imagery alone; the two were highly distinguishable in a simple ratio image.

Summy et al. (2010) found that increases in the intensity of mite damage to leaves were accompanied by progressively higher levels of visible (blue, green and red) reflectance with little or no change in NIR reflectance. The effects of these spectral changes were clearly evident in the ratio image in which increasing intensity of mite damage was accompanied by progressively decreasing ratios of NIR to red wavelengths. The significance of this trend relates to the fact that the undamaged control and the slightly damaged leaf, which were not readily distinguishable in either the RGB or CIR images, were clearly distinguishable in the ratio image.

Numerous studies have indicated the occurrence of spectral changes in stressed plants including those due to nitrogen deficiency and soil salinity in conventional crops. Blackmer et al. (1996) detected nitrogen deficiency in corn (*Z. mays*) in the green region of the spectrum at a wavelength of 550 nm. Osborne et al. (2002) predicted the nitrogen concentration form corn canopies by using reflectance in the green and red regions of the spectrum. Gausman et al. (1985) stated that soil salinity stress in cotton (*Gossypium* spp.) plants cause spectral changes and can be detected using CIR imagery. Leone et al. (2000) was able to detect soil salinity in pepper plants (*Capsicum annuum* L.) using spectral reflectance measurements. Nonetheless, very limited research has been conducted to evaluate the potential of using remote sensing techniques in detecting nitrogen deficiency and soil salinity stresses in greenhouse crops.

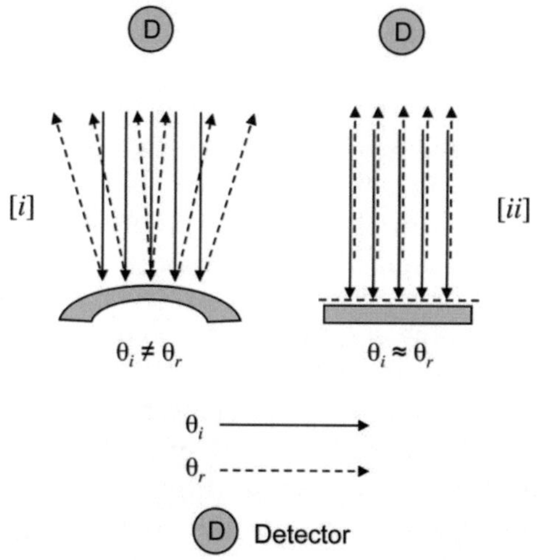

Fig. 3. Reduction of light scattering [*i*] results when leaves exhibiting synclastic Gaussian curvature are compressed [*ii*]. Compression of the leaves using the *in situ* image acquisition template results in light reflected at angles (θ_r) equivalent or nearly so to incident light (θ_i), which improves the quality of sample detection via image acquisition or spectroradiometry.

3. Methodology

In order to assess the contributions of individual leaves to whole plant remote-sensing data, leaf samples were mounted using an *in situ* image acquisition system in which significant turgor loss is not observed (after leaf excision) and light scattering (defined as the variability in angles of reflectance) is reduced after compression of a reflective Gaussian surface (Figures 3 and 4). Light scattering occurs when reflected light deviates significantly from its incident angle ($\theta_i \neq \theta_r$; where θ_i = angle of incidence, θ_r = angle of reflectance) (Figure 3).

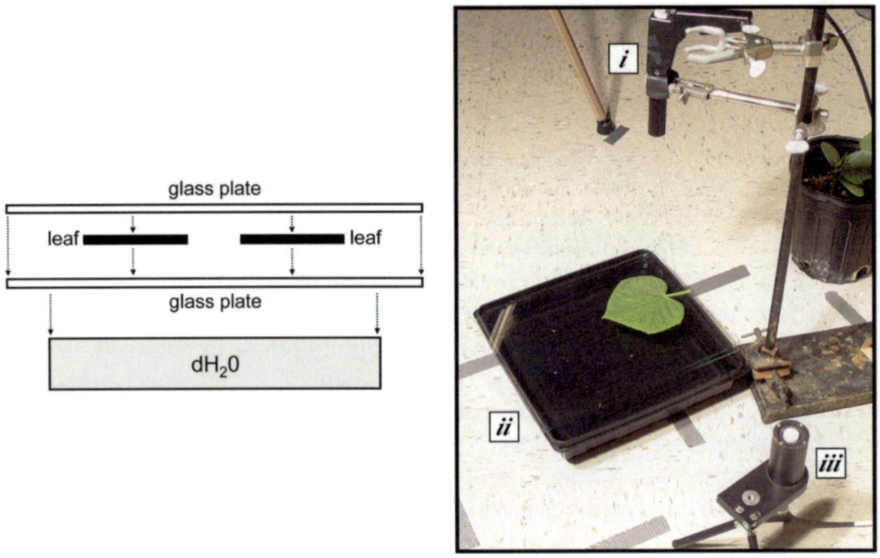

A B

Fig. 4. Diagram of the *in situ* image acquisition template used to examine individual leaves acquired from healthy and stressed whole plants (A). Photo of the image acquisition template demonstrating the use of the [*i*] VNIR sensor, [*ii*] glass plates, and [*iii*] remote cosine receptor used to collect spectrophotometric data (B). A CIR camera may be mounted at the same level as the spectroradiometer VNIR sensor shown above [*i*].

For the studies described in Summy and Little (2008) and Summy et al. (2010), vertical CIR images of individual leaves mounted using a plexiglass template were acquired under natural and artificial lighting conditions (500 W halogen lamps) at a distance of 1.5 m using a DuncanTech MS3110 digital CIR camera. CIR imagery acquired in this manner was imported into an image-processing package (Idrisi32® or Kilamanjaro®) after being converted to ".TIF" files and separated into NIR, red, and green bands using Adobe Photoshop 7. CIR imagery was evaluated to determine the degree to which the color rendition of infected and infested plants of a given species or cultivar differs from healthy controls in the raw (unprocessed) CIR imagery. Conventional CIR photography was also used for some experiments. In this case, a 35 mm Nikon SLR camera equipped with a Wratten 15 (yellow) filter and loaded with Kodak Ektachrome Professional Infrared EIR film were used to obtain the CIR images described in this chapter. All RGB "control" images were captured using a Sony Mavica CD400 digital camera.

In order to obtain NIR/red ratios, simple vegetative indices were generated utilizing the red and NIR bands of images that had been converted from digitized CIR images in Idrisi32®. The resulting images represent a ratio of NIR and red *at each pixel*. Ratio images were contrast stretched where necessary in order to eliminate approximately 20% of the unrepresentative wavelengths. To statistically compare NIR/red ratio images, contrast stretched ratios images were layered with a stratified spatial sample of random points. For individual leaves, 20 random points were selected. NIR/red ratio random point means, from template-mounted leaves, were compared using ANOVA and a means separation test (Tukey's Honestly Significant Difference ($P < 0.05$)).

Spectral measurements of healthy plants and plants within treatment or exposure groups (abiotic and biotic stressors) were obtained under natural and artificial lighting conditions using a FieldSpec VNIR spectroradiometer equipped with a remote cosine receptor (Analytical Spectral Devices, Boulder, CO) to measure incident radiation between the ultraviolet (350 nm) and NIR (1100 nm) regions of the electromagnetic spectrum. The spectroradiometer was equipped with ViewSpec Pro software (Analytical Spectral Devices, Boulder, Colorado). Measurements of radiance were converted to percent reflectance using a Spectralon® reference plate, and reflectance of selected wavelengths in the blue (450 nm), green (550 nm), red (650 nm) and NIR regions (850 nm) were compared using ANOVA and a means separation test (Tukey's HSD, $P < 0.05$).

The *in situ* image acquisition system used in these studies (Figure 4) consisted of a black, plastic plant growth flat filled with distilled water (in order to absorb light and prevent background reflection in images) and two 0.3 x 22 x 30 cm glass plates. Individual leaves were pressed between the glass plates and then remotely sensed using spectroradiometry and CIR imagery (Figure 4). The glass plates used in the "template system" were evaluated for irradiance levels (350 to 1150 nm) to check the relative amount of light attenuation that might occur in various wavebands due to the layer of glass covering a leaf held on the template (Figure 4).

To test the effect of leaf excision, *L. esculentum* and *C. sativus* non-excised and excised leaves were measured with the Field Spec Dual VNIR spectroradiometer when pressed between the glass plates on the *in situ* image acquisition system. Measurements were taken at 0, 1, 2, 3, 4, and 5 minutes after excision. Mean NIR/red ratio values were derived from ratio images (simple vegetation indices, see below) of excised and non-excised *L. esculentum* and *C. sativus* leaves that either were or were not flattened using the image acquisition system (Tables 1 and 2). Individual leaves were flattened between two glass plates using the *in situ* image acquisition system previously described. Spectoradiometer data and CIR imagery were obtained and analyzed. Measurements were taken 10 and 12 minutes after excision.

The quality and interpretability of CIR imagery acquired under an artificial (quartz halogen) lighting source is comparable to that acquired under natural lighting conditions, which clearly demonstrates that ambient lighting conditions do not pose a major constraint to the use of this technology for monitoring pest infestations in the glasshouse environment (Summy et al., 2004).

4. Results and progress

Leaves may be excised and data obtained without loss of spectral and image data quality if data is obtained in a relatively brief period of time. Leaf excision did not significantly reduce spectroradiometric values from either *C. sativus* or *L. esculentum* compared to non-excised leaves. Also, NIR/red ratio means did not differ when comparing non-excised and excised. There was a significant difference between spectroradiometric and NIR/red ratio values between compressed and non-compressed leaves using the *in situ* image acquisition system, whether comparing differences in Gaussian leaf curvature or plant stressors. Specifically, leaf compression generally reduced variability (standard deviations) among the quantitative spectroradiometric and imagery data, which improved the ability to differentiate treatment effects (Tables 1 and 2).

Treatment	NIR/red ratio (Mean ± SD)
Non-excised, non-flattened	2.69 ± 0.33 a*
Non-excised, flattened	2.49 ± 0.21 b
Excised, flattened	2.40 ± 0.15 b

Table 1. Mean NIR/red ratio values derived from ratio images of excised and non-excised *C. sativus* leaves flattened or not flattened using the *in situ* image acquisition system. *Values followed by different letters are significantly different at $P < 0.05$ (Tukey's HSD).

Treatment	NIR/red ratio (Mean ± SD)
Low curvature, non-flattened	2.57 ± 0.67 a*
High curvature, non-flattened	2.18 ± 0.55 bc
Low curvature, flattened	2.31 ± 0.26 ab
High curvature, flattened	1.93 ± 0.21 c

Table 2. Mean NIR/red ratio values derived from ratio images of excised *L. esculentum* leaves exhibiting low or high Gaussian curvature flattened or non-flattened using the *in situ* image acquisition system. *Values followed by different letters are significantly different at $P < 0.05$ (Tukey's HSD).

Treatment	NIR/red ratio (Mean ± SD)
Healthy, non-flattened	2.59 ± 0.14 a*
-N, non-flattened	1.46 ± 0.19 c
Healthy, flattened	2.19 ± 0.15 b
-N, flattened	1.37 ± 0.16 c

Table 3. Mean NIR/red ratio values derived from ratio images of healthy or N deficient (-N) excised *C. sativus* leaves flattened or non-flattened using the *in situ* image acquisition system. *Values followed by different letters are significantly different at $P < 0.05$ (Tukey's HSD).

Use of the *in situ* image acquisition system successfully aided the acquisition of color infrared imagery and spectroradiometric data from *Citrus* spp., *Ficus religiosa, C. sativus*, and *L. esculentum* exposed to biotic stressors, including fungi and insects. The *in situ* image acquisition system described in this chapter and utilized in Summy and Little (2008) and Summy et al. (2010) showed two important features that suggest a potential application to understanding the contributions that individual leaves make to a holistic remote sensing image. Leaves may be excised and data obtained without loss of spectral quality if data is obtained in a relatively brief period of time. Water potential in leaves is regulated by two mechanisms: (1) opening and closing of the stomata and (2) internal osmotic pressure differentials in the vasculature of the plant (and associated cells) (Gutschick, 1999). Leaf excision did not significantly reduce spectroradiometric values from either *L. esculentum* or *C. sativus* compared to non-excised leaves (Figure 5). Also, NIR/red ratio means did not differ when comparing non-excised and excised (Table 1).

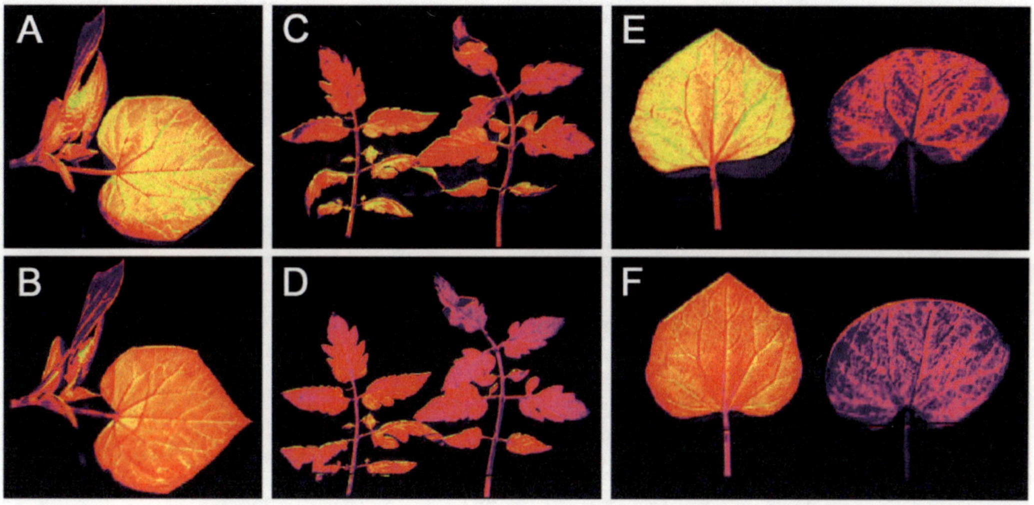

Fig. 5. False-colored near-infrared/red ratio images of non-excised *Cucumis sativus* leaves (A) non-flattened and (B) flattened using the *in situ* image acquisition system (see Fig. 4). Near-infrared/red ratio images of excised (left-side of panels) and non-excised (right-side of panels) *Lycopersicon esculentum* leaves before (C) and after (D) flattening, respectively. Near-infrared/red ratio images of healthy *C. sativus* leaves (left-side of panels) and those exhibiting nitrogen deficiency (right-side of panels) before (E) and after flattening (F).

There was a significant difference between spectroradiometric and NIR/red ratio values between leaves that were and were not flattened using the "template system" whether comparing differences in leaf curvature or plant stress (Figures 5 and 6; Tables 1, 2, and 3). However, it is difficult to visualize the differences when comparing NIR/red ratio images though changes in the uniformity of the images are observed. This increase in uniformity of the flattened leaves is demonstrated by the decrease in variability (eg. standard deviations) among quantitative data derived from the NIR/red ratio images (Tables 1, 2, and 3).

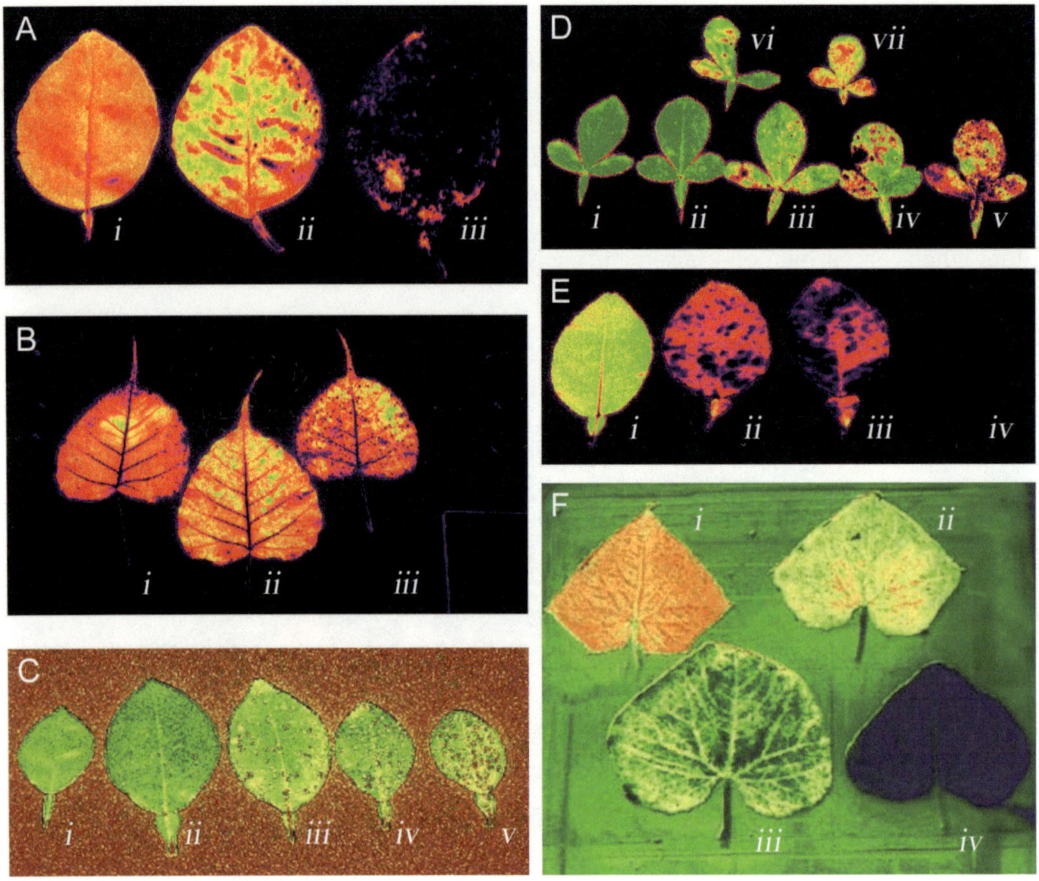

Fig. 6. Examples of false-colored NIR/red waveband ratio images of excised leaves from healthy and stressed plants acquired using the *in situ* image acquisition template. (A) Healthy [*i*], insect honeydew-coated [*ii*], and sooty mold infested [*iii*] 'Valencia' orange [*Citrus sinensis*] leaves; (B) Healthy [*i*], honey-dew coated [*ii*], and sooty mold infested [*iii*] *Ficus religiosa* leaves; (C) 'Valencia' orange leaves non-infested [*i, ii*] and infested [*iii, iv, v*] with California red scale insect armor [*Aonidiella aurantii*]; (D) Healthy [*i, ii*], and sooty mold and citrus mealy bug [*Planococcus citri*] infested [*iii-vii*] trifoliate orange [*Poncirus trifoliata*] leaves. The leaflets in item *v* represent the highest level of infestation; (E) Healthy [*i*] and diseased [*ii-iv*; greasy spot, *Mycosphaerella citri*] grapefruit leaves. Severe chlorosis in item *iv* resulted in a NIR/red ratio coded as black in the false-colored image; (F) Healthy [*i*] and spider mite [*Eutetranychus banksi*] damaged [*ii-iv*] cucumber leaves [*C. sativus*] leaves.

5. Opportunities and constraints

The common use of NIR/red ratio images to detect plant stress is based on the well known fact that stressed plants commonly exhibit both a decrease in NIR reflectance and an increase in reflectance of red wavelengths. Thus, NIR/red ratios tend to be relatively high within areas of imagery representing healthy plant foliage, and generally decrease within areas exhibiting physiological stress. The main exception to this is significant honeydew deposition on leaf surfaces. Ratio images compiled during the research described clearly demonstrate the potential usefulness of this image enhancement technique for identifying certain types of biotic plant stress.

Damage caused by each of the representative pest species discussed herein was accompanied by distinct spectral changes that were readily distinguishable (from healthy foliage) in CIR and/or derivative imagery. By providing a capability to identify small and localized areas of foliar damage (e.g., feeding injury by spider mites) and/or the presence of characteristic pest products on plants (e.g., honeydew), CIR imagery appears to have considerable potential for the detection of incipient infestations of several major groups of glasshouse arthropod pests. Moreover, use of a suitable artificial lighting source (e.g., quartz halogen lamps) facilitates the acquisition of CIR imagery that is equivalent in quality and interpretability to imagery obtained under optimal natural lighting conditions, and thus mitigates a major problem (i.e., poor or unpredictable ambient lighting) that has long represented one of the principal constraints to use of remote sensing in conventional outdoor crops.

Overall it appears that excising and flattening leaves do not severely affect spectroradiometric and CIR image quality. Thus, one of the principal advantages of this method is that it provides a means by which to experimentally compare reflectance values and image ratios (NIR/red) in "side-by-side" comparisons without the vagaries caused by leaf curvature or reflectance from adjacent or underlying leaves. Summy and Little (2008), Summy et al. (2010), and Yousef et al. (2011) discuss the use of this template system for the direct comparison of leaves exhibiting signs and symptoms of sooty mold and fungal pathogens, insect infestations, and nutrient deficiencies and toxicities.

6. Future directions

In order to effectively use a template system such as that described herein for obtaining accurate spectral measurements of excised leaves, the user must ensure that the excision process and handling methods for leaf samples do not adversely affect leaf tissues or cause a degree of desiccation sufficient to affect spectral reflectance (Foley et al., 2006). Although much emphasis has been placed on laboratory handling methods, the procedures used to store samples for transport to the laboratory are equally important. One recent study demonstrated that excised foliage of giant reed, *Arundo donax*, placed within paper bags and stored in a refrigerated ice chest desiccated rapidly and exhibited substantial changes in spectral properties within a period of 24 hours following collection. In contrast, samples of *A. donax* foliage stored within clear plastic zip-lock bags exhibited little evidence of desiccation or significant changes in spectral properties for 72 to 96 hours after collection (Summy et al., *in press*) (Figure 7). The development of field collection and transport methodology for plant foliage is critical to obtaining accurate spectral measurements in the laboratory and represents a fruitful area of future research.

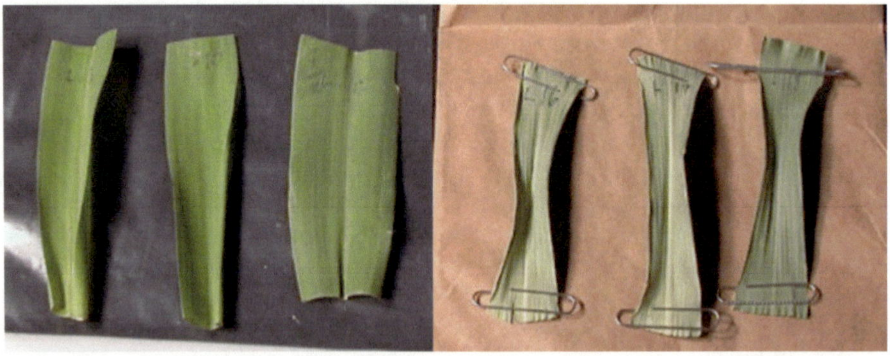

Fig. 7. Samples of *Arundo donax* leaves maintained in plastic zip-lock bags (*left*) and paper bags (*right*) following a 96-hour observation period (from Summy et al., *in press*).

7. Acknowledgements

This book chapter is Contribution No. KAES 12-084-B from the Kansas Agricultural Experiment Station, Manhattan.

8. References

Ancisco, J.R., French, F.V., Skaria, J.W., and Holloway, R. (2002). IPM in Texas citrus. Texas Cooperative Extension Service, B-6121. Texas A&M University, College Station, Texas, USA

Avery, T.E., and Berlin, G.L. (1992). *Fundamentals of remote sensing and airphoto interpretation*, 5th ed. Prentice Hall, ISBN 0-02305-035-7, Upper Saddle River, New Jersey, USA

Babitskaya, V.G., and Shcherba, V.V. (2002). The nature of melanin pigments of several micro- and macromycetes. *Applied Biochemistry and Microbiology*, Vol. 38, No. 3, pp. 411-451

Bell, A.A., and Wheeler, M.H. (1986). Biosynthesis and function of fungal melanins. *Annual Review of Phytopathology*, Vol. 24, No. 1, pp. 411-451

Blackmer, T.M., Schepers, J.S., Varvel, G.E., and Walter-Shea, E.A. (1996). Nitrogen deficiency detection using reflected shortwave radiation for irrigated corn canopies. *Agronomy Journal*, Vol. 88, No. 1, pp. 1-5

Blazquez, C.H., and Horn, F.W. (1980). Aerial color infrared photography: applications in agriculture. National Aeronautics and Space Administration, Reference Publication 1067, Washington, D.C.

Blazquez, C.H., Edwards, G.J., and Horn, F.W. (1979). Aerial color infrared photography - a management tool. *Florida State Horticultural Society Proceedings*, Vol. 92, No. 1, pp. 13-15

Blazquez, C.H., Lowe, O., Sisk, J.R., and Bilbrey, M.D. (1988). Use of aerial color infrared photography, dual color video, and a computer system for property appraisal of citrus groves. Photogrammetry Engineering and Remote Sensing, Vol. 54, No. 2, pp. 233-236

Brenchley, G.H. (1964). Aerial photography for the study of potato blight. *World Review of Pest Control*, Vol. 3, No. 1, pp. 68-84

Campbell, J.B. (2002). *Introduction to remote sensing*, 3rd ed. Guilford Press, ISBN 1-57230-640-8, New York, New York, USA

Colwell, R.N. (1956). Determining the prevalence of certain cereal diseases by means of aerial photography. *Hilgardia*, Vol. 26, pp. 223-226

Cracknell, A.P., and Hayes, L. (2007). Introduction to remote sensing, 2nd ed. CRC Press, ISBN 0-84939-255-1, Boca Raton, Florida, USA

Daughtry, C.S.T., and Biehl, L.L. (1985). Changes in spectral properties of detached birch leaves. *Remote Sensing of the Environment*, Vol. 17, No. 3, pp. 281-289

Everitt, J.H., Drawe, D.L., Little, C.R., and Lonard, R.I. (2011). *Grasses of south Texas: a guide to their identification and value.* Texas Tech University Press, ISBN 0-89672-668-1, Lubbock, Texas, USA

Everitt, J.H., Gerbermann, A.H., and Alaniz, M.A. (1981). Microdensitometry to identify saline rangelands on 70 mm color infrared film. *Photogrammetric Engineering and Remote Sensing*, Vol. 47, pp. 1357-1362

Everitt, J.H., Lonard, R.I., and Little, C.R. (2007). *Weeds in south Texas and northern Mexico: a guide to identification.* Texas Tech University Press, ISBN 0-89672-614-2, Lubbock, Texas, USA

Foley, S., Rivard, B., Sanchez-Azofeifa, and Calvo, J. (2006). Foliar spectral properties following leaf clipping and implications and implications for handling techniques. *Remote Sensing of the Environment*, Vol. 103, pp. 421-425

Forterre, Y., Skotheim, J.M., Dumais, J., and Mahadevan, L. (2005). How the Venus flytrap snaps. *Nature*, Vol. 433, pp. 421-425

Gamon, J.A., and Surfus, J.S. (1999). Assessing leaf pigment content with a reflectometer. *New Phytologist*, Vol. 143, No. 1, pp. 105-117

Gandy, Y.P.P. (2010). Spectral reflectance as an indicator of foliar concentrations of arsenic in common sunflower, *Helianthus annuus. M.S. Thesis*, The University of Texas - Pan American, Edinburg, Texas, USA

Gandy, Y.P., Mamachen, A., Mamachen, A., Lieman, J., Persans, M., Parson, J., Ibrahim, E., Summy, K.R., and Little, C.R. (2011). Techniques to facilitate the acquisition of accurate spectral measurements and multispectral imagery of plant foliage under artificial lighting conditions. *Subtropical Plant Science*, Vol. 63, No. 1 (*in press*)

Gates, D.M., Keegan, J.J., Schleter, J.C., and Weidner, V.R. (1965). Spectral properties of plants. *Applied Optics*, Vol. 4, No. 1, pp. 11-20

Gausman, H.W., Allen, W.A., and Cardenas, R. (1969). Reflectance of cotton leaves and their structure. *Remote Sensing of the Environment*, Vol. 1., No. 1, pp. 110-122

Gausman, H.W. (1985). Plant leaf optical parameters in visible and near-infrared light. *Graduate Studies, Texas Tech University, No. 29*. Texas Tech University Press, ISBN 0-89672-132-9, Lubbock, Texas, USA

Gutschick, V.P. (1999). Biotic and abiotic consequences of differences in leaf structure. *New Phytologist*, Vol. 143, No. 1, pp. 3-18

Hart, W.G., and Myers, V.I. (1968). Infrared aerial color photography for the detection of populations of brown soft scale in citrus groves. *Journal of Economic Entomology*, Vol. 61, No. 3, pp. 617-624

Hart, W.G., Ingle, S.J., Davis, M.R., and Magnum, C. (1973). Aerial photography with infrared color film as a method of surveying for citrus blackfly. *Journal of Economic Entomology*, Vol. 66, No. 1, pp. 190-194

Jensen, J.R. (2004). *Introductory digital image processing: a remote sensing perspective,* 3rd ed. Prentice Hall, ISBN 0-13145-361-0, Upper Saddle River, New Jersey, USA

Jensen, J.R. (2006). *Remote sensing of the environment: an Earth resource perspective,* 2nd ed. Prentice Hall, ISBN 0-13188-950-8, Upper Saddle River, New Jersey, USA

Johannsen, C.J., Carter, P.G., Morris, D.K., Erickson, B., and Ross, K. (1999). Potential applications of remote sensing. *Site-specific Management Guidelines Series, SSMG-22.* Potash and Phosphate Institute, South Dakota State University, Brookings, South Dakota, USA

Lee, K., Avondo, J., Morrison, H., Blot, L., Stark, M., Sharpe, J., Bangham, A., and Coen, E. (2006). Visualizing plant development and gene expression in three dimensions using optical projection tomography. *The Plant Cell*, Vol. 18, No. 9, pp. 2145-2156

Leone, A.P., Menenti, M., and Sorrentino, G. (2001). Reflectance spectrometry to study crop response to soil salinity. *Italian Journal of Agronomy*, Vol. 4, No. 2, pp. 75-85

Lillesand, T.M., Kiefer, R.W., and Chipman, J. (2007). *Remote sensing and image interpretation,* 6th ed. John Wiley and Sons, Inc., ISBN 0-47005-245-7, New York, New York, USA

Liu, Z., Jia, L., Mao, Y., and He, Y. (2010). Classification and quantification of leaf curvature. *Journal of Experimental Botany*, Vol. 61, No. 10, pp. 2757-2767

Myers, V.I. (1970). Soil, water and plant relations. pp. 253-297 In *Remote sensing with special reference to agriculture.* National Academy of Sciences, Washington, D.C., USA

Myers, V.I., Ussery, L.R., and Rippert, W.J. (1963). Photogrammetry for detailed detection of drainage and salinity problems. *American Society of Agricultural Engineers*, Vol. 6, No. 4, pp. 332-334.

Murtha, P.A. (1978). Remote sensing and vegetation damage: a theory for detection and assessment. *Photogrammetry, Engineering & Remote Sensing*, Vol. 44, No. 9, pp. 1147-1158

Nath, U., Crawford, B.C.W., Carpenter, R. and Coen, E. (2003). Genetic control of surface curvature. *Science*, Vol. 299, No. 5611, pp. 1404-1407

Niklas, K.J. (1999). A mechanical perspective on foliage leaf form and function. *New Phytologist*, Vol. 143, No. 1, pp. 19-31

Norman, G.G., and Fritz, N.L. (1965). Infrared photography as indicator of disease and decline in citrus. *Florida State Horticultural Society Proceedings*, Vol. 75, No. 1, pp. 59-63

Osborne, S.L., Schepers, J.S., Francis, D.D., and Schlemmer, M.R. (2002). Detection of phosphorus and nitrogen deficiencies in corn using spectral radiance measurements. *Agronomy Journal*, Vol. 94, No. 6, pp. 1215-1221

Payne, J.A., Hart, W.G., Davis, M.R., Jones, L.S., Weaver, D.J., and Horton, B.D. (1971). Detection of peach and pecan pests and diseases with color infrared photography. *Proceedings of the 3rd Bienniel Workshop on Color Aerial Photography in the Plant Sciences*, Falls Church, Virginia, USA, American Society of Photogrammetry

Perez, J.L., French, J.V., Summy, K.R., Baines, A.D., and Little, C.R. (2009). Fungal phyllosphere communities are altered by indirect interactions among trophic levels. *Microbial Ecology*, Vol. 57, No. 4, pp. 766-774

Riley, P.A. (1998). Melanin. *International Journal of Biochemistry and Cell Biology*, Vol. 29, No. 11, pp. 1235-1239

Prusinkiewicz, P., de Reuille, P.B. (2010). Constraints of space in plant development. *Journal of Experimental Botany*, Vol. 61, No. 8, pp. 2117-2129

Summy, K.R., Lieman, J., Gandy, Y.P., Mamachen, A., Mamachen, A., Goolsby, J., and Moran, P.J. (2011). Effects of leaf excision and sample storage methods on spectral reflectance by foliage of giant reed, *Arundo donax*. Subtropical Plant Science, Vol. 63, No. 1 (*in press*)

Summy, K.R., and Little, C.R. (2008). Using color infrared imagery to detect sooty mold and fungal pathogens of glasshouse-propagated plants. *HortScience*, Vol. 43, No. 5, pp. 1485-1491

Summy, K.R., Little, C.R., French, J.V., Setamou, M., Mata, J., and Everitt, J.H. (2007). Use of ratio images to detect subtle forms of plant stress caused by foliar feeding arthropods. *Proceedings of the 21st Biennial Workshop on Aerial Photography, Videography, and High Resolution Digital Imagery for Resource Assessment*. ISBN 1-60560-375-9, Terre Haute, Indiana, May 2007

Summy, K.R., Little, C.R., Everitt, J.H., Mazariegos, R.A., French, J.V., Setamou, M., and Mata, J. (2010). Detection of incipient pest infestations on glasshouse crops using multispectral imagery and a common vegetation index. *Subtropical Plant Science*, Vol. 62, No. 1, pp. 56-62

Summy, K.R., Little, C.R., Mazariegos, R.A., Everitt, J.H., Davis, M.R., French, J.V., and Scott, A.W. (2003a). Detecting stress in glasshouse plants using color infrared imagery: a potential new application for remote sensing. *Subtropical Plant Science*, Vol. 55, No. 1, pp. 51-58

Summy, K.R., Little, C.R., Mazariegos, R.A., Everitt, J.H., Davis, M.R., French, J.V., and Scott, A.W. (2003b). Technical feasibility of color infrared imagery for monitoring physiological stress in glasshouse crops. *Proceedings of the 19th Biennial Workshop of Color Photography, Videography and Airborne Imaging for Resource Assessment*. ISBN 1-57083-074-6, Logan, Utah, October 2003

Summy, K.R., Little, C.R., Mazariegos, R.A., Hinojosa-Kettelkamp, D.L., Carter, J., Yousef, S., and Valdez, R. (2004). Evaluation of artificial lighting sources for the acquisition of color infrared imagery under glasshouse conditions. *Subtropical Plant Science*, Vol. 56, No. 1, pp. 44-51

Thomas, J.R., and Oerther, G.F. (1977). Estimation of crop conditions and sugar cane yields using photography. *American Society of Sugar Cane Proceedings*, Vol. 6, No. 1, pp. 93-99

Toler, R.W., Smith, D.B., and Harlan, J.C. (1981). Use of aerial color infrared photography to evaluate crop disease. *Plant Disease*, Vol. 75, No. 1 pp. 24-31

Wiegand, C.L., Gausman, H.W., Allen, W.A. (1972). Physiological factors and optical parameters as bases of vegetation discrimination and stress analysis. *Proceedings of the seminar on: Operational Remote Sensing Seminar*, Houston, Texas. American Society of Photogrammetry, Falls Church, Virginia, USA

Wilke, D.S., and Finn, J.T. (1996). Remote sensing imagery for natural resources monitoring. Columbia University Press, ISBN 0-23107-928-1, New York, New York, USA

Yepsen, R.B. (1984). *The encyclopedia of natural insect & disease control.* Rodale Press, ISBN 0-87857-488-3, Emmaus, Pennsylvania, USA

Yousef, S., Summy, K.R., and Little, C.R. (2011) Detection of salt toxicity and nitrogen deficiency in *Cucumis sativus* L. using spectroradiometry and color infrared imagery. *Journal of Plant Nutrition*, Vol. 34, No. 8, pp. 1236-1244

8

A Comparative Study of Some Markov Random Fields and Different Criteria Optimization in Image Restoration

José I. De la Rosa, Jesús Villa, Ma. Auxiliadora Araiza,
Efrén González and Enrique De la Rosa
Laboratorio de Procesamiento Digital de Señales
Facultad de Ingeniería Eléctrica, Universidad Autónoma de Zacatecas
Mexico

1. Introduction

The present chapter illustrates the use of some recent alternative methods to deal with digital image filtering and restoration. This collection of methods is inspired on the use of Markov Random Fields (MRF), which introduces prior knowledge of information that will allow, more efficiently, modeling the image acquisition process. The methods based on the MRF are analyzed and proposed into a Bayesian framework and their principal objective is to eliminate noise and some effects caused by excessive smoothness on the reconstruction process of images which are rich in contours or edges. In order to preserve object edges into the image, the use of certain convexity criteria into the MRF is proposed obtaining adequate weighting of cost functions in cases where discontinuities are remarked and, even better, for cases where such discontinuities are very smooth.

Some image analysis and processing tasks involve the filtering or image recovery $\widehat{x}$ (e.g. restoration) after x passes by a degradation process giving the observed image y (see equation (1)). Such degradation covers the noise perturbations, blurring effects due to focus of the acquisition system lenses or to the bandwidth capacity, and other artifacts that may be added to the correct data. The use of Bayesian methods proposed in the seventies (Besag, 1974; 1986; Geman and Geman, 1984), are nowadays essential at least in the cases of image segmentation and image restoration (Andrews and Hunt, 1977). The basic idea of these methods is to construct a Maximum a posteriori (MAP) estimate of the modes or so called estimator of true images by using MRF into a Bayesian framework. The general approach is based on a robust scheme which could be adapted to reject outliers, tackling situations where noise is present in different forms during the acquisition process (Bertaux et al., 2004; Cai et al, 2008; Chan et al., 2006; Durand and Nikolova, 2006a;b; Nikolova, 2006; 2005; Nikolova and Ng, 2005; Pan and Reeves, 2006).

The restoration or recuperation of an image to its original condition given a degraded image, passes thus by reverting the effects caused by noise or / and a distortion function. In fact, the degradation characteristic is a crucial source of information and its mathematical function must be known or estimated during the inversion procedure. Typically, this is a point spread function (PSF) which can be linked with the probability distribution of the noise contamination or likelihood function. In the case of MAP filters, usually the additive Gaussian noise is considered, however in some applications this noise is non-Gaussian (Bertaux et al., 2004; Cai et al, 2008) or unknown noise probability distribution function (pdf), $p(e) = p(y|x)$, with some partial knowledge. In the latter case, we propose to use the data itself to obtain a non-parametric entropy estimate (EE) of the log-likelihood pdf, $\widehat{p}_{n,h}(e)$ (De la Rosa and Fleury, 2002; De la Rosa et al., 2003; De la Rosa, 2004). Then the log-likelihood will be optimized (e.g. minimized) together with a log-MRF to obtain the MAP image estimation. A variety of applications in signal processing and instrumentation, are based in statistical modeling analysis. One of the most used is the linear regression model (simple or multi-variable in the case of images)

$$y_{i,j} = x_{i,j}^{\top}\theta_{i,j} + e_{i,j}, \text{ with } e \sim p(e), \tag{1}$$

where y represents the response (observed data, acquired data or explained variables), to x explicative variables for $i = 1, \ldots, N$ and $j = 1, \ldots, M$, and a system response parameterized by θ (being θ a linear operator which models the image degradation (or PSF)) which is associated to data (y, x). In some applications θ are functional parameters which will be estimated by an identification procedure if x are known, but if θ are known and x are unknown, the estimation is made about x, or the estimation can be made for both cases (e.g. blind deconvolution). The e variables are independent random processes identically distributed accordingly to $p(e)$. A natural extension of the linear regression model is the non-linear regression model based on a parameterized function $f(x,\theta)$ (see equation (2)). This function is nonlinear with respect to the parameters, and its use is also considered because it has been shown in a large variety of signal processing and control applications that the modeling could be more realistic when using nonlinear functions. The perturbations affecting the analyzed system are also modeled as stochastic processes. Then, for this case:

$$y_{i,j} = f(x,\theta)_{i,j} + e_{i,j}, \text{ with } e \sim p(e). \tag{2}$$

Another source of information which imposes a key rule in the image processing context, is the contextual or spatial information that represents the correlation between the intensity values of a neighborhood of pixels well specified. The modellig, when using MRF, takes into account such spatial interaction and it was introduced and formalized in (Besag, 1974), and extended in some pioneering works (Besag, 1986; Bouman and Sauer, 1993; Geman and Geman, 1984; Sauer and Bouman, 1992). Combining both kinds of information into a statistical framework, the restoration is led by an estimation procedure given the MAP of the true images when the distortion functionals are known. The algorithms implemented in this chapter were developed considering a degraded signal, where the resulting non-linear recursive filters show excellent characteristics to preserve all the details contained in the image and, on the other hand, they smooth the noise components. Some existent optimization methods are commented, since the optimization (e.g. maximization or minimization) task is central during the reconstruction and its performance depends on the structure of the cost functionals. Finally, a comparison between some existent Bayesian schemes and new proposed for noise filtering and image deblurring is presented. Particularly, five MAP estimation schemes are implemented where the first two schemes use two MRF; the semi-Huber (SH) potential function which is proposed as an extension of some previous works (De la Rosa and Fleury, 2006; De la Rosa et al., 2007), and the generalized Gaussian MRF (GGMRF) introduced in (Bouman and Sauer, 1993) in both cases, Gaussian noise is assumed. The other three MAP schemes correspond to new MAP entropy estimators (MAPEE) for image filtering, where unknown noise pdf assumptions are made and the generalized Gaussian MRF is also used.

The rest of this chapter is organized as follows. Section 2 describes the general definition of a MRF and the proposal of the MAP estimator. The potential functions must be proposed to conduct adequately the inversion process, some functions are described in section 3 where the convexity level is the key to formulate an adequate criterion to be maximized or equivalently minimized. In sections 4 and 5 are deduced some MAP estimators and commented some optimization techniques resulting from different MRF structures for Gaussian noise assumptions, and MAPEE estimators for unknown noise pdf. Section 6 introduces the Kernel structures used for MAPEE estimators, while in section 7 results for Gaussian and non-Gaussian restoration are discussed. Finally, some conclusions and comments are given in section 8.

2. MAP estimation and Markov random fields

The problem of image estimation (e.g. restoration) into a Bayesian framework deals with the solution of an inverse problem, where the estimation process is carried out in a whole stochastic environment. The most popular estimators used nowadays are:

Maximum Likelihood estimator (ML): A classical procedure to estimate x when θ is known (from equations (1) and (2)), is based in a cost function or criterion $\mathcal{J}(x)$ which varies in function $\psi(\cdot)$ of residuals or noise $e(x)$, where:

$$e_{i,j}(x) = y_{i,j} - x_{i,j}^{\top}\theta_{i,j} \quad \text{or} \quad e_{i,j}(x) = y_{i,j} - f(x,\theta)_{i,j}, \tag{3}$$

and so

$$\mathcal{J}(x) = \sum_{i=1}^{N}\sum_{j=1}^{M}\psi(e_{i,j}(x)). \tag{4}$$

This is, for example, the case of the maximum likelihood (ML) estimator:

$$\begin{aligned} \widehat{x}_{\mathbf{ML}} &= \arg\max_{x\in\mathbb{X}} p(y|x) = \arg\min_{x\in\mathbb{X}} \left(-\log p(y|x)\right), \\ &= \arg\min_{x\in\mathbb{X}} \left(-\sum_{i=1}^{N}\sum_{j=1}^{M}\log p(e_{i,j}(x))\right). \end{aligned} \tag{5}$$

The ML estimator is optimal when all information about the distribution $p(e)$ is accessible, which is the case for Gaussian noise. When the knowledge about $p(e)$ is imprecise or wrong, the estimator $\widehat{x}_{\mathbf{ML}}$ is possibly suboptimal. Moreover, under certain circumstances, in image processing restoration, it results in an ill-posed problem or produces excessive noise and also causes smooth of edges. The regularization of the ML estimator gives both a more effective approach to reduce noise and smoothness (in fact, it depends on the mathematical structure of the regularization term). In a probabilistic framework, the regularization of the ML estimator leads to the Bayesian approach, where it is important to exploit all known information or so called prior information about any process under study, which gives a better statistical estimator called

Maximum A Posteriori (MAP) estimator:

$$\begin{aligned}\widehat{x}_{\mathbf{MAP}} &= \arg\max_{x\in\mathbb{X}} p(x|y), \\ &= \arg\max_{x\in\mathbb{X}} \left(\log p(y|x) + \log g(x)\right), \\ &= \arg\min_{x\in\mathbb{X}} \left(-\log p(y|x) - \log g(x)\right).\end{aligned} \tag{6}$$

In this case, the estimator is regularized by using a MRF function $g(x)$ which models all prior information as a whole probability distribution, where $\mathbb{X}$ is the set of pixels x capable to maximize $p(x|y)$, and $p(y|x)$ is the likelihood function from y given x.

The Markov random fields (MRF) can be represented in a generic way by using the following equation:

$$g(x) = \frac{1}{Z}\exp\left(-\sum_{c\in\mathbb{C}} V_c(x)\right), \tag{7}$$

where Z is a normalization constant, $\mathbb{C}$ is a set of "cliques" c or local neighborhood of pixels, and $V_c(x)$ is a weighting function given over the local neighborhood. Generally, the "cliques" correspond to the possible set of neighborhoods of pixels. A theorem introduced by Hammersley-Clifford (Besag, 1974; Geman and Geman, 1984) probes the equivalence between the Gibbs distribution and the MRFs. The Markov random fields have the capacity to represent various images sources. The main partial disadvantage using MRFs is that the estimation procedure deals with local minimization schemes (generally it grows the computation time), while the proposal of global minimization schemes has been recently introduced by modifying the local structure of the MRFs in order to establish a better trade-off between quality of reconstruction and computation time. There is a variety of MRF models which depend on the cost functions also known as potential functions that can be used. Each potential function characterizes the interactions between pixels in the same local group. As an example, the following family represents convex functions:

$$\rho(\Delta) = |\Delta|^p \tag{8}$$

where $\Delta = \lambda[x_s - x_r]$, λ is a constant parameter to be chosen, and p takes constant values such as $p \geq 1$ accordingly to the theorem 2 in (Bouman and Sauer, 1993).

3. MRFs and convexity of potential functions

In recent works (Champagnat and Idier, 2004; Ciuciu and Idier, 2002; Ciuciu et al., 2001; Giovannelli et al., 2002; Idier, 2001; Rivera and Marroquin, 2003; 2004; Rivera, 2005) some new potential functions were introduced. Such proposed functions are semi-quadratic functionals or half-quadratic and they characterize certain convexity into the regularization term (Geman and Reinolds, 1992; Geman and Yang, 1995)(eg. extension of penalization) which permits to build efficient and robust estimators in the sense of data preservation which is linked to the original or source image. Also, the necessary computation time decreases with respect to other proposed schemes as shown in (Chan et al., 2006; Durand and Nikolova, 2006a;b; Nikolova, 2006; 2005; Nikolova and Ng, 2005; Nikolova and Chan, 2007) and

(Labat and Idier, 2006; Labat, 2006) in the case of non-convex and convex potential functions. On the other hand, in previous works from (Gibbs, 2000) it has been proposed a way to obtain the posterior distribution of the images; in this case, it is necessary to use sophisticated stochastic simulation techniques based on the Markov Chain Monte Carlo (MCMC) methods (Neal, 1993; Robert and Casella, 2004). If it is possible to obtain the posterior distribution of any image, thus, it is also possible to sample from such posterior distribution and obtain the MAP estimator, or other estimators such as the median estimator which is sensible to be as well as the MAP estimator under certain circumstances imposed by the noise structure, the MAP and the median estimators search the principal mode of the posterior distribution.

In the present chapter two already reported potential functions are revised and their performance is compared. The generalized Guassian MRF introduced in (Bouman and Sauer, 1993; Sauer and Bouman, 1992) is compared with respect to semi-Huber functional used in problems of one dimensional estimation in (De la Rosa and Fleury, 2006).

3.1 Generalized Gaussian MRF (GGMRF)

If one considers to generalize the Gaussian MRF (when $p = q = 2$ one has a GMRF, see equation (15)) as proposed by Bouman, where the generalized potential functions correspond to

$$\rho_1(\Delta) = |\Delta|^p , \quad 1 < p < 2 \tag{9}$$

obtaining the GGMRF

$$\log g(x) = -\lambda^p \left(\sum_{s \in S} a_s x_s^p + \sum_{\{s,r\} \in C} b_{sr} |x_s - x_r|^p \right) + \text{ct}, \tag{10}$$

where ct is a constant term, and theoretically $a_s > 0$ and $b_{sr} > 0$, s is the site or pixel of interest and S is the set of sites into the whole MRF, and r corresponds to the local neighbors. In practice and for Gaussian noise assumptions, it is recommended to take $a_s = 0$, assuring the unicity of $\widehat{x}_{\mathbf{MAP}}$, thus the GGMRF can be written as

$$\log g(x) = -\lambda^p \left(\sum_{\{s,r\} \in C} b_{sr} |x_s - x_r|^p \right) + \text{ct}, \tag{11}$$

and from equation (2), $\log p(y|x)$ is strictly convex and so $\widehat{x}_{\mathbf{MAP}}$ is continuous in y, and in p. On the other hand, the MAPEE approach proposed here takes into account that the noise pdf is unknown or non-Gaussian. For this particular case, it is recommended to take $a_s = 1$, since the likelihood term is not given in terms of quadratic $q = 2$ functional, and in order to relax the possible non-convexity problem it has been used

$$\log g(x) = -\lambda^p \left(\sum_{s \in S} a_s x_s^2 + \sum_{\{s,r\} \in C} b_{sr} |x_s - x_r|^p \right) + \text{ct}, \tag{12}$$

also ensuring that $\log p(y|x)$ is convex and so $\widehat{x}_{\mathbf{MAPEE}}$ is continuous in y, and in p. The choice of p is capital, since it constrains the convergence speed of the local or global estimator, and the quality of the restored image.

3.2 Semi-Huber potential function

In order to assure completely the robustness into the edge preserving image filtering, diminishing at the same time the convergence speed, the Huber–like norm or semi–Huber (SH) potential function is proposed as a half-quadratic (HQ) function. Such functional has been used in one dimensional robust estimation as described in (De la Rosa and Fleury, 2006) for the case of non-linear regression. This function is adjusted in two dimensions according to the following equation:

$$\log g(x) = -\lambda \left(\sum_{\{s,r\}\in\mathbb{C}} b_{sr}\rho_2(x) \right) + \text{ct}, \tag{13}$$

where

$$\rho_2(x) = \frac{\Delta_0^2}{2}\left(\sqrt{1+\frac{4\varphi_1(x)}{\Delta_0^2}}-1\right),$$

and where $\Delta_0 > 0$ is a constant value, b_{sr} is a constant that depends on the distance between the r and s pixels, and $\varphi_1(x) = e^2$ where $e = (x_s - x_r)$. The potential function $\rho_2(x)$ fulfills the following conditions

$$\begin{aligned}
\rho_2(x) &\geq 0,\ \forall x \quad \text{with } \rho_2(0) = 0,\\
\psi(x) &\equiv \partial\rho_2(x)/\partial x, \text{ exists},\\
\rho_2(x) &= \rho_2(-x), \text{ is symmetric},\\
w(x) &\equiv \tfrac{\psi(x)}{2x}, \text{ exists},\\
\lim_{x\to+\infty} w(x) &= \mu,\ 0 \leq \mu < +\infty,\\
\lim_{x\to+0} w(x) &= M,\ 0 < M < +\infty.
\end{aligned} \tag{14}$$

4. MAP estimators for Gaussian noise and optimization

In this section some estimators are deduced. The single problem of filtering noise to restore an observed signal y leads to establish the estimators.

4.1 Image filtering and optimization

The observation equation could be

$$y = x + e, \text{ where } e \sim \mathcal{N}(0, I\sigma_n^2),$$

where I is the identity matrix. For this particular problem when using the GGMRF and under hypothesis of Gaussian noise with variance σ_n^2, the MAP estimator is given by,

$$\widehat{x}_{\mathbf{MAP1}} = \arg\min_{x\in\mathbb{X}} \left\{ \sum_{s\in\mathbb{S}} |y_s - x_s|^q + \sigma^q\lambda^p \sum_{\{s,r\}\in\mathbb{C}} b_{s-r}|x_s - x_r|^p \right\}, \tag{15}$$

the minimization in equation (15) or optimization problem leads to consider various methods (Allain et al., 2006; Chan et al., 2006; Nikolova, 2006; 2005; Nikolova and Ng, 2005; Nikolova and Chan, 2007):

- global iterative techniques such as: the descendent gradient (Nikolova and Chan, 2007), conjugate gradient (Rivera and Marroquin, 2003) (for recent propositions one can consult the work (Labat and Idier, 2006; Labat, 2006)), Gauss-Seidel, Over-relaxed methods, etc.
- local minimization techniques: minimization at each pixel x_s (which generally needs more time, but from our point of view are more precise), where also some of the above methods can be used.

In this work the local techniques were used, the expectation maximization (EM) was not implemented, nor complete half-quadratic scheme as proposed in (Geman and Reinolds, 1992) and in (Geman and Yang, 1995), since all hyper-parameters included into the potential functions were chosen heuristically or according to values proposed in references. Only, the step of minimization with respect to x was implemented to probe convergence of estimators. For example, the local MAP estimator for the GGMRF is given by

$$\widehat{x}_{s1} = \arg\min_{x \in \mathbb{X}} \left\{ |y_s - x_s|^q + \sigma^q \lambda^p \sum_{r \in \partial \mathbf{s}} b_{r-s} |x_s - x_r|^p \right\}, \tag{16}$$

where, according to the value of parameters p and q, the performance of such estimator varies. For example, if $p = q = 2$, one has the Gaussian condition of the potential function where the obtained estimator is similar to the least-squares one (L_2 norm) since the likelihood function is quadratic, with an additional quadratic term of penalization which degrades the estimated image

$$\widehat{x}_s = \frac{y_s + (\sigma\lambda)^2 \sum_{r \in \partial \mathbf{s}} b_{r-s} x_r}{1 + (\sigma\lambda)^2 \sum_{r \in \partial \mathbf{s}} b_{r-s}}. \tag{17}$$

On the other hand, in the case of $p = q = 1$, the criterion is absolute (L_1 norm), and the estimator converges to the median estimator, which in practice, is difficult to implement in a precise way

$$\widehat{x}_s = \text{median}\left(y_s, x_{r_1}, \ldots, x_{r_l}\right). \tag{18}$$

This criterion is not differentiable at zero and this fact causes instability in the minimization procedure. For intermediate values of p and q these estimators become sub-optimal, and the iterated methods can be used to minimize the obtained criterions. Such iterative methods are the sub–gradient, or the Levenberg–Marquardt method of MATLAB 7, the last method was used as optimization technique in this work. For cases where $q \neq p$, for example $q = 2$ and $1 < p < 2$, some studies and different propositions of a priori functions have been proposed in (Durand and Nikolova, 2006a;b; Nikolova, 2006; 2005; Nikolova and Ng, 2005; Nikolova and Chan, 2007), particulary in (Durand and Nikolova, 2006a;b; Nikolova, 2006; Nikolova and Ng, 2005) where non-convex regularized least-squares schemes are deduced and its convergence is analyzed.

The local or global condition of the estimator depends thus on

1) if one has values of $1 < p < 2$: the estimator $\widehat{x}_{min.loc} \to \widehat{x}_{min.glob}$, which means that a local minimum would coincide with a global minimum,

2) moreover, if $p \neq q$, the criterion is not homogeneous, but: $\widehat{x}(\alpha y, \lambda) = \alpha \widehat{x}(y, \alpha^{1-q/p}\lambda)$ is convex, assuring the convergence and existence of the estimator which is continuous with respect to p.

Moreover, when the noise is Gaussian, the value of $q = 2$ is a good choice, but if the noise is non-Gaussian, and if the structure of noise is known, thus the likelihood term changes giving a particular estimator such as that proposed in (Bertaux et al., 2004), or in (Cai et al, 2008), giving some properties of robustness to the minimization procedure. If the structure of noise is supposed unknown, still one could reconsider the GGMRF with values for $q \in (1, 2]$, or consider also another type of MRFs as those described in some works of Idier (Champagnat and Idier, 2004; Ciuciu and Idier, 2002; Ciuciu et al., 2001; Giovannelli et al., 2002) and Nikolova (Nikolova, 2006; 2005; Nikolova and Ng, 2005; Nikolova and Chan, 2007).

A second MAP estimator can be obtained when using the SH potential function, the global estimator can be described by the equation

$$\widehat{x}_{\mathbf{MAP2}} = \arg\min_{x \in \mathbb{X}} \left\{ \sum_{s \in \mathbb{S}} |y_s - x_s|^2 + \lambda \left(\sum_{\{s,r\} \in \mathbb{C}} b_{s-r} \rho_2(x) \right) \right\}. \tag{19}$$

As in the previous MAP estimator, it has been proposed to implement the local estimator which leads to a similar expression for the first local MAP estimator (see equation (16)), that is

$$\widehat{x}_{s2} = \arg\min_{x \in \mathbb{X}} \left\{ |y_s - x_s|^2 + \lambda \left(\sum_{r \in \partial \mathbf{s}} b_{s-r} \rho_2(x) \right) \right\}. \tag{20}$$

The use of a prior distribution function based on the logarithm, with any degree of convexity and quasi-homogeneous, permits to consider a variety of possible choices of potential functions. Maybe, the most important challenges that must be well solved are: the adequate selection of hyper-parameters from potential functions, where different versions of the EM algorithms try to tackle this problem (Champagnat and Idier, 2004; Giovannelli et al., 2002; Idier, 2001; Nikolova and Ng, 2005), another is the minimization procedure which in any sense will regulate the convergence speed as proposed in (Allain et al., 2006; Geman and Reinolds, 1992; Geman and Yang, 1995; Labat and Idier, 2006; Labat, 2006; Nikolova, 2006; 2005; Rivera and Marroquin, 2003), etc.

4.2 Image deconvolution

On the other hand, for the problem of image deblurring to restore an observed signal y, the observation equation used is given by

$$y = \Theta x + e, \text{ with } e \sim \mathcal{N}(0, I\sigma_n^2). \tag{21}$$

Now, for the two previous MAP estimators the likelihood term changes, such that,

$$\widehat{x}_{\mathbf{MAP}_k} = \arg\min_{x \in \mathbb{X}} \left\{ \sum_{s \in \mathbb{S}} |y_s - \Theta x_s|^2 - \log g(x) \right\}, \tag{22}$$

where the matrix Θ is known and given by the following truncated Gaussian blurring function,

$$\theta(i,j) = \exp\left(\frac{-i^2 - j^2}{2\sigma_b^2}\right), \text{ for } -3 \leq i,j \leq 3, \tag{23}$$

as used also in (Nikolova et al., 2010), with $\sigma_b = 1.5$. And $k = 1,2$ according to the GGMRF, and the SH potential functions. Here, the results were improved combining ideas introduced in a similar Bayesian way by Levin (Levin et al., 2007a;b) adding a Sparse prior (SP) for filtering and then reconstructing the image.

5. MAP entropy estimators (EE) for unknown noise pdf

Our proposition for a new MAP scheme is to use a generalized Gaussian MRF introduced in section 3.1, together with three kernel estimators used in (De la Rosa and Fleury, 2002; De la Rosa et al., 2003; De la Rosa, 2004) to obtain cost functionals or criterions based on the entropy of the approximated likelihood function (first term of equation (6)) $\widehat{p}_{n,h}(e)$. Thus, $-\log p(y|x)$ is built on the basis of the entropy of an estimate (EE) version $\widehat{p}_{n,h}(e)$ of the distribution $p(e)$. A first proposition is due to Pronzato and Thierry (Pronzato and Thierry, 2000a;b; 2001). The approximation is obtained using the classical kernel estimators which uses the empirical distribution of the random vector $e_1(x), \ldots, e_n(x)$. The next expression denote such estimators:

$$\widehat{p}_{n,h}(e) = \widehat{p}_{n,h}(e|e_1(x), \ldots, e_n(x)) = \frac{1}{n}\sum_{i=1}^{n} K_h\left(e - e_i\right). \tag{24}$$

This expression assumes the hypothesis that $p(e)$ is symmetric, two times differentiable and positive, indeed, it is assumed that $K(z)$ is a kernel weighted function which satisfies some imposed conditions treated in (Masry, 1983) and subsequently taken back by Devroye (Devroye, 1992; 1989; Devroye and Krzyzàk, 1999; Devroye, 1997), Berlinet (Berlinet and Devroye, 1994), and Loader (Loader, 1999) in some of their research work. The bandwidth $h = h_n$ is given in function of the sample size n. This parameter could be considered as a sequence of positive numbers that must satisfy: $h_n \to 0$ and $nh_n \to \infty$ when $n \to \infty$. The strong uniform consistency of $\widehat{p}_{n,h}(e)$ and its convergence toward $p(e)$, depend on a convenable procedure of bandwidth selection. A simple and faster procedure which has been retained in this work is the technique proposed and developed by Terrell (Terrell, 1990; Terrell and Scott, 1985). In the two dimensional kernel cases, the previous idea has been extended in this work accordingly to the equation:

$$\begin{aligned}\widehat{p}_{n,h}(e) &= \widehat{p}_{n,h}(e|e_{1,1}(x), \ldots, e_{n,n}(x)) \\ &= \frac{1}{n^2}\sum_{k=1}^{n}\sum_{l=1}^{n} K_h\left(e - e_{k,l}\right).\end{aligned} \tag{25}$$

If the convergence and consistence of $\widehat{p}_{n,h}(e)$ are assumed, such that $\widehat{p}_{n,h}(e) \to p(e)$, then the entropy criterion over $\widehat{p}_{n,h}(e)$ can be approximated to $-\log p(y|x)$. The fact that the entropy of any probability density function is invariant by translation, leads to consider one practical artifact to build a suitable criterion. An extended criterion $\widehat{p}_{n,h}(e_E)$ is based on the residuals or noise extended vector which is given by: $\boldsymbol{e}_E = \{e_{1,1}(x), \ldots, e_{n,n}(x), -e_{1,1}(x), \ldots, e_{n,n}(x)\}$

and on a suitable choice of h:

$$\mathcal{J}_e(x) = \mathrm{H}_A\left(\widehat{p}_{n,h}(\boldsymbol{e}_E)\right) \approx -\log p(y|x), \tag{26}$$

where $\mathrm{H}_A(f) = -\int_{-A_n}^{A_n} f(x)\log f(x)dx$. Finally, if we assume that the EE is a version of the log-likelihood function into the MAP estimator, then a general version of the MAP-entropy estimator (MAPEE) which assumes unknown noise pdf can be constructed from the fact that $-\log p(y|x)$ can be approximated by the entropy of an estimate version $\widehat{p}_{n,h}(e)$ of the distribution $p(e)$, that is $\mathrm{H}_A\left(\widehat{p}_{n,h}(e_E)\right)$, thus:

$$\widehat{x}_{\mathbf{MAPEE}} = \arg\min_{x\in\mathbb{X}} \left\{\mathrm{H}_A\left(\widehat{p}_{n,h}(e_E)\right) - \log g(x)\right\}. \tag{27}$$

Now, substituting a particular $\log g(x)$ such as the GGMRF into the equation (27) one could obtain at least three MAPEE estimators given by

$$\widehat{x}_{\mathbf{MAPEE}_m} = \arg\min_{x\in\mathbb{X}} \left\{\mathrm{H}_A\left(\widehat{p}_{n,h}(e_E)\right) - \lambda^p\left(\sum_{s\in\mathbb{S}} a_s x_s^2 + \sum_{\{s,r\}\in\mathbb{C}} b_{sr}|x_s - x_r|^p\right)\right\}, \tag{28}$$

for $m = 1,2,3$ according to the three following kernels: Normal, cosine and Hilbert.

6. Kernel structures

A function of the form $K(z)$ is assumed as a fixed kernel $K_h(z) = 1/(h^d)K(z/h)$, where h is called the kernel bandwidth and $h > 0$. The fundamental problem in kernel density estimation lies in both the selection of an appropriate value for h and the selection of the kernel structure. The choice of $K(z)$ could depend on the smoothness of $p(e)$. Three different kernels or nonparametric schemes are reviewed in this section to approximate $\widehat{p}_{n,h}(e_E)$. The gaussian kernel, which has proved to give good performance when h is selected by using the over-smoothed principle introduced by Terrell (Terrell, 1990; Terrell and Scott, 1985) when the errors vector is generally of finite length n. Second kernel is the cosine based weights functions, where h is viewed in a different way. Finally, the third kernel is obtained from a recent class of Hilbert kernels (Devroye and Krzyżak, 1999). It avoids the bandwidth h selection and its performance depends on other parameters, whose selection is very easy (parameters d and k are defined in section 6.3).

6.1 Normal or gaussian kernel

Among the different classical kernels (Berlinet and Devroye, 1994), the gaussian kernel has been chosen since it is one of the most popular and easy to implement estimator. The following expression resumes this estimator by a sum of exponentials:

$$\widehat{p}_{n,h}(z) = \frac{1}{n^2 h\sqrt{2\pi}} \sum_{k=1}^{n}\sum_{l=1}^{n} \exp\left(-\frac{(z - z_{k,l})^2}{2h^2}\right). \tag{29}$$

In such a case, and considering that a fixed kernel structure has been chosen, Terrell (Terrell, 1990) proposes to use an over-smoothed bandwidth h that corresponds to:

$$h = 3\left(\frac{1}{2\sqrt{\pi}(35)}\right)^{\frac{1}{5}} \sigma n^{-\frac{1}{5}},$$

this bandwidth value guarantees the minimization of the Mean Integrated Squared Error (MISE), σ is the standard deviation of the sample z, and $\int K(z)^2 dz = \frac{1}{(2\sqrt{\pi})}$. Under mild conditions, the kernel density estimates based on the over-smoothing principle are consistent and for sufficiently large sample sizes, they will display all information present in the underlying errors density $p(e)$, we chose $n \times n$ array of samples $z_{k,l}$ near z.

6.2 Cosine based weights functions

A sequence of special weight cosine functions

$$c_q(z) = 1/(A_q)\cos^{2q}(z/2)$$

requires only $O(q^2 n)$ arithmetic operations, where q is a slowly growing function that increases without bound together with n (i.e. $q(n) < n$ or $q(n) > n$). This estimator is similar to the kernel classical estimators and evaluates a series expansion in a more efficient way. The role of h is replaced by q ($c_q(z) \equiv K_h(z)$) and the efficiency is attained (according to the time of calculus), since the selection of q is generally more simple than h. Thus (25) is equivalent to

$$\widehat{p}_{n,q}(z) = \frac{1}{n^2 A_q} \sum_{k=1}^{n} \sum_{l=1}^{n} \left(\frac{1+\cos(z - z_{k,l})}{2}\right)^q, \tag{30}$$

where the A_q value could be approximated by

$$A_q \approx \frac{2\sqrt{\pi}}{\sqrt{q}}.$$

Sufficient consistency and convergence conditions are given in (Eğecioğlu and Srinivasan, 2000) for the one dimensional case.

6.3 The Hilbert kernel

Finally, other kernel density estimates called the Hilbert kernel estimate is used. The equation $K_h(z) = 1/(h^d)K(z/h)$ is considered equivalent to $K(u) = 1/\|u\|^d$, where the smoothing factor h is canceled obtaining:

$$\widehat{p}_n(z) = \frac{1}{n^2} \sum_{k=1}^{n} \sum_{l=1}^{n} \frac{1}{\|z - z_{k,l}\|^d}. \tag{31}$$

The Hilbert estimates are viewed as a universally consistent density estimate whose expected performance (L_1, L_∞, pointwise) is monotone in n (at least in theory) for all densities. The consistency of this class of estimators is proved in Devroye and Krzyżak (1999)(see theorem 2). The Hilbert density estimate of order k ($k > 0$) is a redefined subclass that avoids the infinite peaks produced during estimation, in one dimensional case and using the value of $k = 2$ the kernel estimate is given by:

$$\widehat{p}_n(z) = \sqrt{\frac{4}{V_d^2 \pi n(n-1)\log n} \sum_{1 \leq i < j \leq n} \frac{1}{\mathrm{Den}_{i,j}}}, \tag{32}$$

where $\mathrm{Den}_{i,j} = \|z - z_i\|^{2d} + \|z - z_j\|^{2d}$ and V_d is the volume of the unit ball in $\mathbb{R}^b$. This last expression is also called Cauchy density estimate, due to its similarity to the multivariate Cauchy density, $\|\cdot\|$ denotes the L_2 metric on $\mathbb{R}^d$. Finally, it is assumed that $\widehat{p}_n(z) \to p(z)$ at least in probability for almost all z. For a suitable choice of A_n and alternatively of h_n, q, or d and k, these estimators could be "blind asymptotically efficient". The asymptotic properties and the strong consistency of the truncated entropy estimators were analyzed in (Pronzato and Thierry, 2000a;b; 2001). More over, in some other papers, the power of these nonparametric tools have been largely used for different signal processing problems (Pronzato et al., 2004), (Wolsztynski et al., 2004a) – (Wolsztynski et al., 2005c).

7. Denoising and deblurring experiments

Results presented in this section were obtained experimenting extensively with four images: synthetic, Lena, Cameraman, and Boat (shown in Figure 1), to probe the performance of the presented estimators.

7.1 Image filtering for Gaussian noise

Some estimation results are presented when images are contaminated by Gaussian noise, and there are no other type of distortions (all $\theta_{i,j} = 1$). The first experiment was made considering that $\sigma_n = 5, 10, 15$. In the work (De la Rosa et al., 2003) some results were previously presented based on the analysis of a synthetic image and the standard image of "Lena", different levels of noise were added to the images: $e \sim \mathcal{N}(0, I\sigma_n^2)$, the values of σ_n are given such that the obtained degradation is perceptible and difficult to eliminate. The obtained results were compared using different values for p and λ preserving $q = 2$ (MAP1), and different values for Δ_0 and with $\lambda = 1$ (MAP2). Generally, with the two MAP estimators the filtering task gives good visual results preserving contours and smoothing noise (see Figures 2 and 3), but the computation time is different between them, the fastest estimator in general is the MAP2 (see image 2(d)), while the slowest is the MAP1 with $p = 1.2$. Table 1 shows the performance of the MAP estimators for the problem of filtering Gaussian noise for different images, where an objective evaluation is obtained accordingly to the peak signal to noise ratio (PSNR). Also the computation times in MATLAB are shown in Table 1. Such comparative evaluation shows that our proposed approach MAP2, gives better or similar performance with respect to MAP1. Some interesting applications of robust estimation are particulary focused in phase recovery from fringe patterns as presented in the work Villa et al. (2005), phase unwrapping, and some other problems in optical instrumentation. In this sense, some filtering results were thus obtained using the presented MAP estimators with similar results to those reported here. On the other hand, the use of half-quadratic potential functions permits flexibility for the computation time (Durand and Nikolova, 2006a;b; Nikolova and Ng, 2005). But still is a challenge to tune correctly the hyper-parameters to obtain a better performance in the sense

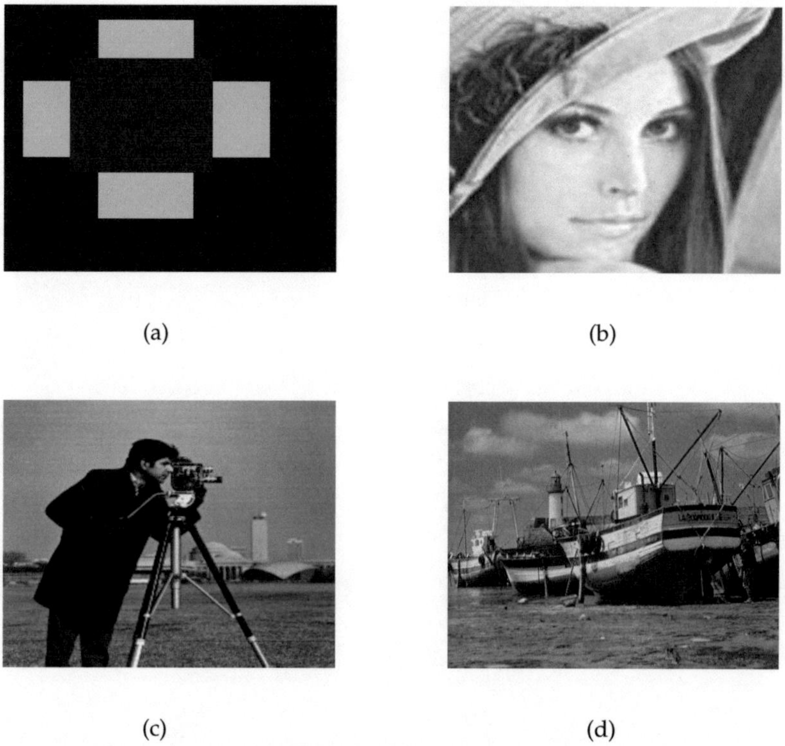

Fig. 1. The figure shows: (a) synthetical probe image; (b) the classical Lena image; (c) the classical Cameraman image; (d) the classical Boat image.

\	$\sigma_n = 15$	MAP1	MAP2
synthetic	PSNR noise	24.6	24.7
35 × 35	PSNR filt.	27.6	28.8
	Time (sec)	7.6	5.9
Lena	PSNR noise	24.5	24.5
120 × 120	PSNR filt.	28.9	29.1
	Time (sec)	80.6	75.3
Cameraman	PSNR noise	24.7	24.6
256 × 256	PSNR filt.	28.8	28.9
	Time (sec)	355.9	341.7
Boat	PSNR noise	24.6	24.6
512 × 512	PSNR filt.	29.5	29.4
	Time (sec)	1,545.5	1,243.3

Table 1. Results obtained when evaluating the filtering capacity of the two MAP estimators.

of restoration quality, the most simple potential function to tune is the semi-Huber (MAP2). Also, making the correct hypothesis over the noise could help to improve the performance of the estimator. This could be directly reflected by proposing a more adapted likelihood

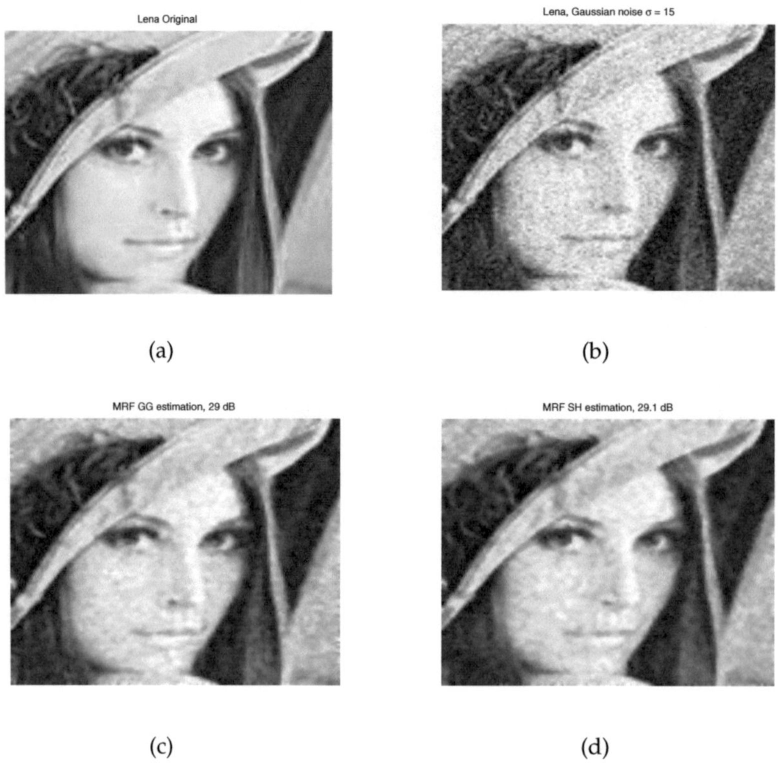

Fig. 2. Results for Lena standard image: (a) describes the original Lena image; (b) describes the noisy image using Gaussian noise with $\sigma_n = 15$; (c) filtered image using MAP1 (with $\lambda = 30$, $p = 1.2$); (d) filtered image using MAP2 (with $\Delta_0 = 20$).

function, as proposed in section 5 for cases of non-Gaussian noise or unknown pdf. More over, also the problem could be solved by using variational and partial differential equations as illustrated in the famous work of Perona and Malik (Perona and Malik, 1990), and some recent related works.

7.2 Image deconvolution

Now, for the problem of image deconvolution some estimation results are presented when images are contaminated by Gaussian noise, and Gaussian distortion (with $\sigma_b = 1.5$) blurring the image. This second experiment was carried out considering that $\sigma_n = 3, 5, 7$. The results were also compared using different values for Δ_0 and with $\lambda = 1$ (MAP2), different values for p and λ preserving $q = 2$ (MAP1). Figure 4 shows a comparison of results obtained for the Cameraman image accordingly to the two MAP estimators. One can notice that preserving values of hyper-parameters near those for the filtering case, the estimators smooth the noise but does not made a good recuperation of edges into the image. One must change the hyper-parameters values searching a trade of between the granularity of the noise and the sharpness of the image. Figure 5 shows the results obtained on the Cameraman image when using a combination of proposed estimators together with a Sparse prior (SP) deconvolution technique introduced in (Levin et al., 2007a;b), the improvement in restoration is visible. In

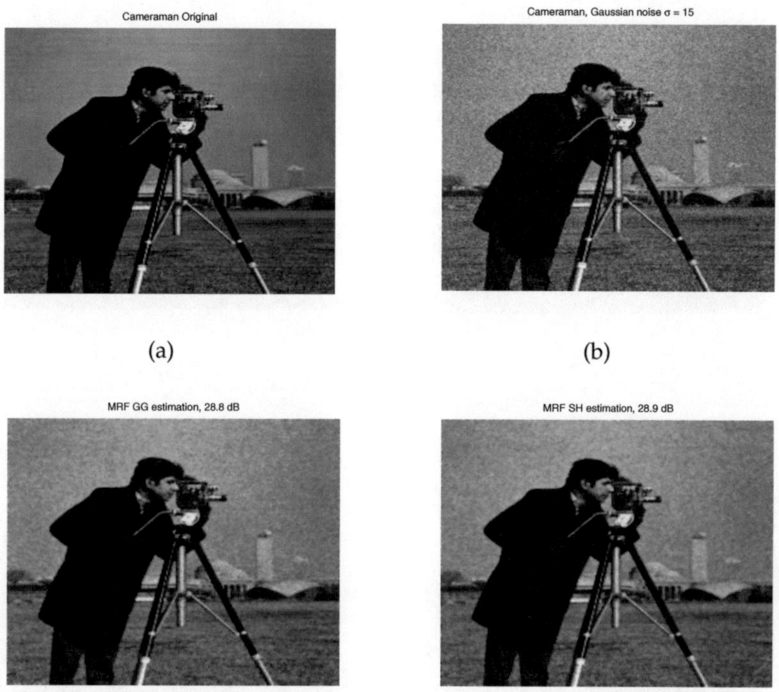

(a) (b) (c) (d)

Fig. 3. Results for Cameraman standard image: (a) describes the original Cameraman image; (b) describes the noisy image using Gaussian noise with $\sigma_n = 15$; (c) filtered image using MAP1 (with $\lambda = 30$, $p = 1.2$); (d) filtered image using MAP2 (with $\Delta_0 = 20$).

the first stage only the SP deconvolution is obtained (see image 5(b)), where some ringing and granularity artifacts occur due to noise and they cannot be correctly smoothed. Then, applying first the filtering of noise and then the SP deconvolution, the images 5(c) and 5(d) are obtained. In Table 2 it is shown the performance of the MAP estimators together with the SP deconvolution for three images giving similar results. An objective evaluation is made using the PSNR measure and also computation times in MATLAB are shown.

7.3 Image filtering for non-Gaussian noise

Now, for the problem of filtering non-Gaussian noise, some estimation results were obtained when images are contaminated by Gamma, Beta, Uniform and impulsive noise. Here, it is assumed that there are not other type of distortions (all $\theta_{i,j} = 1$). The observation equation then could be

$$y = x + e, \text{ where } e \sim \mathcal{G}(\alpha, \beta), e \sim \mathcal{B}(\alpha, \beta), \ldots$$

A third experiment was made considering Gamma noise where $\alpha = 1.5, 3.5, 7$ and $\beta = 1, 2, 3$, and also two factors of amplification of noise were used $\sigma_a = 5, 10$ ($\sigma_a \mathcal{G}(\alpha, \beta)$). The values of α and β are given in such a way that the obtained degradation is perceptible and difficult to eliminate.

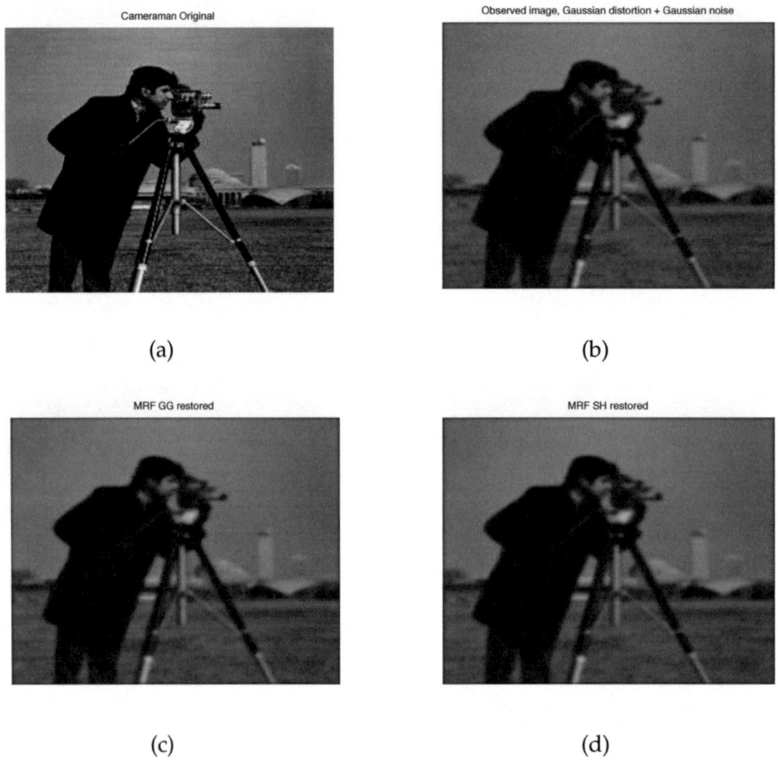

Fig. 4. Results for Cameraman standard image: (a) describes the original Cameraman image; (b) describes the distorted image using Gaussian noise with $\sigma_n = 3$; (c) partially restored image using MAP1 ($\lambda = 30$, $p = 1.2$); (d) partially restored image using MAP2 ($\Delta_0 = 20$).

	$\sigma_n = 3$	MAP1	MAP2
Lena	PSNR distorted	17.4	17.4
120 × 120	PSNR rest.	17.6	17.5
	PSNR rest. SP	20.8	20.8
	Time (sec)	91.3	58.9
Cameraman	PSNR distorted	19.3	19.3
256 × 256	PSNR rest.	19.4	19.4
	PSNR rest. SP	22.3	22.5
	Time (sec)	408.0	257.7
Boat	PSNR distorted	20.4	20.4
512 × 512	PSNR rest.	20.5	20.5
	PSNR rest. SP	25.8	25.6
	Time (sec)	1,606.5	1,014.9

Table 2. Results obtained when evaluating the deconvolution capacity of the two MAP estimators.

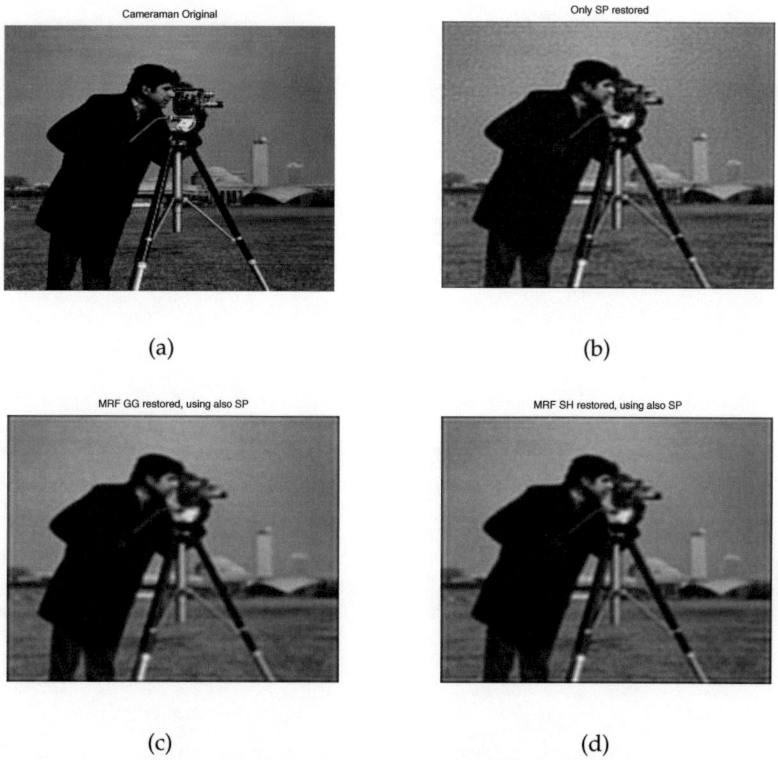

Fig. 5. Results for Cameraman standard image: (a) describes the original Cameraman image; (b) describes restored image using only a Sparse prior (SP) deconvolution technique Levin et al. (2007a); (c) restored image using MAP1 and SP ($\lambda = 0.15, p = 1.2$); (d) restored image using MAP2 and SP ($\Delta_0 = 20$).

Figure 6 shows the filtering of the synthetical image using the three MAPEE estimators introduced in section 5 for parameters $\lambda = 10$, $p = 1.2$ of the GGMRF. Generally, with the three estimators the filtering task gives good performing results (see also Figure 7 where a three dimensional-3D view is shown), but the computation times are different between them, the fastest estimator was MAPEE3 (image 6(d)). Some objective measurements were obtained for all probe images, such as the PSNR depicted in Table 3 which agree with the visual results. Also all times of computation are shown in Table 3. On the other hand, in the filtering case of the Cameraman and the Boat images the results coincide with those obtained for synthetic and Lena images. Visually one can see in Figures 8 and 9 the robustness performance of MAPEE estimators. Some other experiments were conducted for Beta and impulsive noise. For the case of Beta noise generation we choose $\alpha = 1.5, 2.5, 5, 7.5$ and $\beta = 1$, and also two factors of amplification of noise were used $\sigma_a = 10, 20$ ($\sigma_a \mathcal{B}(\alpha, \beta)$). The filtering results are promising for non-Gaussian noise, the obtained results for the Beta noise filtering also confirm the robustness of the proposed approach. Moreover, as one can see for impulsive noise with a 15% of outliers in Figures 10 and 11, the robustness is assured when using the three MAPEE estimators, where for instance, in the synthetic image case the PSNR was improved from 11.45 dB to 17.1 dB.

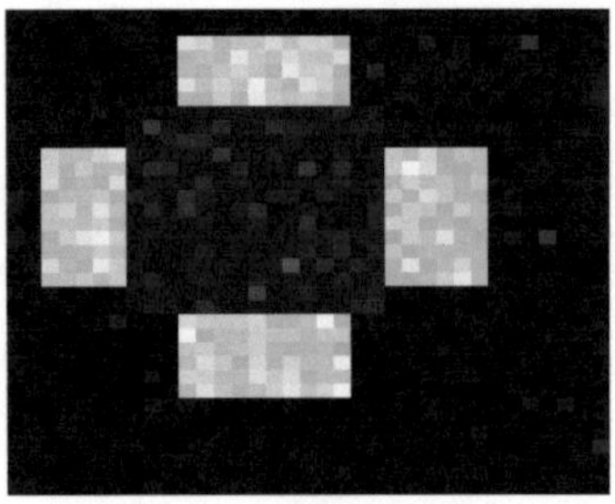

(a)

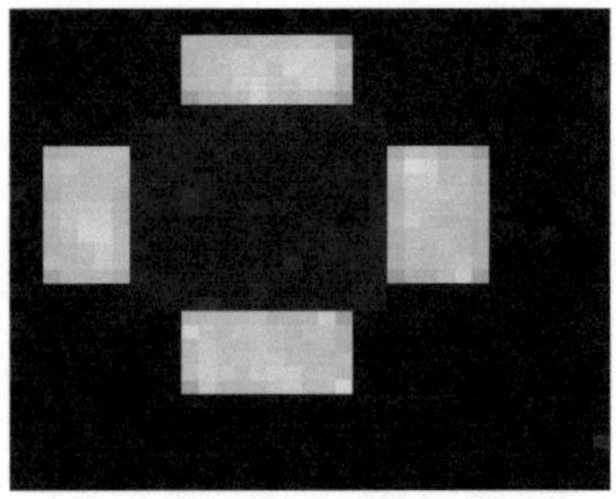

(b)

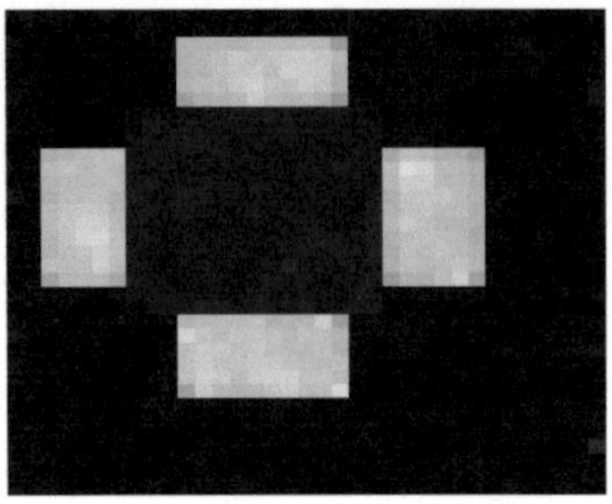

(c)

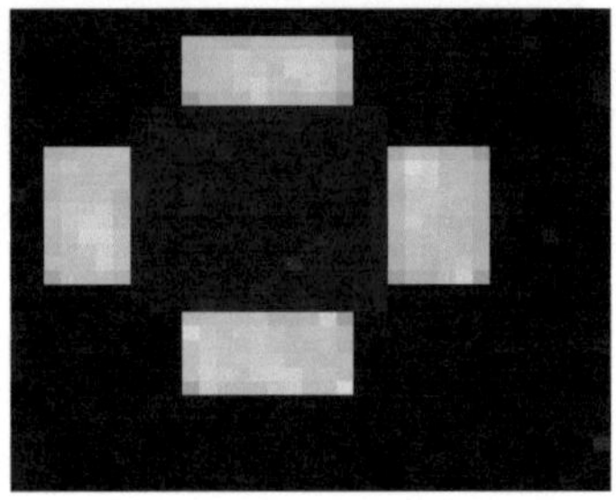

(d)

Fig. 6. Results for synthetical probe image: (a) describes the noisy synthetical image, for Gamma noise with $\alpha = 1.5$ and $\beta = 2$, and $\sigma_a = 5$; (b) filtered image using MAPEE1 (with Normal kernel); (c) filtered image using MAPEE2 (with cosine kernel); and, (d) filtered image using MAPEE3 (with Hilbert kernel).

	$\alpha = 1.5, \beta = 2$	MAPEE1	MAPEE2	MAPEE3
synthetic	PSNR noise	22.2	22.4	22.6
35×35	PSNR filtered	24.1	24.1	24.4
	Time (sec)	10.6	12.1	9.3
Lena	PSNR noise	16.3	16.2	16.3
120×120	PSNR filtered	17.9	17.9	18
	Time (sec)	123.6	141.6	109.8
Cameraman	PSNR noise	16.4	16.4	16.4
256×256	PSNR filtered	18.5	18.5	18.5
	Time (sec)	563.2	644.8	499.9
Boat	PSNR noise	16.3	16.4	16.4
512×512	PSNR filtered	18.7	18.7	18.8
	Time (sec)	2,340.1	2,569.8	2,063.5

Table 3. Results obtained in evaluating the filtering capacity of the three MAPEE estimators for Gamma $\mathcal{G}(\alpha, \beta)$ noise, with $\sigma_a = 10$.

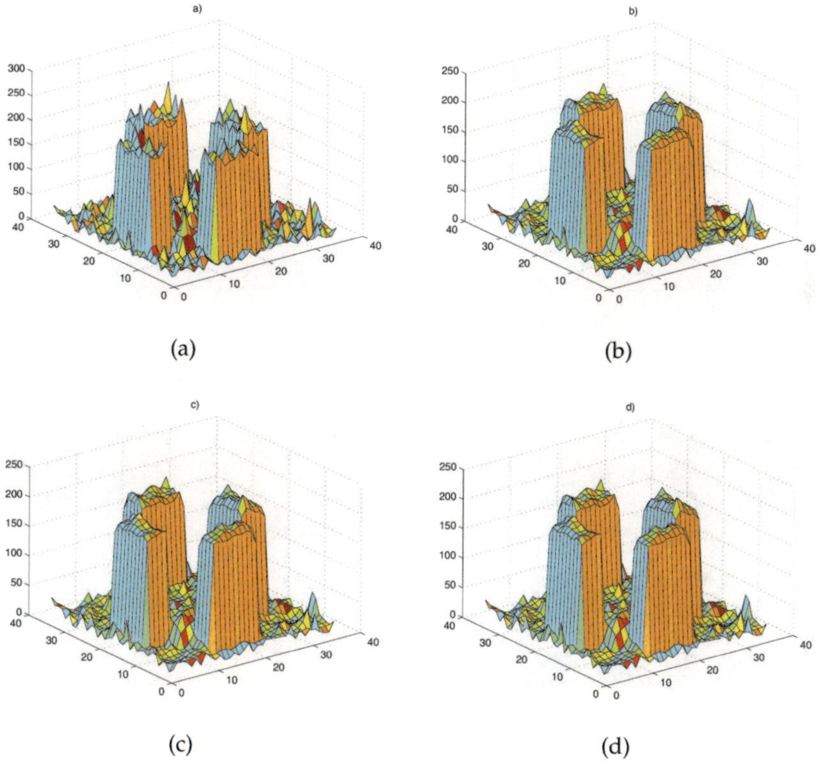

(a) (b)

(c) (d)

Fig. 7. Results for synthetical image (3-D view): (a) describes the noisy synthetical image, for Gamma noise; (b) filtered image using MAPEE1 (with Normal kernel); (c) filtered image using MAPEE2 (with cosine kernel); and, (d) filtered image using MAPEE3 (with Hilbert kernel).

Fig. 8. Results for Cameraman image: (a) describes the noisy Cameraman image, for Gamma noise with $\alpha = 3.5$ and $\beta = 2$, and $\sigma_a = 10$; (b) filtered image using MAPEE1 (with Normal kernel); (c) filtered image using MAPEE2 (with cosine kernel); and, (d) filtered image using MAPEE3 (with Hilbert kernel).

(a)

(b)

(c)

(d)

Fig. 9. Results for Boat image: (a) describes the noisy Boat image, for Gamma noise; (b) filtered image using MAPEE1 (with Normal kernel); (c) filtered image using MAPEE2 (with cosine kernel); and, (d) filtered image using MAPEE3 (with Hilbert kernel).

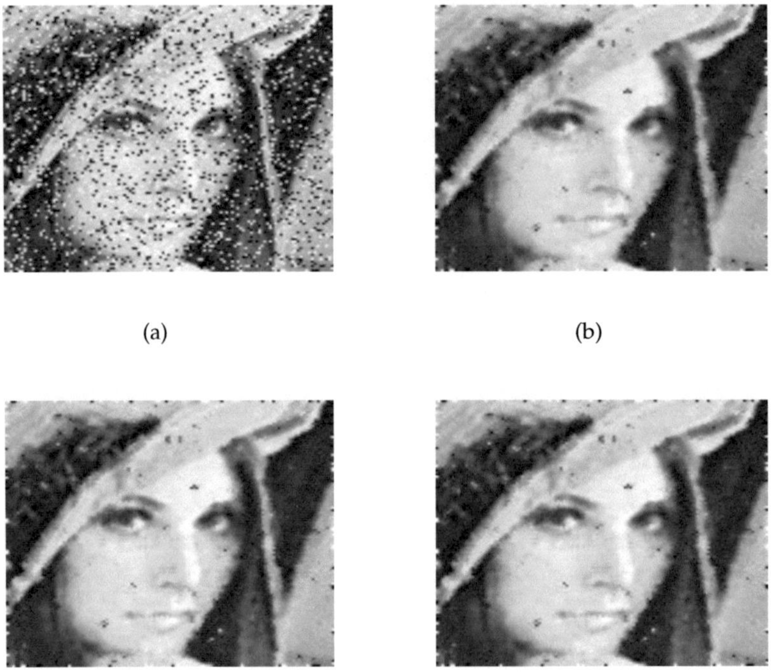

(a) (b)

(c) (d)

Fig. 10. Results for Lena image: (a) describes the noisy Lena image, for impulsive noise; (b) filtered image using MAPEE1 (with Normal kernel); (c) filtered image using MAPEE2 (with cosine kernel); and, (d) filtered image using MAPEE3 (with Hilbert kernel).

(a) (b)

(c) (d)

Fig. 11. Results for Cameraman image: (a) describes the noisy Cameraman image, for impulsive noise; (b) filtered image using MAPEE1 (with Normal kernel); (c) filtered image using MAPEE2 (with cosine kernel); and, (d) filtered image using MAPEE3 (with Hilbert kernel).

8. Conclusions and comments

Some advantages on the use of GGMRF as prior information into the Bayesian estimation (MAP1) are: the continuity of the estimator is assured as a function of the data values when $1 < p \leq 2$ even for Gaussian and non-Gaussian noise assumptions. The edge preserving is also assured, over all when $p \to 1$ and obviously it depends on the choice between the interval $1 < p < 2$. The use of other semi-quadratic or half-quadratic potential functions such as SH (MAP2) also presents some advantages: the convexity of these functions is relaxed with respect to the GGMRF. This fact gives as a result the decrement of the computation time, which is a good advantage over the GGMRF, since the tuning of hyper-parameters in the GGMRF is more complicated, one has more degrees of freedom. However, this problem can be solved as argued by Idier (Champagnat and Idier, 2004) and Rivera (Rivera and Marroquin, 2003) by implementing more sophisticated algorithms. The robustness in both cases is assured. Moreover, the advantages presented by those estimators could overcome the disadvantages, by experimenting largely with them, and establishing the aim to implement more sophisticated algorithms with the compromise to reduce computation time and better quality in restoration as recently exposed by Ruimin Pan (Pan and Reeves, 2006).

On the other hand, the performance and improvement of the MAPEE estimators for non-Gaussian noise filtering, could be classified in terms of simplicity and in terms of filtering quality. The obtained results for the three proposed estimators are favorable in general in the sense of robustness, and the fastest convergence is obtained for the MAPEE1 and MAPEE3 estimators (in the case of the MAPEE2 estimator $q = 40$, and for MAPEE3, $k = 2$, $d = 1$, and $V_d = 0.7071$. The value of q was changed alternatively in the range of $30 \leq q \leq 90$, and some performance improvement has been noticed). A general scheme for MAPEE estimators has been introduced and it works in real frameworks, where the nonlinearity conditions of some systems could be present. For future works it exists the interest to implement procedures of Bayesian estimation into high level programming that will be characterized into algorithms to be used in DSP cards, and tasks such as image reconstruction and segmentation. Also, one can probe to use MAPEE to processing real signals issued from real instrumentation or signal processing problems. The final objective of this work has been to contribute with a series of software tools for image analysis, focused for instance, in optical instrumentation tasks such as those treated in the works (Villa et al., 2005)–(Villa et al., 2010b) and (Rivera and Marroquin, 2004; Rivera, 2005) obtaining competitive results in filtering and reconstruction.

9. Acknowledgements

We would like to express our deep gratitude to the Secretaría de Educación Pública (SEP) of Mexico, this work was partially supported through the PIFI Mexican Program (PIFI 2010-2011).

10. References

Allain, M.; Idier, J. and Goussard, Y. (2006). On global and local convergence of half-quadratic algorithms, *IEEE Trans. Image Processing*, Vol. 15, No. 5, pp. 1130–1142.

Andrews, H. C. and Hunt, B. R. (1977). *Digital image restoration*, Prentice-Hall, Inc., New Jersey.

Berlinet, A. and Devroye, L. (1994). A comparison of kernel density estimates, *Publications de l'Intitut de Statistique de l'Université de Paris*, Vol. 38, No. 3, pp. 3–59.

Bertaux, N.; Frauel, Y.; Réfrégier, P. and Javidi, B. (2004). Speckle removal using a maximum-likelihood technique with isoline gray-level regularization, *J. Opt. Soc. Am. A*, Vol. 21, No. 12, pp. 2283–2291.

Besag, J. E. (1974). Spatial interaction and the statistical analysis of lattice systems, *J. Royal Stat. Soc. Ser. B*, Vol. B-36, pp. 192–236.

Besag, J. E. (1986). On the statistical analysis of dirty pictures, *J. Royal Stat. Soc. Ser. B*, Vol. B-48, pp. 259–302.

Bouman, C. and Sauer, K. (1993). A generalizaed Gaussian image model for edge-preserving MAP estimation, *IEEE Trans. on Image Processing*, Vol. 2, No. 3, pp. 296–310.

Cai, J.-F.; Chan R. H., and Nikolova, M. (2008). Two-phase approach for deblurring images corrupted by impulse plus Gaussian noise, *Inverse Problems and Imaging*, Vol. 2, No. 2, pp. 187–204.

Champagnat, K. and Idier, J. (2004). A conection between half-quadratic criteria and EM algorithms, *IEEE Signal Processing Letters*, Vol. 11, No. 9, pp. 709–712.

Chan, T. F.; Esedoglu, S. and Nikolova, M. (2006). Algorithms for finding global minimizers of image segmentation and denoising models, *SIAM J. on Applied Mathematics*, Vol. 6, No. 5, pp. 1632–1648.

Ciuciu, P. and Idier, J. (2002). A half-quadratic block-coordinate descent method for spectral estimation, *Journal of Signal Processing*, Vol. 82, pp. 941–959.

Ciuciu, P.; Idier, J. and Giovannelli, J.-F. (2001). Regularized estimation of mixed spectra using circular Gibbs-Markov model, *IEEE Trans. on Signal Processing*, Vol. 49, No. 10, pp. 2202–2213.

De Campos Velho, H. F.; Ramos, F. M.; Chalhoub, E. S.; Stephany, S.; Carvalho, J. C. and De Sousa, F. L. (2007). Inverse problems in space science and technology, *Inverse Problems in Science and Engineering*, Vol. 15, No. 4, pp. 359–372.

De la Rosa, J. I. and Fleury, G. (2002). On the Kernel selection for Minimum-Entropy estimation, *Proc. of the IEEE Instrumentation and Measurement Technology Conference*, Vol. 2, pp. 1205–1210, Anchorage, AK (USA).

De la Rosa, J. I.; Fleury, G., and Davoust, M.-E. (2003). Minimum-Entropy, pdf approximation and Kernel selection for measurement estimation, *IEEE Trans. on Instrum. Meas.*, Vol. 52, No. 4, pp. 1009–1020.

De la Rosa, J. I. (2004). Convergence of Minimum-Entropy robust estimators: Applications in DSP and Instrumentation, *Proc. of the XIV International Conference on Electronics, Communications, and Computers - CONIELECOMP'04*, pp. 98–103, Veracruz, Ver. (Mexico).

De la Rosa, J. I., and Fleury, G. (2006). Bootstrap methods for a measurement estimation problem, *IEEE Trans. on Instrum. Meas.*, Vol. 55, No. 3, pp. 820–827.

De la Rosa, J. I.; Villa, J. J. and Araiza, Ma. A. (2007). Markovian random fields and comparison between different convex criteria optimization in image restoration, *Proc. XVII International Conference on Electronics, Communications, and Computers - CONIELECOMP'07*, Cholula, Puebla, (Mexico).

Devroye, L. (1992). A note on the usefulness of superkernels in density estimation, *The Annals of Statistics*, Vol. 20, pp. 2037–2056. URL : //jeff.cs.mcgill.ca/~luc/

Devroye, L. (1989). The double kernel method in density estimation, *Annales de l'Institut Henri Poincaré*, Vol. 25, pp. 533–580.

Devroye, L., and Krzyzàk, A. (1999). "On the Hilbert kernel density estimate," *Statistics and Probability Letters*, Vol. 44, pp. 299–308.

Devroye, L. (1997). Universal smoothing factor selection in density estimation: theory and practice, *Test*, Vol. 6, pp. 223–320.

Durand, S. and Nikolova, M. (2006). Stability of the minimizers of least squares with a non-convex regularization. Part I: Local behavior, *Journal of Applied Mathematics and Optimization*, Vol. 53, No. 2, pp. 185–208.

Durand, S. and Nikolova, M. (2006). Stability of the minimizers of least squares with a non-convex regularization. Part II: Global behavior, *Journal of Applied Mathematics and Optimization*, Vol. 53, No. 3, pp. 259–277.

Eğecioğlu, Ö., and Srinivasan, A. (2000). Efficent non-parametric density estimation on the sphere with applications in fluid mechanics, *SIAM Journal on Scientific Computing*, Vol. 22, No. 1, pp. 152–176.

Geman, S. and Geman, D. (1984). Stochastic relaxation, Gibbs distribution, and the Bayesian restoration of images, *IEEE Trans. Pattern Anal. Machine Intell.*, Vol. PAMI-6, pp. 721–741.

Geman, D. and Reinolds, G. (1992). Constrained restoration and the recovery of discontinuities, *IEEE Trans. Pattern Anal. Machine Intell.*, Vol. 14, No. 3, pp. 367–383.

Geman, D. and Yang, C. (1995). Nonlinear image recovery with half-quadratic regularization, *IEEE Trans. Image Processing*, Vol. 4, No. 7, pp. 932–946.

Gibbs, A. L. (2000). *Convergence of Markov Chain Monte Carlo algorithms with applications to image restoration*, Ph.D. Thesis, Department of Statistics, University of Toronto, URL : www.utstat.toronto.edu.

Giovannelli, J.-F.; Idier, J.; Boubertakh, R. and Herment, A. (2002). Unsupervised frequency tracking beyond the Nyquist frequency using Markov chains, *IEEE Trans. on Signal Processing*, Vol. 50, No. 12, pp. 2905–2914.

Idier, J. (2001). Convex half-quadratic criteria and interacting auxiliary variables for image restoration, *IEEE Trans. on Image Processing*, Vol. 10, No. 7, pp. 1001–1009.

Labat, C. and Idier, J. (2006). Convergence of truncated half-quadratic algorithms using conjugate gradient, *technical repport*, IRCCyN, August (France).

Labat, C. (2006). *Algorithmes d 'optimisation de critères pénalisés pour la restauration d 'images. Application à la déconvolution de trains d 'impulsions en imagerie ultrasonore*, Ph.D. Thesis, École Centrale de Nantes, Nantes, December (France).

Levin, A.; Fergus, R.; Durand, F. and Freeman, W. T. (2007). Image and depth from a conventional camera with a coded aperture, Massachusetts Institute of Technology, Computer Science and Artificial Intelligence Laboratory, SIGGRAPH, *ACM Transactions on Graphics*, August.

Levin, A.; Fergus, R.; Durand, F. and Freeman, W. T. (2007). Deconvolution using natural image priors, Massachusetts Institute of Technology, Computer Science and Artificial Intelligence Laboratory, SIGGRAPH.

Loader, C. M. (1999). Bandwidth selection: classical or plug-in?, *The Annals of Statistics*, Vol. 27, No. 3, pp. 415–438.

Masry, E. (1983). Probability density estimation from sampled data, *IEEE Trans. on Information Theory*, Vol. IT-29, No.5, pp. 697–709.

Neal, R. M. (1993). Probabilistic inference using Markov chain Monte Carlo methods, Tech. Rep., CRG-TR-93-1, Department of Computer Science, University of Toronto (CA). URL : www.cs.toronto.edu/~radford.

Nikolova, M. (2006). *Functionals for signal and image reconstruction: properties of their minimizers and applications,* Research report to obtain the Habilitation à diriger des recherches, CMLA (CNRS UMR 8536), ENS Cachan, Paris (France).

Nikolova, M. (2005). Analysis of the recovery of edges in images and signals by minimizing nonconvex regularized least-squares, *SIAM Journal on Multiscale Modeling and Simulation*, Vol. 4, No. 3, pp. 960–991.

Nikolova, M. and Ng, M. (2005). Analysis of half-quadratic minimization methods for signal and image recovery, *SIAM Journal on Scientific computing*, Vol. 27, No. 3, pp. 937–966.

Nikolova, M. and Chan, R. (2007). The equivalence of half-quadratic minimization and the gradient linearization iteration, *IEEE Trans. on Image Processing*, Vol. 16, No. 6, pp. 1623–1627.

Nikolova, M.; Ng, M. K. and Tam, C.-P. (2010). Fast nonconvex nonsmooth minimization methods for image restoration and reconstruction, *IEEE Trans. on Image Processing*, Vol. 19, No. 12, pp. 3073–3088.

Pan, R. and Reeves, S. J. (2006). Efficent Huber-Markov edge-preserving image restoration, *IEEE Trans. on Image Processing*, Vol. 15, No. 12, pp. 3728–3735.

Perona, P. and Malik, J. (1990). Scale-space and edge detection using anisotropic diffusion, *IEEE Trans. Pattern Anal. Machine Intell.*, Vol. 12, No. 7, pp. 629–639.

Pronzato, L., and Thierry, E. (2000). A minimum-entropy estimator for regression problems with unknown distribution of observation errors, *MaxEnt 2000*, Edited by A. Mohammad-Djafari, American Institute of Physics, pp. 169–180.

Pronzato, L., and Thierry, E. (2000). A minimum-entropy estimator for regression problems with unknown distribution of observation errors, Tech. Rep. 00-08, Laboratoire I3S, CNRS-Université de Nice-Shopia Antipolis (France).

Pronzato, L., and Thierry, E. (2001). Entropy minimization of parameter estimator with unknown distribution of observation errors, *Proc. of the IEEE International Conference in Acoustics, Speech and Signal Processing*, Vol. 6, pp. 3993–3996.

Pronzato, L.; Thierry, E., and Wolsztynski, E. (2004). Minimum entropy estimation in semi-parametric models: a candidate for adaptive estimation?, *Proceedings of the 7th Int. Workshop on Advances in Model-Oriented Design and Analysis*, Kapellerput, Nederlands, 14-18 june, pp. 125–132. A. Di Bucchianico, H. Laüter and H.P. Wynn (eds.), Physica Verlag, Heidelberg.

Rivera, M. and Marroquin, J. L. (2003). Efficent half-quadratic regularization with granularity control, *Image and Vision Computing*, Vol. 21, No. 4, pp. 345–357.

Rivera, M. and Marroquin, J. L. (2004). Half-quadratic cost functions for phase unwrapping, *Optics Letters*, Vol. 29, No. 5, pp. 504–506.

Rivera, M. (2005). Robust phase demodulation of interferograms with open or closed fringes, *J. Opt. Soc. Am. A*, Vol. 22, No. 6, pp. 1170–1175.

Robert, C. P. and Casella, G. (2004). *Monte Carlo Statistical Methods*, Springer Verlag, 2nd Edition.

Sauer, K. and Bouman, C. (1992). Bayesian estimation of transmission tomograms using segmentation based optimization, *IEEE Trans. on Nuclear Science*, Vol. 39, No. 4, pp. 1144–1152.

Terrell, G. P. (1990). The maximal smoothing principle in density estimation, *Journal of the American Statistical Association*, Vol. 85, pp. 470–477.

Terrell, G. P., and Scott, D. W. (1985). Oversmoothed nonparametric density estimation, *Journal of the American Statistical Association*, Vol. 80, pp. 209–214.

Villa, J. J.; De la Rosa, J. I.; Miramontes, G. and Quiroga, J. A. (2005). Phase recovery from a single fringe pattern using an orientational vector field regularized estimator, *J. Opt. Soc. Am. A*, Vol. 22, No. 12, pp. 2766–2773.

Villa, J. J.; Quiroga, J. A. and De la Rosa, J. I. (2009). Regularized quadratic cost-function for directional fringe pattern filtering, *Optics Letters*, Vol. 37, No. 11, pp. 1741–1743.

Villa, J. J.; Rodríguez-Vera, R.; Quiroga, J. A.; De la Rosa, J. I. and González, E. (2010). Anisotropic phase-map denoising using a regularized cost-function with complex-valued Markov-random-fields, *Optics and Lasers in Engineering*, Vol. 48, No. 6, pp. 650–656.

Villa, J. J.; Quiroga, J. A.; Servín, M.; Estrada, J. C. and De la Rosa J. I. (2010). N-dimensional regularized fringe direction-estimator, *Optics Express*, Vol. 18, No. 16, pp. 16567–16572.

Wolsztynski, E.; Thierry, E., and Pronzato, L. (2004). Minimum entropy estimation in semi parametric models, *Proc. of the IEEE International Conference in Acoustics, Speech and Signal Processing - ICASSP'2004*, 17-21 may, Montreal, Canada, Vol. II, pp. 1045–1048.

Wolsztynski, E.; Thierry, E., and Pronzato, L. (2004). Consistency of a Minimum-Entropy Estimator of Location, Research Report I3S/RR-2004-38-FR Projet TOpMODEL, Laboratoire I3S, CNRS-Université de Nice-Shopia Antipolis (France), 30 pages.

Wolsztynski, E.; Thierry, E., and Pronzato, L. (2005). Estimation semi-paramétrique robuste par minimisation de l'entropie des résidus, application en traitement d'images, *Proc. GRETSI'05*, pp. 149–152, Louvain-la-Neuve (Belgium).

Wolsztynski, E.; Thierry, E., and Pronzato, L. (2005). Minimum Entropy Estimators in Semiparametric Regression Problems, *Proc. 11th Int. Symp. on Applied Stochastic Models and Data Analysis*, pp. 882–889, 17-20 mai, Brest (France), J. Jansen and P. Lenca (eds.).

Wolsztynski, E.; Thierry, E., and Pronzato, L. (2005). Minimum entropy estimation in semi parametric models, *Signal Processing*, Vol. 85, pp. 937–949.